THE EVERYTHING®
BRAZILIAN COOKBOOK

Dear Reader,

I grew up in Tennessee, eating biscuits and country ham, far from Brazil. And though I loved to cook and bake, I was not very adventurous. I had a collection of favorite recipes, and I was content with what I knew how to do. But then our family moved to South America for several years, and I began to think about food differently.

At first, the food seemed very exotic. But gradually I discovered many similarities between the traditional cooking from my part of the world and the cooking of Latin America. There are big differences, of course, but there are many connections. Learning how to cook the food of another culture teaches you a lot about why you cook the way you do. You gain new skills and techniques that you can apply to your oldest, most favorite recipes. You see new possibilities in everything and start to think like a chef.

I hope you will discover the fun of cooking Brazilian food through this book. The recipes are approachable and designed for someone new to Brazilian cuisine. Brazilian food is both exotic and familiar, comforting yet interesting, and definitely worth discovering!

Marian Blazes

Welcome to the EVERYTHING® Series!

These handy, accessible books give you all you need to tackle a difficult project, gain a new hobby, comprehend a fascinating topic, prepare for an exam, or even brush up on something you learned back in school but have since forgotten.

We give you everything you need to know on the subject, but throw in a lot of fun stuff along the way, too.

We now have more than 400 Everything® books in print, spanning such wide-ranging categories as weddings, pregnancy, cooking, music instruction, foreign language, crafts, pets, New Age, and so much more. When you're done reading them all, you can finally say you know Everything®!

PUBLISHER Karen Cooper

MANAGING EDITOR, EVERYTHING® SERIES Lisa Laing

COPY CHIEF Casey Ebert

ASSISTANT PRODUCTION EDITOR Alex Guarco

ACQUISITIONS EDITOR Lisa Laing

SENIOR DEVELOPMENT EDITOR Brett Palana-Shanahan

EVERYTHING® SERIES COVER DESIGNER Erin Alexander

Visit the entire Everything® series at *www.everything.com*

THE EVERYTHING®

BRAZILIAN COOKBOOK

Marian Blazes

Adamsmedia

Avon, Massachusetts

An Everything® Series Book.
Everything® and everything.com® are registered trademarks of F+W Media, Inc.

Published by
Adams Media, a division of F+W Media, Inc.
57 Littlefield Street, Avon, MA 02322. U.S.A.
www.adamsmedia.com

ISBN 10: 1-4405-7938-5
ISBN 13: 978-1-4405-7938-7
eISBN 10: 1-4405-7939-3
eISBN 13: 978-1-4405-7939-4

Printed in the United States of America.

10 9 8 7 6 5 4 3 2 1

Library of Congress Cataloging-in-Publication Data

Blazes, Marian.
  The everything Brazilian cookbook / Marian Blazes.
    pages cm. -- (An everything series book)
  Includes index.
  ISBN 978-1-4405-7938-7 (pbk.) -- ISBN 1-4405-7938-5 (pbk.) -- ISBN 978-1-4405-7939-4 (ebook) -- ISBN 1-4405-7939-3 (ebook)
  1. Cooking, Brazilian. 2. Cooking--Brazil. I. Title.
  TX716.B6B58 2014
  641.5981--dc23

                    2014012977

Photographs by Morena Escardo and Morena Cuadra.
Cover photographs © Morena Escardo; © StockFood/Poplis, Paul.

*This book is available at quantity discounts for bulk purchases.
For information, please call 1-800-289-0963.*

Contents

Acknowledgments

Thank you to my husband, Dave, who has always supported me in every endeavor and inspires me in so many ways. He gives me honest and helpful advice about my cooking and writing, and I value his opinion above all others on matters of food and life. Thank you also to our three wonderful children, who willingly try unfamiliar foods and unusual recipe combinations for dinner, when they would really probably rather have Chipotle. Thanks to my family and my husband's family, who have also cheerfully tasted experimental recipes, especially over the holidays, and were always encouraging.

Thank you especially to Lisa Laing, and to everyone at Adams Media who worked to get this cookbook ready for publication. Thank you for letting me be a part of the Everything® series.

Introduction

IF YOU WERE TO imagine a vacation trip to Brazil, you might think of Rio de Janeiro, gorgeous beaches, skimpy bikinis, Carnaval, and samba dancing. With regard to the food, you might envision sipping a *caipirinha*, the famous Brazilian cocktail, while having dinner at a *churrascaria*, a restaurant that serves all-you-can-eat grilled meats. That would be a good start, but it is only the tip of the iceberg of what Brazil has to offer. Brazilian cuisine is an exotic mix of indigenous, Portuguese, and African cuisines, with a bit of the Middle East, Italy, Germany, and Japan thrown into the mix. Ever since the Portuguese explorers first encountered indigenous tribes, Brazilian cuisine has evolved as a fusion of different cultures and culinary traditions.

The most basic meal in Brazil is rice and beans, which most Brazilians eat every day. Another staple is manioc root (cassava), which is enjoyed in countless incarnations. Brazilian markets offer a wide variety of tropical fruits and exotic Amazonian ingredients. There is excellent street food on every corner and delicious bar snacks to enjoy while watching soccer (*futebol*). There is fresh seafood, sushi, and a selection of world-class restaurants. There are cheese breads, cakes, and elaborate European-style desserts to sample. It's really hard to know where to begin. Because of the unique blend of cultures, geographic and climate diversity, and wide variety of ingredients, Brazilian food has something for everyone.

Though Brazilian food may sound exotic, it is also very approachable. Brazilians might eat fried ants, tripe, and jungle herbs that make their mouths tingle, but they also enjoy beans and rice, pasta, soup, salads, pizza, cake, and hamburgers. Many of the recipes in this cookbook will seem familiar, yet with an interestingly different spin on the traditional. Brazilians have a welcoming, comforting, yet creative way of cooking. Even if you never make a soup with Amazonian herbs or have access to specialty Brazilian ingredients, there are many things you can learn from this cuisine that will carry over into your everyday cooking.

Brazil is a developing country and most Brazilians still cook from scratch with local ingredients. Prepared foods are more expensive and less widely available, and commercial fast food is pricy and reserved for special occasions (though this is beginning to change). Most recipes in this book tend to start with fresh ingredients, instead of relying on prepared or packaged foods. This "back to basics" way of cooking is easier and less time-consuming than most people think, and the results taste better and are far more nutritious.

The recipes in this book are meant to represent a broad sample of Brazilian cuisine, and are chosen partly because they adapt well to the North American kitchen. Trying recipes from other countries is a great way to see your own cooking in a new light, and new ideas and ingredients inevitably become part of your regular repertoire. Cooking and eating bring people together. Jump in and explore the world of Brazilian food and see what it has to offer. *Bom apetite!*

CHAPTER 1

Introduction to Brazilian Food

Brazil is a true melting pot of people and cultures. This vibrant mix is the perfect recipe for a cuisine that is remarkably unique and constantly evolving. Brazilian cooking draws on ingredients and techniques from both indigenous and immigrant influences, blending them together in a distinctly Brazilian way. To understand how all of this came to be, it's helpful to learn a bit about Brazil's history, geography, climate, and culture. Then when you are ready to try the recipes, you'll understand what they represent and the stories that go with them.

A Bit of Brazilian History

Brazil is a very large country with distinct geographic regions. Each region has its own cuisine, based on locally available ingredients and the people who settled there. Brazil has great biological diversity, with no shortage of exciting ingredients to explore. Some of these ingredients are indigenous, like tropical fruit, Amazonian herbs, manioc (the root of the cassava plant), potatoes, corn, and seafood. Other ingredients, such as *dendê* (palm) oil, okra, olives, beef, chicken, and sugarcane, came to Brazil with immigrants from Portugal, Africa, Italy, Germany, the Middle East, and Asia. While immigrants brought new foods along with them, they also learned how to use what was available in the New World to make the dishes they missed from home. Invention born of necessity often leads to great things, like cornmeal "couscous" and cheese puffs made with tapioca starch (*pão de queijo*). These culinary inventions have become staples in the Brazilian kitchen over time.

In Brazil, you'll find many examples of fusion cuisine—two or more cuisines coming together in one dish. Taken as a whole, all of Brazilian cuisine could be called fusion cuisine, at least since the arrival of the first European explorers. The national dish *feijoada*, for example, demonstrates how many influences can come together in one pot. *Feijoada* is a dish of slow-cooked black beans with smoked meats and sausages, served with white rice, collard greens, and *farofa* (toasted manioc meal). One explanation of the history of this dish is that it was invented by African slaves, who had to find creative ways to cook the less desirable pieces of meat that were left to them. But *feijoada* is similar to European cassoulet, so the Portuguese are also thought to have had a role in how the dish came to be what it is today. Rice and beans were staples of the West African diet, and though beans had long been cultivated in South America by the time the Portuguese arrived, both the Portuguese and the African immigrants are credited with introducing rice to Brazilian cuisine. Many influences played a role in the making of the dish that is called *feijoada* today.

The Europeans Arrive

The melting pot that is contemporary Brazilian cuisine began in 1500 with the arrival of Pedro Álvares Cabral to the shores of South America, making him the first European to colonize the land that is now Brazil. At that time there were hundreds of native tribes in Brazil, mostly hunter-gatherers, who practiced limited agriculture. Some of these civilizations are thought to have been there for as long as 10,000 years, though they are not as well studied as the ones to the west of the Andes. Many of these indigenous people died of diseases that came with the Europeans, but the traditional cooking methods and native foods of those that survived became a part of the local cuisine in areas where they lived, particularly in the Amazon.

Sugarcane and West Africa

In the sixteenth century, Portuguese land owners began to grow sugarcane in their new world and imported slaves from Africa to work on their plantations. Africans brought their own culinary traditions with them and made use of locally available ingredients to cook stews, like *moqueca*, and other dishes based on West African cuisine. The state of Bahia in northeastern Brazil is recognized today for its unique Afro-Brazilian cuisine. Thanks to the sugarcane legacy, Brazil is well known for its distinctive white rum–like spirit called *cachaça*, which is distilled from fermented sugarcane juice.

The Brazilian gold rush began in the eighteenth century, when gold was discovered in the mountains of the area that is now the state of Minas Gerais. The discovery led to a massive influx of population to the area. The Portuguese brought more slaves to build infrastructure and to mine, and many sugarcane plantations were abandoned. Minas Gerais became a cultural center of Brazil and developed its own regional cuisine, one that is still prized today. Minas Gerais is particularly known for its cheeses and Portuguese-style sweets, as well as the famous cheese bread *pão de queijo*.

More Immigration

Other European immigrants arrived in the nineteenth century, particularly Germans and Italians. The Germans came earlier in the century, around the time Brazil became independent from Portugal, and settled mostly in the south. The majority of the Italian immigrants arrived later in the century, escaping poor economic conditions at home. Both populations had major influences on the cuisines of the areas where they settled.

Lebanese and Syrian immigrants came to Brazil in the late nineteenth and early twentieth centuries. Many were Christians fleeing religious persecution and quickly assimilated into Brazilian society. São Paulo has many Lebanese restaurants, and many Middle Eastern dishes are part of Brazilian cuisine today.

One more immigration wave with significant culinary impact occurred in the early twentieth century, when many Japanese came to Brazil, to escape rural poverty and to find work on the Brazilian coffee plantations. Many eventually settled in São Paulo, which now has a large Japanese district with many Asian restaurants and food markets.

Indigenous Foods

Manioc (cassava) is a native root vegetable (known as *mandioca* or *aipim* in Brazil) that was an essential staple of indigenous people and remains one of the staple foods of Brazil today. The native people knew how to process the root to remove the natural toxins before eating it, knowledge they shared with the Portuguese and other immigrants. They ground the manioc root into flour, extracted the starch, and boiled the extracted liquid to make *tucupi*, an essential ingredient in the famous Amazonian soup called *tacacá*.

Manioc is used in a variety of ways in modern Brazilian cuisine. *Farofa* is seasoned and toasted manioc meal, and is an essential condiment for many Brazilian dishes. Manioc starch is used for baking, and is the key ingredient in the famous cheese bread called *pão de queijo*. Manioc can be boiled, mashed, fried, and even made into gelatinous tapioca pearls.

Other native foods that are still a part of contemporary Brazilian cuisine include *guaraná* (a fruit whose seeds contain twice as much caffeine as coffee beans), *açaí* (the dark purple fruit of the açaí palm tree), *jambú* (an herb that makes the mouth tingle and turn numb), *pirão* (a gravy-like condiment made with fish broth and cassava), *canjica* (hominy corn), and *pamonhas* (fresh corn tamales wrapped in corn husks).

Portuguese Cuisine

The Portuguese arrived with their own fully developed cuisine, and it wasn't long before they found ways to make their beloved dishes in the New World, substituting locally available ingredients for foods they did not have from home. Guavas filled in for quince to become guava paste candy. Brazil nuts and peanuts substituted for almonds and walnuts in cookies and pastries. Manioc flour replaced wheat flour.

The Portuguese eventually brought domesticated farm animals to the New World, including chickens, sheep, goats, horses, and cows. They brought new crops like rice, olives, wheat, and apples. They made their favorite foods—sweet bread (*pão doce*), sausages, beer, wine, and sweets. They brought new cooking techniques, such as a penchant for heavy earthenware pots and for starting every dish with a *refogado* of garlic and onions. Over time, all of these things became incorporated into Brazil's national cuisine.

African Flavors

African immigrants were initially brought to Brazil in great numbers as slaves. They had an enormous influence on the cuisine. Like the Portuguese, they attempted to make their traditional West African dishes from the ingredients they could find on hand. From this improvisation came many of the traditional dishes of the renowned Bahian cuisine, such as *acarajé* (black-eyed pea and shrimp fritters), *moqueca* (a seafood stew flavored with coconut milk and *dendê* oil), and *caruru* (a condiment made of okra, peanuts, and shrimp). African immigrants also brought foods from home that became established crops in Brazil, including yams, okra, *dendê* (palm) oil, and hot peppers.

Pasta and Sausages

German immigrants began to settle in Brazil starting in the early nineteenth century and had a large influence on food and culture, especially in the south of Brazil. There are still *Oktoberfest* celebrations in southern cities like Blumenau in Santa Catarina. German-style cakes (*kuchen*) are known as *cuca* in Portuguese. Germans brought their beer expertise and established some of the earliest breweries in Brazil.

Most Italian immigrants settled in the states of São Paulo and Minas Gerais to work on coffee plantations, though a fair number went to the south (and eventually established vineyards there). The Italian immigrants in São Paulo assimilated rapidly, and many moved to the cities and prospered. They had a large influence on the cuisine in this region, and many traditional Italian dishes are well established in Brazilian cuisine, such as *macarrão* (pasta), *risotto*, *panettone*, *milanesa*, and *polenta*.

Middle Eastern Food

Middle Eastern immigrants, primarily from Lebanon and Syria, worked as traders, selling textiles and other goods. But some opened restaurants and soon Brazilians became familiar with dishes such as *sfihas* (pastries with ground beef or lamb known as *esfihas* or *esfirra*s in Brazil), tabbouleh, hummus, and kibbeh. Middle Eastern–style couscous dishes are also very popular, though they are often prepared with a specially processed cornmeal (*milharina*) instead of actual couscous.

Sushi and Pastels

Many Japanese immigrants were mistreated on the coffee plantations, where they came to work in the early twentieth century. Some fled to cities and opened Chinese restaurants, a cuisine that was more socially acceptable to Brazilians than Japanese food. One of the great culinary legacies of this period is the Brazilian *pastel*, a fried wonton-like pastry that is a very popular street food. Pastels (*pastéis*) have Brazilian-style fillings in a Chinese wonton crust, and are sold by Japanese vendors even today. Today Japanese-Brazilian cuisine is very trendy, and there is an explosion of restaurants serving creative fusion sushi and other Asian-Brazilian dishes.

Brazil by Region

Brazil is a large country, divided into twenty-six states and the federal district that contains the capital, Brasília. These states can be grouped into five different geographic regions. Each region has its own distinctive cuisine, influenced by population, geography, history, climate, and agriculture.

Northern Brazil: The Amazon

The Amazon region is of course one of the most biologically diverse regions of the world, and it's no surprise that many of Brazil's most unique dishes and ingredients come from the jungle. One of the most unusual ingredients is *jambú*, a medicinal plant that causes a tingling, numbing sensation in the mouth and is a key ingredient in famous Brazilian dishes like *pato no tucupi* (duck stewed in wild manioc juice), and is even used as a pizza topping. The chef Alex Atala has been recognized around the world for featuring exotic and previously unknown Amazonian ingredients in his São Paulo restaurant, D.O.M.

Fish and dried shrimp are a big part of the Amazonian diet. *Pirarucu*, the largest freshwater fish in South America (6 feet long), is one of the many Amazonian fish species that are prized as delicacies. This species is so valued that it has suffered from overfishing.

Amazonian cuisine is also known for its hot chili peppers, Brazil nuts (*castanhas*), *pirão* (a condiment made of manioc meal and fish stock), fish and shrimp stews, banana dishes, and manioc.

Northeastern Brazil: Land of Sugarcane

The northeastern part of Brazil includes the state of Bahia, famous for its Afro-Brazilian cuisine. The region has dry plains and low plateaus, and includes the northeastern coast. Some of the typical foods of this region are seafood, coconuts, cashews, plantains, *dendê* (palm) oil, chili peppers, and *cachaça* (a white rum–like spirit). One notable dish from this region is *moqueca*, a seafood stew made with coconut milk and flavored with *dendê* oil, a bright orange oil from a West African palm species. *Moqueca* is often described as a stew of native Brazilian ingredients seasoned with African spices and cooked in Portuguese pots (*panela de barro*). Other famous dishes from this region include *acarajé* (black-eyed pea and shrimp fritters fried in *dendê* oil), *vatapá* (seafood chowder), and *bobó de camarão* (shrimp and manioc stew).

Pernambuco, a coastal state in northeastern Brazil, is famous for certain dishes such as *bolo de rolo* (a guava roll cake), *cartola* (a dessert of fried bananas and cheese), and *bolo souza leão* (a rich Portuguese-style cake made with manioc).

Central Western Brazil: The Wild West

This region of Brazil includes the states of Mato Grosso, Mato Grosso do Sul, and Goiás. It has traditionally been somewhat isolated from the rest of the country, though the relocation of the capital, Brasília, to the eastern part of the region in the 1950s caused an increase in population there. This region is known for its national parks and wide range of ecosystems, including jungle, plains, forests, and the world's largest tropical wetlands (the Pantanal). It is also home to the indigenous Bororo people.

Central Brazil is known for its fish and game, including piranha and even alligator meat. Grilled meats (*churrasco*) and the culture of the *gaúchos* (cowboys) are also important in this region. Dried beef (*carne seca*), manioc, and plantains are staple foods. The region borders both Paraguay and Bolivia, and is influenced by the cuisine of both countries. *Sopa paraguaya* (Paraguayan-style corn bread) and *chipa* (Bolivian cheese bread) are popular dishes.

Southeastern Brazil: Mining, Big Cities, and Beaches

Southeastern Brazil encompasses two of the most important cities in Brazil, Rio de Janeiro and São Paulo. In addition to its beautiful beaches and famous statue, Rio de Janeiro is famous for *feijoada*, the national dish of Brazil, which is a stew of black beans cooked with smoked meats. Other well-known dishes include *sopa leão veloso* (seafood chowder), *cozido à carioca* (traditional Portuguese-style stew), and *peixada* (fish stew).

São Paulo is most known for its diverse and cosmopolitan cuisine. It is the largest city in Brazil and more international in flavor. Italian and Middle Eastern foods are very popular. One very famous dish is *cuscuz paulista*, a beautifully decorated ring of cornmeal "couscous" filled with chicken, seafood, and vegetables.

The state of Espírito Santo is renowned for its seafood, and has its own version of *moqueca* called *moqueca capixaba*, which is flavored with achiote (a red seed used for seasoning and color, also known as annatto) and is not made with coconut milk like the Bahian version. People from this region are known to say "*Moqueca é capixaba, o resto é peixada*," meaning the only true *moqueca* comes from this region, and everything else is just fish stew (*o resto é peixada*).

Minas Gerais is another state in this region with a very distinctive cuisine. It's home to many coffee plantations and is famous for its cheese (*queijo minas*) and milk production. *Pao de queijo* (cheese bread), *angu* (cornmeal), guava paste, beans, and pork are popular foods in this region. A typical dish is *tutu de feijão*, or refried beans, which are often served with *torresmos* (fried pork rinds).

Southern Brazil: *Gaúchos*

The state of Rio Grande do Sul lies at the southernmost tip of Brazil, and the cuisine of this region is related to that of Argentina and Uruguay, which share the same *pampas* (plains) culture. This is the land of the *gaúchos* (Brazilian cowboys), who travel long distances on horseback tending their cattle, and are experts at grilling meat (*churrasco*). Those famous cattle-driving horsemen perfected a method of cooking their meat on spits over a campfire. One legend about the *gaúchos* is that the Native Americans taught them how to carry meat under their saddles, so that the sweat from their horses would salt the meat and preserve it. This may be the only region in the world where drinking tea is considered very macho, as long as it is mate tea (*chimarrão*), sipped from a gourd.

Many Italians and Germans settled in southern Brazil, so Italian food, beer, sausage, and German-style cakes and desserts are also well known in this region.

Staples of the Brazilian Kitchen

Most of the ingredients needed for the recipes in this book are widely available in North American grocery stores. If you live in a city that has Latin American grocery stores or markets, you will have even more ingredients available to you. Major cities often have a Brazilian grocery, where you can buy real Brazilian cheeses, frozen Brazilian fruits and vegetables, and boxed mixes for Brazilian cheese bread, cakes, and candy.

Manioc (*Mandioca*)

Manioc is the edible root that is a huge part of the Brazilian diet. In the United States, you might find it labeled as cassava or yucca. You can buy fresh manioc root in the produce section of many grocery stores. Goya brand sells frozen manioc root that is peeled and ready to cook. Tapioca starch (*polvilho de mandioca*) is commonly available in the baking section of North American supermarkets as well, though it is typically the "sour" (slightly fermented) version. There is also sweet tapioca starch (*polvilho doce*), which has a milder taste. Manioc meal (*farinha de mandioca*) is processed manioc that has been dried and ground into a coarse meal that is excellent at soaking up flavor from fats like butter and bacon grease. Seasoned, toasted manioc meal, or *farofa*, is an essential condiment for *feijoada* and other traditional dishes. Tapioca pearls (like those used for making tapioca pudding) are made of processed manioc starch, and are used in certain Brazilian dishes.

Beans and Rice

Most Brazilians eat beans and rice every day. They prefer white rice, and though black beans are associated with the national dish *feijoada*, many other kinds of beans are popular. Most Brazilian households have a pressure cooker for cooking beans more efficiently.

Corn and Potatoes

Fresh corn is called *milho verde*, and is a key ingredient many different dishes. Cornmeal (*fubá*) is widely used in cakes and breads. *Canjica* is a white hominy corn that is used to make a sweet corn pudding associated with the June Festival (*Festa Junina*). *Milharina* is cornmeal that is processed into coarse flakes, which are steamed and eaten like couscous.

Potatoes are not quite as popular as manioc, but potato salad (*maionese*) is a popular side dish for grilled meat (*churrasco*), and for some reason Brazilians love to put potato sticks (the packaged potato chip kind) on everything!

Cheese

Brazil has a large dairy industry and has several important cheeses that appear in many dishes. *Requeijão* (or *Catupiry*) cheese is a mild cheese spread, which is used very much in the same way that cream cheese is used in the United States. It's often paired with chicken on pizzas and in fried pastels. *Queijo coalho* is a firm, nonmelting white cheese that is similar to Greek halloumi cheese (it even squeaks). *Queijo coalho* is often grilled on a stick and sold as a street food snack, since it keeps its shape when heated. *Queijo minas* is the famous cow's milk cheese from Minas Gerais. There are three kinds of minas cheese: *frescal* (very fresh, like queso fresco), *meia-cura* (partly cured), and *curado* (aged). *Queijo prato* is another cheese from Minas Gerais. It is a yellow Dutch-style soft cheese, a legacy from Dutch colonization.

Fruit and Nuts

Brazilian markets display a spectacular array of tropical fruits, many of which are essentially unavailable in the United States, or only available frozen. Some of the fruits widely used in Brazilian cuisine that are available in North America include pineapple, papaya, bananas, plantains, citrus fruits, mango, strawberries, and coconut.

Slightly more exotic fruits that are widely used in Brazilian cooking include passion fruit and açaí (pronounced *"ah-sigh-EE"*) Açai is a dark purple berry that is thought to have healthful properties and is often added to smoothies. Frozen açaí and passion fruit pulp are fairly easy to find in the United States. Another important fruit in Brazil is *cajú*, or the fruit of the cashew nut (not widely available in the United States). You can find soda and syrup made with *guaraná*, another jungle fruit that happens to be naturally caffeinated.

Brazilians do not cook with lemons but instead use the tart, thin-skinned, juicy limes that are widespread in South America. Mexican limes are very similar. Cashews, peanuts, Brazil nuts, and walnuts are widely used in Brazilian cooking, as are olives, raisins, and other dried fruits.

Vegetables

Nearly every Brazilian recipe starts by sautéing onions in oil, then adding some garlic, then adding chopped tomatoes, which is a Portuguese trick called a *refogado*. It's the basic seasoning of everything from seafood stews to pasta sauces. In addition to onions, garlic, and tomatoes, some of the most widely used vegetables are hearts of palm, pumpkin, squash, eggplant, zucchini, carrots, cauliflower, and okra.

Seafood (*Frutos do Mar*)

Brazil has a lot of coastal regions, and the inland areas are rich with freshwater fish, so Brazilians consume a lot of seafood. The Amazon boasts an amazing variety of tasty freshwater fish, such as *pacu* and the large *pirarucu*. Dried shrimp are very important in Bahian cuisine. *Bacalhau*, or Portuguese dried salt cod, is eaten throughout Brazil.

Meat

Brazilians are known for their meat consumption. Beef, pork, and chicken are all standard at the feast of grilled meats known as *churrasco*. Portuguese-style sausages such as *chouriço* and *linguiça* are very popular. Dried beef is a specialty of Brazil, dating back to the times of the *carreteiros*, or mule drivers, who traveled for long distances and had to carry nonperishables like sun-dried beef (*carne de sol*), beans, and manioc meal. It is hard to find a good substitute for Brazilian dried beef in the United States. Some people use chipped beef or pastrami, but they are not quite the same.

Sweets

Many Brazilian desserts are variations of Portuguese sweets. If you stock your pantry with several cans of condensed milk, sugar, and plenty of eggs, you will have the basic ingredients for many Brazilian desserts. Brazilians make many candies with condensed milk, adding chocolate, fruit, or nuts. Dulce de leche (*doce de leite*), or milk caramel, is very popular. Brazilians love cake, which they bake in the shape of a ring, and sweet breads. Flan, rice pudding, and other creamy desserts are very popular.

Cachaça

Cachaça is a rum-like liquor that is made by distilling fermented sugarcane juice. *Cachaça* is the key ingredient in the *caipirinha*, Brazil's national cocktail, and is also used in many recipes and as a marinade for meats. One story about the *caipirinha* cocktail is that it was invented as a flu remedy, during the Spanish flu epidemic of 1918. The word *caipira* means "country bumpkin" or "hillbilly", and *caipirinha* is the diminutive form of the word, so the name of this cocktail translates to "Little Hillbilly."

CHAPTER 2

Appetizers (*Tira-Gostos*)

Chicken Croquettes (*Coxinha*)

These creamy chicken croquettes were originally made with chicken thighs, but these days they are simply shaped to resemble them. Mashed potatoes and mozzarella cheese are tasty additions to this snack. Add 1 cup of mashed potatoes and ½ cup shredded mozzarella to the shredded chicken.

INGREDIENTS | MAKES 25

2 tablespoons butter
2 large onions, peeled and chopped
2 cloves garlic, minced
1 large carrot, peeled and diced
1 pound boneless, skinless chicken breasts
1 bay leaf
4 cups chicken broth
Juice of 1 medium lime
¾ teaspoon salt, divided
½ teaspoon freshly ground black pepper
8 ounces cream cheese, softened
3½ cups all-purpose flour
2 large eggs
2 cups finely grated bread crumbs
3 cups vegetable oil

1. Heat butter in a medium skillet over medium heat. Sauté onions, garlic, and carrot for about 8 minutes, or until the onions are fragrant and translucent. Set aside half of the onion mixture, and place the other half in a large saucepan with the chicken and the bay leaf. Cover the chicken with the broth.

2. Bring broth to a boil over medium-high heat, then reduce heat to medium-low. Simmer for about 10 minutes, or until the chicken's internal temperature reaches 160°F. Remove chicken from broth and set aside to cool. Strain and reserve the broth.

3. Shred the chicken in a food processor. In a large bowl, mix the chicken with the reserved onion mixture, lime juice, ½ teaspoon salt, pepper, and cream cheese.

4. Return 3½ cups of the broth to the saucepan. Whisk flour and remaining salt into the broth. Heat over medium heat, stirring until it thickens into a stiff dough. Remove from heat and let cool.

5. With floured hands, divide the dough into 25 pieces. Roll each piece into a ball. Make an indentation in the center of the dough, and add 1 tablespoon of the chicken filling. Wrap the dough around the filling, forming it into the shape of a teardrop. Repeat with remaining dough and filling.

6. Whisk the eggs together in a bowl, and place the bread crumbs in a separate bowl. Dip each *coxinha* into the egg mixture (letting excess drip off) and then into the bread crumbs.

7. Heat the oil in a deep skillet or large heavy saucepan to 350°F. Cook the *coxinhas* in batches, turning occasionally, until they are golden brown. Remove with a slotted spoon and drain on paper towels. Serve warm. *Coxinhas* can be reheated in a 200°F oven for 10–15 minutes.

Salt Cod Croquettes (*Bolinho de Bacalhau*)

Salt cod is still wildly popular in Brazil, but it can be difficult to find in the United States (though you can order it online). Some people substitute fresh fish, but the dried fish has a characteristic flavor that can't be recreated. The dried cod must be soaked in water for 24 hours to remove the excess salt, so plan ahead.

INGREDIENTS | MAKES 25

1 clove garlic, minced

½ cup mayonnaise

1 tablespoon lime juice

1 teaspoon smoked paprika

½ pound salt cod, desalted and shredded (see sidebar)

2 cups mashed potatoes

1 tablespoon all-purpose flour

¼ cup chopped fresh parsley

2 large eggs, lightly beaten

½ teaspoon freshly ground black pepper

3 cups vegetable oil

Preparing Salt Cod

Rinse the fillet under cold water to remove the salty crust. Cut the fillet into 2" pieces, and place them in a bowl. Cover the fish with cold water and refrigerate for 24 hours (cover bowl with plastic wrap), changing the water every 4–6 hours. Taste a piece of the fish for saltiness. Soak longer if needed. When desired flavor is obtained, drain the fish, pat dry with paper towels, and shred.

1. In a small bowl, mix garlic, mayonnaise, lime juice, and smoked paprika. Chill until ready to serve.

2. Place the shredded fish in a medium bowl. Add the mashed potatoes, flour, parsley, eggs, and black pepper. Mix well.

3. Heat the oil in a deep skillet or large heavy saucepan to 350°F. Using 2 large tablespoons, scoop up a portion of the potato/fish mixture. Carefully drop the batter into the oil, using one spoon to help slide the batter off of the other spoon, in order to make an oblong croquette. Cook the croquettes in batches until well browned and crispy.

4. Remove the croquettes from the oil with a slotted spoon and drain on paper towels. Serve warm with the garlic mayonnaise for dipping.

Hearts of Palm Empanadas (*Empanada de Palmito*)

These traditional pastries are similar to baked empanadas, except that they are made in a muffin tin, giving them their characteristic domed shape.

INGREDIENTS | SERVES 12

3 cups all-purpose flour

1½ teaspoons salt, divided

6 tablespoons cold vegetable shortening

9 tablespoons cold butter, divided

3 egg yolks, divided

3–4 tablespoons cold water

1 clove garlic, minced

1 large onion, peeled and chopped

2 (14-ounce) cans hearts of palm, drained and chopped into ½" pieces

1 large tomato, seeded and diced

½ cup sliced green olives

½ cup heavy cream

1 cup frozen green peas, thawed

¼ cup chopped fresh parsley

Nomenclature

If you make these pastries in regular- or large-size muffin tins, they are called *"empadas."* If you make them in small muffin tins, they are *"empadinhas."* In Portuguese, when you want to describe something as small, you can add the suffix *"inha"* to the end of the word. To describe something that is really big, you can add the suffix *"ão."* So if you were to make this recipe into one big pie, you might call it an *"empadão de palmito."*

1. Place the flour and ½ teaspoon salt in a large bowl. Cut the vegetable shortening and 8 tablespoons butter into small pieces and add them to the flour. Use your fingers to mix the butter and shortening into the flour, until the mixture resembles coarse meal. Add 2 egg yolks and 1–2 tablespoons cold water and knead mixture until it comes together into a smooth dough, adding more water if mixture is too dry. Wrap dough with plastic wrap and chill for 30 minutes, or until ready to use (dough can be made 1 day ahead).

2. Melt the remaining tablespoon of butter in a medium skillet over low heat. Add the garlic and onion and cook until onion is translucent, about 10 minutes. Add the hearts of palm and tomato to the skillet and cook for 5 minutes more, stirring often. Add the olives and cream and cook for 5–10 minutes longer. Add the peas and cook for 2–3 minutes more. Remove from heat and stir in the parsley. Let cool.

3. Preheat oven to 350°F. Divide the dough into 2 portions, one twice as big as the other. Divide each portion into 12 pieces. Roll each piece of dough into a ball. Press one large dough ball into each well of a 12-cup muffin tin, covering the bottom and pressing dough up sides to cover. Fill the dough with enough filling to mound up over the top of the muffin tin slightly. Using your fingers or a rolling pin, flatten each of the remaining small dough balls into a circle. Place a circle of dough to cover each *empada*. Press the edges of the dough together to seal and trim away any excess.

4. Beat the remaining egg yolk and brush over the tops of the *empadas*. Bake for 25–30 minutes until golden brown. Serve warm or at room temperature.

Beef and Bulgur Croquettes (*Kibe*)

These football-shaped croquettes are made with ground beef and bulgur wheat, and are seasoned with mint. Serve them with lime wedges and Yogurt Tahini Dressing (see recipe in Chapter 9) for a great appetizer or snack.

INGREDIENTS | MAKES 15

1½ cups bulgur wheat

3 cups beef broth

3 cups plus 1 tablespoon vegetable oil, divided

1 pound lean ground beef

1 medium onion, peeled and finely minced, divided

1 teaspoon salt, divided

½ teaspoon ground black pepper

¼ cup chopped mint leaves

1 clove garlic, minced

1 teaspoon dried oregano

Kibe Meatloaf

Kibe is sometimes prepared as a meatloaf or casserole. To make *kibe en forno* (oven-baked *kibe*), mix the soaked wheat, ground beef, onions, salt, pepper, mint, garlic, and oregano, and add the juice of a small lime. Layer half of the mixture in a 9" square baking dish. Place 1 cup grated mozzarella cheese and several tomato slices on top, then cover with the other half of the beef mixture. Bake at 350°F for 35–45 minutes, or until the meat is browned and cooked through. Cut into squares to serve.

1. Place the bulgur wheat in a medium heatproof bowl. Heat the beef broth to almost boiling and pour it over the wheat. Soak wheat for 1 hour, then drain well and set aside.

2. Heat 1 tablespoon vegetable oil in a large skillet over medium heat. Add ground beef and half the minced onion. Cook, stirring often, until the meat is well browned, about 5 minutes. Drain fat, and season beef with ½ teaspoon salt and black pepper. Set aside.

3. Place the drained wheat, mint leaves, garlic, oregano, remaining onion, and remaining salt in the bowl of a food processor. Pulse mixture to mix, adding a tablespoon of water or broth if needed until mixture starts to clump together.

4. Take 2 tablespoons of the wheat mixture at a time and shape into balls. Make a well in the center of each and fill it with a spoonful of beef. Fold the wheat around the filling, seal, and form croquette into an oblong shape with pointed ends.

5. Heat the remaining vegetable oil in a deep skillet or large heavy saucepan to about 350°F. Cook the *kibe* in batches, turning once or twice, until they are well browned and crispy. Drain on paper towels. Serve warm.

Beef and Cornmeal Empanadas (*Pastel de Milho*)

These fried empanadas are a specialty of the Minas Gerais region of Brazil.
The crispy cornmeal dough is filled with seasoned ground beef.

INGREDIENTS | MAKES 25

3 cups cornmeal

⅔ cup cornstarch

2 teaspoons salt, divided

2 tablespoons butter

½ teaspoon baking soda

4–6 cups boiling water

1 tablespoon olive oil

½ cup chopped onion

1 clove garlic, minced

1 pound ground beef

1 large baking potato, peeled, boiled until tender, and cubed

½ cup beef stock

3 cups vegetable oil

1. Place the cornmeal, cornstarch, 1 teaspoon salt, butter, and baking soda in the bowl of a standing mixer. Gradually add some of the boiling water to the cornmeal mixture while mixing at low speed with the paddle attachment. Add just enough water to make a smooth dough that does not crack or crumble when kneaded. Wrap the dough in plastic wrap and set aside.

2. Heat the olive oil in a large skillet over medium-high heat. Add onion, garlic, remaining salt, and ground beef. Cook until beef is well browned, about 5 minutes. Add the potato and beef stock. Bring to a boil, then reduce heat to low and simmer mixture for 5–10 minutes, until most of the liquid has evaporated.

3. On a floured surface, roll out the dough to about ¼" thick. Cut out 5" circles of dough. Reroll the dough scraps and cut more circles of dough. Place a tablespoon of filling in the center of each circle. Fold the circle of dough in half to enclose the filling and press the edges with your fingers to seal.

4. Heat the vegetable oil in a deep skillet or large heavy saucepan to 350°F. Working in batches, cook the *pastéis* in the hot oil, turning occasionally, until they are deep golden brown in color. Carefully remove *pastéis* from the oil with a slotted spoon and place them on paper towels to drain. Serve warm.

Lebanese-Style Lamb Pastries (*Esfiha*)

Traditionally the lamb (or beef) and onions are not cooked before the pastry goes into a very hot wood-burning oven, but for the home cook it's best to sauté the meat before baking.

INGREDIENTS | MAKES 20

1 cup milk

2 teaspoons sugar

2¼ teaspoons active dry yeast

3½ cups all-purpose flour

1 tablespoon butter, softened

2 teaspoons salt, divided

1 tablespoon olive oil

½ cup chopped onion

½ cup finely diced red bell pepper

1 pound ground lamb or beef

½ teaspoon freshly ground black pepper

½ cup tomato sauce

1 tablespoon molasses

2 tablespoons lemon juice

1 egg yolk, lightly beaten

Pizza-Style *Esfihas*

For a variation, roll the dough into a log and slice it crosswise into ½" slices. On a floured surface, use a rolling pin to flatten each slice of dough into a 3" circle. Let dough rest for 5 minutes. Press 2 table-spoons of the beef filling into each circle of dough, while flattening the dough with the back of a spoon into a slightly larger circle and leaving a ¼" of dough around the edges. Let rise for 1 hour before baking.

1. In a small saucepan, warm the milk over medium heat until it is just hot. Stir sugar into the milk, then sprinkle the yeast over the milk and set aside for 5 minutes.

2. Add flour, butter, and 1 teaspoon salt to the bowl of a standing mixer. Knead mixture with the dough hook attachment while gradually adding the milk/yeast mixture to the flour. Knead until smooth, adding a bit more milk if dough seems too stiff, or a bit more flour if dough is too sticky. Place dough in an large bowl, lightly oiled with vegetable oil, and let dough rise in a warm place, loosely covered, for about 1 hour.

3. Heat 1 tablespoon olive oil in a medium skillet over medium-low heat. Sauté onion and red pepper about 5–8 minutes or until soft. Add the ground meat, black pepper, and remaining salt and sauté until just browned, about 5 minutes. Stir in tomato sauce, molasses, and lemon juice and remove from heat.

4. Preheat oven to 350°F. Line a baking sheet with parchment paper.

5. Punch down the dough and divide it into 20 pieces. Roll each piece into a ball. Using a rolling pin, flatten each ball into a small (5–6") circle and place 1 tablespoon of the filling in the middle of each. Fold the lower third of the circle toward the middle to cover the filling, then fold the left and the right thirds over, forming a triangle. Pinch the ends together to seal and place each pastry seam side down on the baking sheet.

6. Brush the pastries with egg yolk and let them rest for 30 minutes before baking. Bake for about 30 minutes, or until golden brown.

Ham and Cheese Crescent Rolls
(*Enroladinho de Presunto e Queijo*)

These rolls are surprisingly easy to make from scratch. Store-bought, refrigerated crescent roll dough is a great substitute when you're pressed for time.

INGREDIENTS | MAKES 16

1 cup milk

1 tablespoon sugar

2¼ teaspoons active dry yeast

4½ cups all-purpose flour, plus more for the baking sheet

1 teaspoon salt

8 tablespoons butter, melted

1 large egg

1 small tomato, diced

½ cup diced green olives

2 teaspoons dried oregano, divided

¼ cup grated Parmesan cheese, divided

16 slices smoked ham

16 slices mozzarella cheese

1 egg yolk, lightly beaten

Brazilian Ham

Presunto is a type of Portuguese dry-cured ham, similar to country ham or Spanish *jamón*. Many Brazilians use the word "*presunto*" to describe all kinds of ham, including deli-style hams. Any type of ham will work in these rolls, but when using the dry-cured ham it's best to chop the ham rather than slice it so that it will roll up more easily.

1. In a small saucepan, warm the milk over medium heat until it is just hot to the touch. Stir sugar into milk, then sprinkle yeast over milk and set aside for 5 minutes.

2. Add flour, salt, and butter to the bowl of a standing mixer. Knead mixture with the dough hook attachment, gradually adding the egg and the milk/yeast mixture to the flour. Knead until smooth, adding a bit more milk if dough seems too stiff, or a bit more flour if dough is too sticky. Place dough in a large bowl, lightly oiled with vegetable oil, and let rise, covered, for 1 hour.

3. In a small bowl, stir together tomato, olives, 1 teaspoon oregano, and 1 tablespoon Parmesan. Place mixture in a strainer to drain excess liquid until ready to use.

4. Preheat oven to 350°F. Dust a baking sheet with flour.

5. Punch down the dough and divide it into 16 equal pieces. On a floured surface, use a rolling pin to flatten each piece of dough into a rectangle, about 3½" × 7". Place a slice of ham and a slice of cheese on each rectangle, and spread a teaspoon of the tomato/olive mixture on top of the cheese. Roll up each rectangle, starting from a short side, enclosing the filling. Place the rolls seam side down on the baking sheet.

6. Brush rolls with egg yolk and sprinkle with remaining oregano and Parmesan. Let the rolls rest in a warm place for 20 minutes before baking. Bake for 25–30 minutes, or until puffed and golden brown.

Couscous Fish Cakes
(*Cuscuz de Peixe*)

These creative appetizers are made from a tasty mixture of couscous and sautéed fish that is shaped into attractive individual servings using a muffin tin.

INGREDIENTS | MAKES 12

2 cups chicken or fish stock

2 cups instant couscous

2 tablespoons olive oil

2 cloves garlic, minced

¼ cup minced onion

½ teaspoon salt

Juice of 1 medium lime

Hot pepper sauce (such as Tabasco), to taste

½ pound fish fillets, such as flouder or haddock

1 tablespoon vegetable oil

2 large hard-cooked eggs, shelled and thinly sliced into rounds

Fresh parsley leaves, for garnish

Brazilian Couscous

Middle Eastern and African immigrants brought their love of couscous to Brazil. When they couldn't find prepared couscous, they substituted a special kind of dried cornmeal called *milho amarelo*, which is coarsely ground and flaked in appearance. If you see the word *"cuscuz"* on a Brazilian menu, you will probably be served this special flaked cornmeal rather than traditional Middle Eastern–style couscous.

1. In a large saucepan over medium-high heat, bring the stock to a simmer and stir in the couscous. Remove from heat, cover, and set aside.

2. Heat olive oil in a medium skillet over medium heat. Add garlic, onion, and salt and cook until onion is soft and fragrant, about 5 minutes. Add lime juice and hot sauce to taste.

3. Add fish and cook, turning once, until cooked through and flaky, 2–3 minutes per side, depending on thickness. Remove fish mixture from skillet and use a fork to break the fish into pieces.

4. Stir the fish mixture into the couscous, and toss gently with a fork to mix. Generously brush the wells of a regular-size muffin pan with vegetable oil. Place a slice of egg in the bottom of each well. Evenly distribute the couscous mixture between the wells and press down gently with the back of a spoon to pack the couscous firmly. Set aside for 5 minutes.

5. Gently unmold the couscous cakes with a knife. Garnish with parsley and serve.

Plantain Chips (*Chips de Banana da Terra*)

Thin slices of green plantain are deep-fried in oil until crispy and golden.

INGREDIENTS | SERVES 6

4 green plantains, peeled

2 cups vegetable oil

1 teaspoon sea salt

1 teaspoon curry powder

How to Peel Green Plantains

Use a sharp paring knife to cut off both tips. Slit the peel lengthwise in several places, making sure to only cut through the skin. Pull the stiff sections of skin away from the plantain flesh.

1. Working quickly, use a mandoline or very sharp knife to cut the peeled plantain lengthwise into the thinnest slices possible. (You can also cut the plantain crosswise at a slight angle, which is easier if you don't have a mandolin.)

2. Heat the oil in a deep skillet or large heavy saucepan to 350°F. Working in batches, cook the plantain slices until golden brown and crispy, about 3–4 minutes.

3. Remove plantain slices from the oil with a slotted spoon and drain on paper towels. Sprinkle with sea salt and curry powder and serve warm or at room temperature.

Cheese Crackers with Guava Paste (*Biscoito de Queijo com Goiabada*)

The famous combination of cheese and guava paste typically appears in desserts and sweets. This savory version combines a rich cheesy cracker with sweet guava paste.

INGREDIENTS | MAKES 20

8 tablespoons salted butter, slightly softened

6 ounces grated sharp Cheddar cheese

1½ cups all-purpose flour

4 ounces guava paste

Piping Guava Paste

In a small saucepan, heat the guava paste with 2 tablespoons of water or lime juice over low heat, stirring, until it softens and becomes spreadable. Fit a pastry bag with a ¼" piping tip and fill bag with the warm guava paste. Pipe small portions of guava paste onto the baked crackers.

1. Place butter and cheese in a food processor and pulse several times until well mixed. Add flour and pulse until mixture comes together in a dough. Roll the dough into a log and chill for 30 minutes.

2. Preheat oven to 350°F. Slice the chilled dough crosswise into 20 rounds and place them on an ungreased baking sheet. Bake until crackers start to brown around the edges, about 12 minutes. Remove from oven and let cool.

3. Serve crackers topped with slices of guava paste, or pipe softened guava paste onto the crackers.

Chicken and Cheese Croquettes (*Risoles de Frango*)

Brazilian risoles resemble empanadas, but they are battered in crispy bread crumbs before they are fried.

INGREDIENTS | MAKES 15

3 tablespoons butter, divided

2 cubes chicken bouillon, divided

1¼ cups milk

2⅓ cups all-purpose flour

1 small onion, peeled and minced

1 clove garlic, minced

½ cup diced red bell pepper

2 tablespoons all-purpose flour or cornstarch

1 cup shredded cooked chicken (roasted or poached)

1 cup chicken stock

⅓ cup cream cheese

½ cup grated cheese (Cheddar or mozzarella or both)

2 tablespoons grated Parmesan cheese

2 large eggs

½ teaspoon sugar

½ teaspoon salt

2 cups very fine bread crumbs

3 cups vegetable oil

Risole Variations

You can use the same dough and bread-crumb technique to make a variety of *risoles* with different fillings. A simple cheese filling is delicious. Ground beef and olives, ham and cheese, and creamy shrimp are also popular in Brazil.

1. Melt 2 tablespoons of butter with 1 bouillon cube in a medium saucepan over low heat. Add milk and bring to a simmer. Mix in 2⅓ cups flour and cook over low heat, stirring, until mixture thickens into a stiff batter and pulls away from the sides of the saucepan, about 3–4 minutes. Set dough aside to cool.

2. Heat remaining butter in a medium skillet over medium-high heat. Add onion, garlic, and red pepper. Sauté vegetables about 8 minutes. Add 2 tablespoons flour or cornstarch and cook for 1 minute.

3. Add chicken, remaining bouillon cube, and chicken stock to the vegetable mixture. Reduce heat to medium and cook for 2–4 minutes, stirring, until mixture thickens. Remove from heat and stir in the cheeses.

4. Knead the dough briefly and add some extra flour if it is too sticky. Divide the dough into 15 pieces and roll each piece into a ball. On a floured surface, use a rolling pin to flatten each ball into a 5" circle.

5. Place 1–2 tablespoons of the chicken filling in the center of each circle of dough. Fold dough in half to enclose filling and seal edges tightly with your fingers.

6. In a medium bowl, whisk the eggs together with the sugar and salt. Place the bread crumbs on a plate.

7. Dip each pastry in the egg wash, and then into the bread crumbs. (Pastries may be refrigerated at this point for several hours before frying.)

8. Heat the oil in a deep skillet or large heavy saucepan to 350°F. Fry *risoles* in batches, turning once, until they are golden brown. Drain on paper towels and serve warm.

Breaded Shrimp (*Camarão Empanado*)

These fried shrimp are prepared with a clever technique that makes them extra crunchy on the outside and creamy on the inside.

INGREDIENTS | MAKES 18

18 large shrimp, peeled, with tails
Juice of 2 limes
½ teaspoon salt
1 tablespoon butter
1 clove garlic, minced
¼ cup minced onion
1 cup chicken broth
1½–2 cups all-purpose flour, divided
1½ cups milk
4 tablespoons mayonnaise
1 cube chicken bouillon
½ teaspoon salt
2 large eggs
1½ cups panko or regular bread crumbs
3 cups vegetable oil
1 cup tartar sauce, for dipping

Potato Shrimp

One interesting variation on this dish is to coat the shrimp with shredded potatoes instead of bread crumbs. Prepare the shrimp in the same way. Mix the cooking liquid with enough flour (about ½ cup) to obtain a thick batter. Peel 1 large potato and finely grate it using a food processor. Toss grated potato with salt and pepper. Dip the shrimp in the batter and roll them in the shredded potatoes. Fry the shrimp in hot oil until potatoes are crispy.

1. In a large bowl, marinate the shrimp in the lime juice and salt for 30 minutes.

2. In a large skillet, heat butter over medium heat. Sauté garlic and onion about 5 minutes, or until soft. Add the shrimp and the chicken broth and cook for 3–4 minutes. Remove shrimp and let cool. Strain and reserve the cooking liquid.

3. Place the reserved cooking liquid in a medium saucepan. Whisk ½ cup flour into the cooking liquid and heat the mixture over low heat. Whisk in milk, mayonnaise, bouillon, and salt. Add another cup of flour and cook for several minutes, stirring. Add more flour as needed to form a soft dough. Remove from heat.

4. Divide the dough into 18 pieces. Wrap each shrimp in one of the pieces of dough, leaving tail uncovered. Whisk eggs in a shallow bowl. Place bread crumbs in another shallow bowl. Dip each dough-wrapped shrimp in the egg wash and then in the bread crumbs to coat.

5. Heat the oil in a deep skillet or large heavy saucepan to 350°F. Fry shrimp in batches, turning occasionally, until shrimp are golden brown. Remove shrimp carefully with a slotted spoon and drain on paper towels. Serve warm with tartar sauce.

Rice Croquettes with Sausage (*Bolinho de Arroz com Salsicha*)

These irresistible croquettes are a great way to use up leftover rice.

INGREDIENTS | MAKES 25

4 cups cooked rice

2 large eggs

3 tablespoons minced fresh parsley

½ cup grated Parmesan cheese

½ teaspoon salt

½ teaspoon freshly ground black pepper

1 cup very fine bread crumbs

4 cooked sausage links, or 1 cup crumbled cooked sausage

3 cups vegetable oil

1. In a large bowl, mix together rice, eggs, parsley, Parmesan, salt, and pepper.

2. Place bread crumbs in a shallow bowl.

3. Dice the sausage links into ½" pieces. Form the rice mixture into walnut-size balls, and press a piece of sausage in the middle of each. Close rice mixture around the sausage and shape into a smooth ball. Roll each ball in the bread crumbs to coat.

4. Heat the oil in a deep skillet or large heavy saucepan to 350°F. Fry the croquettes in the oil until golden brown. Drain the croquettes on paper towels and serve warm.

Crispy Meatballs (*Bolinho de Carne Moída*)

These are not your ordinary meatballs. In Brazil, meatballs are deep-fried for an extra-crispy exterior.

INGREDIENTS | MAKES 15

1 pound ground beef

¼ cup minced onion

3 cloves garlic, peeled and crushed

1 teaspoon salt

½ teaspoon freshly ground black pepper

1 tablespoon grated Parmesan cheese

1 teaspoon dried oregano

1 tablespoon minced fresh parsley

1 medium French bread roll, or 5" piece of baguette, cut into cubes

¼ cup milk

½ cup all-purpose flour, panko, or very fine bread crumbs

3 cups vegetable oil

2 limes, cut into wedges, for garnish

1. Place the ground beef in a large bowl with the onion, garlic, salt, pepper, Parmesan, oregano, and parsley. Mix gently with your hands until evenly combined.

2. In another large bowl, soak the bread cubes in the milk for 5 minutes, then crumble them and add to the meat mixture.

3. Divide meatball mixture into 20–25 portions, and roll them between your palms to make smooth balls, without compressing them too much. Place the flour or bread crumbs in a shallow bowl and gently roll the meatballs in the flour to coat.

4. Heat the oil in a deep skillet or large heavy saucepan to 350°F. Fry the meatballs in batches until well browned and cooked through (about 8 minutes). Serve warm with lime wedges.

Cheese Croquettes (*Bolinho de Queijo*)

These cheese croquettes have a layer of savory dough surrounding a pocket of melted mozzarella and are seasoned with oregano and Parmesan cheese.

INGREDIENTS | MAKES 25

2 cups chicken stock

4 tablespoons butter, divided

2 cups all-purpose flour

¾ teaspoon salt

½ teaspoon smoked paprika

10 ounces mozzarella cheese

1 large egg

1 tablespoon water

2 cups very fine bread crumbs

½ cup finely grated Parmesan cheese

1 teaspoon dried oregano

Bolinho de Mandioca

Fried balls of seasoned, cooked manioc (*yuca*) are another popular type of *bolinho*. Cook 2 pounds of peeled manioc in salted water, drain, and pass through a ricer. Mix with 2 eggs, 1 tablespoon of butter, and chopped parsley, chives, salt, and pepper to taste. Shape into round or oblong croquettes, roll in bread crumbs, and fry in oil until golden.

1. Place the chicken stock in a heavy saucepan with 1 tablespoon of butter. Add flour, salt, and smoked paprika and cook over medium-low heat, stirring until mixture stiffens and pulls away from the sides of the pot, about 5 minutes. Remove from heat and let cool.

2. Divide the dough into 25 walnut-size balls. Cut mozzarella into 25 small cubes. Wrap each piece of dough around a cube of mozzarella and roll between the palms of your hands to make a smooth ball.

3. In a small bowl, whisk egg with water. In a shallow bowl, mix bread crumbs with Parmesan and oregano. Dip the croquettes into egg and then into bread crumbs to coat.

4. Heat the oil in a deep skillet or large heavy saucepan to 350°F. Fry the croquettes in the oil until golden brown. Drain on paper towels and serve warm.

CHAPTER 3

Salads (*Saladas*)

Hearts of Palm Salad (*Salada de Palmito*)

Hearts of palm show up frequently in Brazilian salads, which tend be artfully arranged on platters rather than tossed in a bowl.

INGREDIENTS | SERVES 6

1 medium shallot, peeled and finely minced

3 tablespoons fresh-squeezed lime juice, divided

1 tablespoon honey

1 teaspoon Dijon mustard

¼ teaspoon cumin

½ teaspoon salt, divided

¼ teaspoon ground black pepper

¼ cup olive oil

1 large head romaine lettuce, torn or chopped into bite-size pieces

1 (14-ounce) can hearts of palm, drained and sliced crosswise into ½" slices

2 medium ripe avocados, peeled and diced

1 cup diced fresh pineapple

½ cup chopped honey-roasted peanuts

1. In a small bowl, whisk the shallot together with 2 tablespoons lime juice, 1 tablespoon honey, mustard, cumin, ¼ teaspoon salt, and pepper. Gradually add the olive oil, whisking vigorously until dressing is well mixed. Set aside.

2. Place the lettuce on a serving platter. Arrange the hearts of palm on top of the lettuce.

3. Toss the avocado with remaining lime juice and salt. Place the avocado on top of the hearts of palm, along with the pineapple.

4. Just before serving, drizzle the dressing over the salad and scatter the peanuts on top.

Hearts of Palm

Hearts of palm are harvested from the stems of young palm trees. The inner core of the stem is the edible portion and is considered a delicacy. Stems of domesticated palm trees can be cut from the same tree from year to year, because cultivated palms produce more than one stem. Harvesting the stem of most wild palm varieties, however, kills the tree. One Brazilian species of wild palm is facing extinction for this reason.

Green Salad with Tomatoes (*Salada de Folhas Verdes*)

This healthy green salad, dressed with a simple vinaigrette, is often on the menus of Brazilian restaurants in one form or another.

INGREDIENTS | SERVES 4

5 cups assorted green lettuces or mesclun mix

1 cup small cherry tomatoes

1 cup sun-dried tomatoes or Oven-Dried Tomatoes (see sidebar)

1 cup cubed mozzarella cheese (or small balls)

½ cup sliced black or green olives

8 hard-cooked quail eggs, peeled and halved lengthwise

1 clove garlic, minced

3 tablespoons red wine vinegar or balsamic vinegar

½ teaspoon salt

½ teaspoon freshly ground black pepper

½ cup olive oil

1. Arrange lettuce on a platter.

2. Arrange the cherry tomatoes, dried tomatoes, mozzarella cheese, olives, and quail eggs on the lettuce.

3. In a small bowl, whisk together the garlic, vinegar, salt, and pepper. Add the olive oil gradually, whisking constantly until dressing is well mixed.

4. Drizzle some of the dressing over the salad, and serve the remaining dressing on the side.

Oven-Dried Tomatoes

Slice 10 ripe plum tomatoes in half lengthwise. Place the tomatoes cut side up on a baking sheet lined with parchment paper. Sprinkle with 1 teaspoon coarse salt, 1 teaspoon dried oregano, and ½ teaspoon black pepper. Bake at 200°F for 2–3 hours until dry and somewhat shriveled. Use tomatoes immediately, or place them in a jar with 1 or 2 peeled garlic cloves, cover with olive oil, and store in refrigerator for up to 2 weeks.

Brazilian-Style Potato Salad (*Maionese de Batata*)

One distinctive characteristic of Brazilian potato salad is the addition of lime juice, which seems like a small thing but is surprisingly different and good.

INGREDIENTS | SERVES 6

4 large potatoes, peeled and cut into ½" pieces

4 medium carrots, peeled and diced

½ cup frozen green peas

3 large hard-cooked eggs, peeled and diced

1 tablespoon fresh lime juice

3 tablespoons olive oil

1 teaspoon Dijon mustard

1 teaspoon Worcestershire sauce

1 tablespoon sugar

1 teaspoon salt

½ teaspoon freshly ground black pepper

¾ cup mayonnaise

¼ cup chopped fresh parsley

3 tablespoons minced fresh chives or green onions

1. Bring a pot of salted water to a boil and add the potatoes. Boil the potatoes for 5 minutes, then add the carrots. Boil for 10 minutes, or until potatoes and carrots are tender. Add the peas and boil for 2–3 minutes longer. Remove from heat, drain, and place in a large bowl. Gently stir in the eggs.

2. In a small bowl, whisk together the lime juice, olive oil, mustard, Worcestershire sauce, sugar, salt, and pepper. Whisk the mayonnaise into the olive oil mixture until smooth.

3. Add the mayonnaise mixture to the vegetables. Add the parsley and chives and toss everything together to mix well. Chill potato salad for 2–3 hours before serving.

Brazilian Chicken Salad (*Salpicão*)

The potato sticks add the perfect bit of crunch and saltiness.

INGREDIENTS | SERVES 6

8 ounces cooked boneless, skinless chicken breasts (roasted or poached)

½ cup cooked green peas

½ cup sliced black or green olives

1 apple, peeled, cored, and diced

½ cup diced pineapple, fresh or canned

⅓ cup chopped celery

¼ cup minced onion

2 medium carrots, peeled and grated

2 tablespoons fresh lime juice

1 cup mayonnaise

¼ teaspoon salt

½ teaspoon freshly ground black pepper

1½ cups potato sticks

2 tablespoons chopped fresh parsley

1. Finely shred the chicken and place in a large bowl.

2. Add the peas, olives, apple, pineapple, celery, onion, and carrots to the chicken.

3. In a small bowl, whisk the lime juice with the mayonnaise, and add to chicken. Toss everything well to mix. Season with salt and pepper.

4. Place salad in a serving bowl and chill in refrigerator for a half-hour or until ready to serve. Just before serving, garnish salad with potato sticks and parsley.

Warm Sweet Potato Salad (*Salada Quente de Batata Doce*)

This warm spiced salad is nice accompaniment for winter meals.

INGREDIENTS | SERVES 6

4 medium sweet potatoes

3 slices bacon

2 teaspoons cumin seed

1 teaspoon ground coriander

½ cup chopped walnuts

½ teaspoon salt

½ teaspoon freshly ground black pepper

½ cup crumbled goat cheese

1. Place the sweet potatoes in a large pot of salted water and bring to boil. Cook the potatoes until they are fork tender. Drain the potatoes and let them cool. Peel the potatoes and cut them into 1" cubes. Set aside.

2. Cook the bacon in a large skillet over medium-high heat until crispy. Remove bacon from skillet and drain on paper towels. Remove all but 1 tablespoon of bacon grease from the skillet. Add the cumin seed, coriander, and walnuts to the skillet and cook for 2–3 minutes.

3. Add the sweet potato, salt, and pepper and cook for 4–6 minutes, stirring, until potatoes start to brown.

4. Remove potatoes to a platter or bowl. Chop the bacon and sprinkle over warm potatoes along with the crumbled cheese. Serve warm.

Kale Salad with Mango (*Salada de Couve com Manga*)

Salads such as this one made with shredded kale are very common in Brazil.

INGREDIENTS | SERVES 6

1 bunch kale, stems removed and chopped into very thin ribbons

1 medium ripe mango, peeled, pitted, and chopped

1 medium red bell pepper, seeded and chopped

¼ cup minced red onion

3 tablespoons orange juice

1 tablespoon rice vinegar

1 tablespoon honey

1 teaspoon minced fresh ginger

½ teaspoon salt

½ teaspoon freshly ground black pepper

4 tablespoons olive oil

¼ cup toasted sunflower seeds or pumpkin seeds

1. Place kale in a large bowl. Add mango, bell pepper, and onion.

2. In a small bowl, whisk the orange juice, rice vinegar, honey, ginger, salt, and black pepper. Add the olive oil gradually and whisk to mix.

3. When ready to serve, toss the kale with the dressing and garnish with the seeds.

Fruit Salad with Passion Fruit Dressing
(*Salada de Fruta com Molho de Maracujá*)

Tropical fruits like pineapple, papaya, kiwi, and mango are delicious in this salad, but use whatever fruit you have available in your local market.

INGREDIENTS | SERVES 4

½ cup passion fruit pulp

2 tablespoons sugar

1 tablespoon vinegar

⅓ cup fresh or frozen raspberries

2 tablespoons papaya seeds (optional)

¼ teaspoon salt

1 tablespoon fresh lime juice

1 cup chopped fresh pineapple

1 cup diced mango

1 cup diced papaya

1 cup sliced banana

½ cup sliced kiwi

1. Place the passion fruit pulp in a small saucepan with the sugar. Bring to a gentle simmer over medium heat and cook, stirring, for 2–3 minutes or until sugar dissolves. Remove from heat and let cool.

2. Add the passion fruit mixture to a blender with vinegar, raspberries, papaya seeds (if using), salt, and lime juice. Blend until smooth. Use immediately or store in the refrigerator until ready to use.

3. Place the fruit in a large bowl. Toss with the dressing. Chill until ready to serve.

Lentil Salad (*Salada de Lentilha*)

Small cooked beans (especially white beans) make a great substitute for the lentils in this salad.

INGREDIENTS | SERVES 4

1 cup dried lentils

1 clove garlic, peeled and halved

3 cups vegetable stock

1 medium carrot, peeled and sliced into coins

12 small cherry tomatoes, halved

1 cup sliced hearts of palm or artichoke hearts

1 cup sliced green or black marinated olives

¼ cup olive oil

2 tablespoons red wine vinegar

1 teaspoon coarse salt

½ teaspoon freshly ground black pepper

1 tablespoon chopped fresh rosemary leaves

2 cups assorted lettuce leaves

1. Place the lentils, garlic, and stock in a medium saucepan. Simmer over low heat, covered, for about 25–30 minutes or until they are tender (but still firm and not mushy). Add the carrots for the last 5 minutes of cooking time.

2. Drain the lentils and carrots well and place them in a large bowl. Remove and discard the garlic. Add cherry tomatoes, hearts of palm, and olives to the lentils.

3. Drizzle the olive oil and vinegar over the lentils and vegetables. Sprinkle with salt, pepper, and rosemary and toss well to mix. Arrange lettuce on a platter and top with lentil mixture. Serve at room temperature.

Orange Vinaigrette (*Molho de Laranja*)

This tasty citrus dressing is excellent on leafy green salads.

INGREDIENTS | MAKES ¾ CUP

2 tablespoons olive oil

¼ cup minced red onion

2 tablespoons red wine

2 tablespoons strawberry jam

6 tablespoons freshly squeezed orange juice

1 tablespoon fresh lime juice

1 teaspoon orange zest

1 teaspoon Dijon mustard

½ teaspoon salt

1 teaspoon freshly ground black pepper

1. Heat oil in a small saucepan over low heat. Add onion and sauté until soft, about 5–8 minutes. Remove from heat and stir in wine, jam, orange juice, lime juice, orange zest, mustard, salt, and pepper.

2. Place mixture in a blender or food processor and blend until smooth.

3. Refrigerate dressing until ready to use, or up to 1 week.

Spicy Mango Dressing (*Molho Picante de Manga*)

This creamy mango dressing has a bit of a kick, and is delicious on both fruit and vegetable salads or as a marinade for chicken or fish.

INGREDIENTS | MAKES 1 CUP

1 cup low-fat plain yogurt

1 medium ripe mango, peeled and chopped, or ½ cup mango purée

1 tablespoon honey

1 tablespoon rice wine vinegar

½ teaspoon salt

½ teaspoon red pepper flakes

2 scallions, trimmed

Place all of the ingredients in a blender or food processor. Blend until smooth. Store dressing in the refrigerator until ready to use, or up to 3 days.

Marinated Eggplant Salad (*Salada de Berinjela*)

This salad is very similar to Italian caponata salad, but with some Brazilian touches.

INGREDIENTS | SERVES 6

2 medium eggplants, trimmed and cut into 1" cubes

4 medium shallots or 1 medium onion, peeled and thinly sliced

1 medium green bell pepper, seeded and chopped into 1"pieces

1 medium red bell pepper, seeded and chopped into 1" pieces

½ cup olive oil, divided

1 teaspoon kosher salt

1 teaspoon freshly ground black pepper

1 cup coarsely chopped fresh basil leaves, divided

¼ cup raisins

½ cup diced oven-dried or sun-dried tomatoes

½ cup sliced black olives

1 teaspoon dried oregano

2 tablespoons red wine vinegar

1. Preheat oven to 400°F.

2. Toss eggplant, onion, and bell peppers with 2 tablespoons olive oil, salt, black pepper, and half the basil. Spread vegetables in a single layer on a baking sheet (use two baking sheets if needed). Roast the vegetables for 20–30 minutes, or until they begin to brown and caramelize on the edges. Remove from oven and let cool on baking sheets for 5 minutes.

3. Add the roasted vegetables to a large bowl. Add the raisins, tomatoes, olives, oregano, vinegar, and remaining olive oil. Toss everything well to mix and refrigerate salad overnight.

4. Bring salad to room temperature and toss with the remaining basil just before serving.

Black-Eyed Pea Salad (*Salada de Feijão-Fradinho*)

This fresh and nutritious salad is quick to prepare with frozen black-eyed peas (though Brazilians would probably cook the dried beans in a pressure cooker), and is a great at a barbecue.

INGREDIENTS | SERVES 6

1 medium red onion, peeled

1 (16-ounce) package frozen black-eyed peas or (15-ounce) can black-eyed peas

½ cup plus 2 tablespoons apple juice, divided

1 teaspoon salt

1 cup halved cherry tomatoes

½ cup chopped celery

1 tablespoon minced fresh cilantro

1 tablespoon minced fresh parsley

2 scallions, trimmed and chopped

1 teaspoon minced jalapeño pepper

6 tablespoons olive oil

2 tablespoons mustard

2 tablespoons apple cider vinegar

1 large hard-cooked egg, peeled and sliced, for garnish

1. Cut the onion in half. Dice one half and place it in a medium saucepan. Reserve other half.

2. Add the frozen black-eyed peas to the saucepan, along with ½ cup apple juice. Add enough water to cover the beans by 1 inch. Simmer over medium low heat until just tender, about 45 minutes. Drain beans and place in a large bowl. (If using canned black-eyed peas, omit the cooking step. Just drain and rinse the beans and place in a bowl.) Toss beans with the salt.

3. Slice the reserved onion crosswise into thin curved strips. Add to black-eyed peas, along with tomatoes, celery, cilantro, parsley, scallions, and jalapeño. Toss to mix.

4. In a small bowl, whisk together olive oil, mustard, vinegar, and 2 tablespoons of apple juice. Pour dressing over salad and mix well. Chill for 1 hour or until ready to serve. Toss salad and garnish with slices of egg just before serving.

Cooking Dried Black-Eyed Peas

Cooking dried beans is easy and economical. South American cooks do not typically presoak the beans overnight. Place ½ pound of beans in a large pot and cover with 2 inches of water or vegetable stock. Add a couple of cloves of garlic, ½ medium onion sliced, a bay leaf, and a piece of smoked ham or ham hock. Cook the beans at a gentle simmer for 2–3 hours (adding more water or stock if needed) or until beans are tender. Season with salt to taste. Drain beans before using in salad recipe.

Toasted Manioc Salad (*Salada de Farofa*)

This salad is similar to Italian-style bread salads, and the manioc meal soaks up the flavor of the vegetables and the dressing. If you can't find manioc meal, substitute very small croutons or coarsely ground and toasted bread crumbs.

INGREDIENTS | SERVES 6

2 cloves garlic, minced, divided

½ cup olive oil, divided

3 cups manioc meal (*farinha de mandioca torrada*)

1½ teaspoons kosher salt, divided

1 medium yellow bell pepper, seeded and cut into 1" pieces

2 medium ripe tomatoes, cut into 1" chunks

1 medium red onion, peeled and thinly sliced

½ cup sliced black olives

3 tablespoons capers

1 teaspoon Dijon mustard

3 tablespoons balsamic vinegar

½ teaspoon salt

½ teaspoon freshly ground pepper

½ cup coarsely chopped fresh basil leaves

1 large hard-cooked egg, peeled and sliced, for garnish

1. Place half the garlic in a medium skillet with 3 tablespoons olive oil. Cook garlic over medium-low heat until fragrant, about 2 minutes. Add manioc meal and 1 teaspoon salt to the skillet and cook for 2–3 minutes, stirring constantly. Remove from heat and place in a large bowl.

2. Add bell pepper, tomatoes, and onion (reserving a few slices for garnish) to the bowl with the manioc meal. Add olives (reserving a few for garnish) and capers and toss to mix.

3. In a small bowl, whisk the remaining minced garlic with mustard, vinegar, salt, and pepper. Slowly whisk in the remaining olive oil until well mixed. Pour dressing over salad and mix well. Add the basil leaves and toss to mix.

4. Garnish the salad with slices of egg and the reserved onion slices and olives.

Manioc Meal

When shopping for manioc meal for this salad or for *farofa* (the most common dish made with manioc meal), look for the yellowish coarsely ground meal that is labeled "*farinha de mandioca torrada*." In Brazil there are varying degrees of coarseness available, even manioc "flakes" that resemble corn flakes. Another common staple is manioc starch (*polvilho de mandioca*), which is very finely ground like cornstarch and would not be suitable for this salad.

Chayote Salad with Oranges and Avocado
(*Salada de Chuchu*)

Chayote squash grows all over Brazil, where it is called chuchu (pronounced shoo-shoo).
Brazilians typically cook the squash even for salads.

INGREDIENTS | SERVES 6

1 small head butter lettuce, torn into bite-size pieces

3 chayote squash, peeled, sliced, and seeded

2 cups orange juice

2 tablespoons fresh lime juice

4 tablespoons olive oil

1 teaspoon salt

1 teaspoon freshly ground black pepper

2 oranges, peeled and cut into segments

2 avocados, peeled and sliced

¼ cup chopped scallions

2 tablespoons chopped fresh parsley

¼ cup finely chopped green olives (optional)

1. Place lettuce in a serving bowl and set aside.

2. Place the chayote slices in a large saucepan with the orange juice and bring to a simmer. Cook until just tender, but not mushy, about 8–10 minutes. Drain and place in a large bowl to cool.

3. In a small bowl, whisk together the lime juice, olive oil, salt, and pepper.

4. Add the oranges, avocados, scallions, and parsley to the bowl with the squash. Add the dressing and toss gently to mix.

5. Arrange salad on top of the lettuce in the serving bowl. Sprinkle with chopped olives, if using. Chill until ready to serve.

Tropical Cobb Salad (*Salada Tropical*)

The name "tropical salad" is used to describe an assortment of different salads, including this chopped salad. A creamy yogurt dressing ties everything together.

INGREDIENTS | SERVES 6

2 cups chopped red lettuce leaves

2 cups chopped green lettuce leaves

1 cup chopped red cabbage

1 cup chopped hearts of palm

1 mango, peeled, cored, and diced

1 apple, peeled, cored, and diced

1 cup diced fresh pineapple

⅓ cup raisins

6 ounces sliced deli-style turkey, chopped into ½" pieces

1 cup cubed farmers cheese or mozzarella

½ cup low-fat plain yogurt

¼ cup mayonnaise

2 tablespoons fresh lime juice

1 tablespoon honey

1 teaspoon mustard

½ teaspoon salt

½ teaspoon freshly ground black pepper

1 cup croutons

⅓ cup grated Parmesan cheese

2 tablespoons fresh parsley leaves

1. Arrange lettuces, cabbage, and hearts of palm in a shallow bowl or platter.

2. In a medium bowl, combine mango, apple, pineapple, raisins, turkey, and cheese. Chill until ready to serve.

3. In a small bowl, whisk together the yogurt, mayonnaise, lime juice, honey, mustard, salt, and pepper. Chill until ready to serve.

4. Just before serving, add the croutons and the Parmesan to the fruit mixture. Toss mixture with half of the dressing and place on top of the lettuce. Garnish salad with parsley leaves and serve remaining dressing on the side.

CHAPTER 4

Soups and Stews
(*Sopas e Ensopados*)

Black Bean Stew with Smoked Meats (*Feijoada Completa*)

Feijoada is Brazil's most famous dish. It's an elaborate meal that's meant to be leisurely shared with friends and family. Authentic feijoada takes two days to prepare, and is traditionally served on a weekend afternoon at home.

INGREDIENTS | SERVES 10

20 ounces dried black beans

1 pound *carne seca* (or plain beef jerky), chopped into small pieces

1 ham hock

4 cloves garlic, divided

6 cups beef or chicken stock

3 tablespoons olive oil

½ pound *chouriço* or chorizo sausage

½ pound smoked sausage (*linguiça* or similar), cut into ½" slices

1 pound pork shoulder, cut into 1" pieces

1 large onion, peeled and thinly sliced

½ cup chopped fresh parsley

2 teaspoons cumin

1 teaspoon salt

1 teaspoon freshly ground black pepper

Accompaniments

Feijoada is always served with certain traditional side dishes. Rice is essential, of course, as well as sautéed kale or collard greens (*couve a mineira*). Toasted manioc meal (*farofa*) should be available as a condiment for the *feijoada*, along with hot-pepper sauce (*molho de pimento*). Fresh orange segments are served on the side as a refreshing contrast to the heavy stew.

1. Place the beans and *carne seca* in a large bowl. Cover with cold water and soak overnight.

2. Drain the beans and beef and place them in a large stew pot. Add the ham hock, 1 clove of peeled garlic, and the stock. Add enough water to the liquid to cover the beans by 2 inches if necessary. Bring to a boil, then cover and simmer over low heat for 2 hours, or until beans are tender. Remove ham hock.

3. Heat the olive oil in a large skillet over medium heat. Remove *chouriço* from casings and crumble it into the skillet. Cook sausage until well browned, about 5 minutes then add it to the beans.

4. Sauté the *linguiça* and the pork shoulder in the same skillet that was used to cook the *chouriço* until browned, about 5 minutes. Add to the beans. Simmer beans over low heat for another hour or so, or until pork shoulder is very tender, adding more water or stock as needed.

5. Peel and mince the remaining 3 garlic cloves. Add to the skillet with onion, parsley, and cumin. Cook over medium heat until onions are soft and translucent, about 5–8 minutes.

6. Spoon several ladlefuls of the beans into the skillet with the onions and garlic. Mash the beans with a potato masher and mix everything together well. Add beans and onion mixture to the large pot of beans and mix well. Simmer for 5 minutes more. Season with salt and pepper to taste and serve.

Potato and Kale Soup with Sausage (*Caldo Verde*)

Caldo verde *is nourishing and quick to prepare. The sausage is optional—leave it out to make a vegetarian version. Serve this soup with corn bread on the side.*

INGREDIENTS | SERVES 6

3 tablespoons olive oil

2 *linguiça* sausages, sliced crosswise into ½" disks

1 medium onion, peeled and chopped

2 cloves garlic, minced

4 medium white potatoes, peeled and cut into 1" cubes

4 cups vegetable or chicken stock

¼ cup chopped fresh parsley

1 teaspoon salt

1 teaspoon freshly ground black pepper

1 bunch kale, stems removed and cut into thin ribbons

About Brazilian Sausages

Linguiça is a Portuguese smoked sausage that is seasoned with garlic and paprika. Brazilians enjoy several kinds of *linguiça*, including a spicier, Italian-style version called *linguiça calabresa*. *Linguiça calabresa* is similar to pepperoni and is enjoyed on pizza. Any smoked sausage that is not overly spicy will work well for this soup.

1. Heat the olive oil in a stockpot over medium heat. Add the sausage and sauté in the oil until lightly browned, about 5 minutes. Remove sausage from skillet and set aside.

2. Add the onion and garlic to the pot and cook until onion is fragrant and translucent, about 5–8 minutes.

3. Add the potatoes to the pot and sauté for 2–3 minutes. Add the stock and bring to a simmer. Cover and cook until potatoes are tender, about 10–15 minutes.

4. With a slotted spoon, remove potatoes and pass them through a potato ricer. Add them back to the soup along with the parsley and the sausage. Simmer for 5 minutes. Season with salt and pepper to taste. Soup can be made ahead to this point and reheated when ready to serve.

5. Add the kale to the soup and simmer for 3–5 minutes just before serving.

Creamy Hearts of Palm Soup (*Creme de Palmito*)

This classic and delicious Brazilian soup is sure to be a crowd pleaser.

INGREDIENTS | SERVES 6

2 tablespoons butter

2 cloves garlic, minced

1 small onion, peeled and chopped

1 (15-ounce) can hearts of palm, drained, rinsed, and cut into ½" disks

2 tablespoons cornstarch

½ teaspoon salt

½ teaspoon freshly ground black pepper

2 cups chicken or vegetable stock

1½ cups heavy cream

¼ cup shredded mozzarella cheese

¼ cup grated Parmesan cheese

2 scallions, chopped

1. Melt the butter in a large saucepan over medium-low heat and add the garlic and onion. Cook until onion is soft and translucent, about 5–8 minutes. Add the hearts of palm and cook for 2–3 minutes more. Add the cornstarch, salt, and pepper and cook, stirring, for 1–2 minutes.

2. Add the stock to the vegetables and bring to a simmer, stirring constantly. Simmer for 5–8 minutes, or until soup starts to thicken.

3. Remove from heat and stir in cream and both cheeses. Stir until smooth. Serve warm, garnished with the scallions.

Brazilian Beef Stew (*Picadinho de Carne*)

Picadinho is a rich stew made with diced beef (carne picada) and seasoned with tomatoes. Serve this stew with white rice, farofa (toasted manioc meal), and Fried Bananas (Bananas à Milanesa; see recipe in Chapter 7).

INGREDIENTS | SERVES 6

2 pounds beef rump roast or stewing beef, cut into ½" pieces

1 teaspoon salt

1 teaspoon freshly ground black pepper

2 tablespoons olive oil

1 small onion, peeled and finely chopped

2 cloves garlic, minced

2 tomatoes, seeded and diced

¼ cup chopped fresh parsley

1 tablespoon soy sauce

1 teaspoon Worcestershire sauce

1 tablespoon tomato paste

4 cups beef stock

1. Season beef with salt and pepper.

2. Heat the oil in a stockpot over medium-high heat. Add the beef and sauté until browned on all sides, about 3–5 minutes. Remove beef with a slotted spoon and set aside.

3. Add the onion and garlic to the pot and cook until onion is translucent and starting to brown, about 5–8 minutes. Add the tomatoes and cook until they are soft, about 3–5 minutes.

4. Add the parsley, soy sauce, Worcestershire sauce, tomato paste, and stock and bring mixture to a boil. Add the beef, reduce heat to low, and simmer until the beef is very tender, about 1 hour, adding more stock or water if needed.

Creamy Shrimp Soup (*Caldo de Camarão*)

This rich and creamy soup is bursting with shrimp flavor. It's delicious as a first course but substantial enough to enjoy as a meal.

INGREDIENTS | SERVES 6

1 pound medium shrimp, peeled and cleaned

4 tablespoons fresh lime juice

1 clove garlic, minced

¼ cup minced fresh cilantro, divided

1 teaspoon salt

2 tablespoons butter

1 medium tomato, diced

¼ cup fresh parsley

2 tablespoons all-purpose flour

3 cups water or seafood stock

1 cup heavy cream

½ cup sour cream

How to Clean Shrimp

Cut or pull the head and the legs off the shrimp. Starting at the head end, peel the shell off of the shrimp, including the tail (for some dishes the tail can be left on for decorative purposes). To devein the shrimp, use a sharp knife to cut about ¼" deep along the top back of the shrimp. Scrape out the exposed vein with the tip of the knife and discard.

1. Place shrimp in a large bowl with lime juice, garlic, ⅛ cup cilantro, and salt. Toss to mix well, cover, and marinate in the refrigerator for 30 minutes to 1 hour.

2. Heat butter in a medium soup pot over medium heat. Add the shrimp and marinade and sauté for several minutes, until the shrimp just turn pink. Remove shrimp and set aside.

3. Add the tomato and the parsley to the pot and cook over medium heat until softened, about 3 minutes. Once the tomato is soft, add 2 tablespoons flour and cook for 1 minute, stirring.

4. Add the stock, increase heat to high, and bring to a boil. Reduce heat to medium-low and simmer soup, stirring frequently, until it thickens slightly, about 10 minutes. Remove from heat and whisk in the cream and the sour cream.

5. Add a few shrimp to each serving bowl, and ladle the soup over the shrimp. Garnish with remaining cilantro.

Beef Stew in a Clay Pot (*Barreado*)

If you are going to serve this stew for a weekend lunch, start it the night before because it needs to cook for 8–9 hours. Serve this stew hot over manioc meal, with white rice and fresh banana slices on the side.

INGREDIENTS | SERVES 10

4 pounds stewing beef, cut into 2" pieces
2 teaspoons kosher salt
2 teaspoons ground black pepper
4 cloves garlic, minced, divided
2 teaspoons cumin
6 ounces bacon, cut into cubes
2 tablespoons olive oil
2 large onions, peeled and finely chopped
2 medium tomatoes, peeled and diced
1 cup chopped fresh parsley, divided
½ cup chopped scallions
2 teaspoons dried oregano
1 bay leaf
8 cups beef stock
5 cups manioc flour or all-purpose flour
Boiling water

1. Place beef in a large bowl with salt, pepper, half the garlic, and cumin. Cover and marinate for 30 minutes in the refrigerator.

2. Add the bacon to a large clay pot or heavy stockpot (with a well-fitting lid) and heat the pot gradually, slowly bringing the heat up to medium-high. Cook the bacon until crisp. Remove the bacon and reserve.

3. Add the beef and marinade to the pot and brown on all sides (cooking in batches if necessary), about 5 minutes per side. Remove beef to the plate with the bacon and set aside.

4. Add olive oil and onion to the pot. Lower heat to medium and cook until onion is soft and translucent, about 5 minutes. Add the remaining garlic and cook for 1 minute more. Add the tomatoes, ½ cup parsley, scallions, and oregano and cook until tomatoes are soft, about 10 minutes.

5. Add the beef and bacon back to the pot, along with the bay leaf and stock. Reduce heat to low.

6. Place 2½ cups of the flour in a large heatproof bowl. Add boiling water gradually to the flour, and stir/knead until the flour comes together into soft dough. Roll the dough into a rope and fit it along the top edge of the pot. Place the top on the pot, and press the rope of dough around the edge of the pot lid to completely cover the seal where the lid meets the pot.

7. Cook over very low heat for 4–5 hours. Break the seal and check the level of the liquid, which should be about an inch over the meat. Add liquid if needed. Reseal the lid with more dough. Cook for 4 hours more over very low heat. (If cooking overnight, leave the pot to cool after the first 4–5 hours of cooking, still sealed. Open it in the morning to check liquid level, adding more if needed, then cook for remaining 4 hours.)

8. Remove lid and check stew. Simmer uncovered for 20–30 minutes to thicken sauce slightly if desired. Just before serving, stir in the remaining parsley and season to taste.

Black Bean Soup (*Caldinho de Feijão Preto*)

The traditional method for this soup is to soak the dried beans overnight, and then cook them in a pressure cooker. This recipe is a quick version with canned beans.

INGREDIENTS | SERVES 6

2 tablespoons olive oil

4 pieces smoked bacon, diced

2 smoked sausages, diced

4 cloves garlic, minced

1 medium yellow onion, peeled and minced

1 teaspoon cumin

1 teaspoon smoked paprika

2 (15-ounce) cans black beans, drained and rinsed

4 cups chicken stock

¾ teaspoon salt

¼ teaspoon red pepper flakes

1 small tomato, diced

4 scallions, chopped

Torresmos

Torresmos are fried pieces of pork rind—also known as cracklings. Pork skin is cooked to render the lard, producing crispy leftovers that are a popular bar snack in Brazil. *Torresmos* are customarily served with certain dishes, such *feijão tropeiro* and this black bean soup.

1. Heat olive oil in a large soup pot over medium heat. Add bacon and sausage and cook until bacon is crispy and sausage is browned, about 5–8 minutes. Remove bacon and sausage from the pot and drain on paper towels.

2. Add garlic, onion, cumin, and smoked paprika to the pot. Reduce heat to medium-low and sauté until the garlic and onions are soft and fragrant, about 5 minutes.

3. Add beans and stock and increase heat to medium-high. Bring to a boil, then reduce heat to medium-low. Simmer for 15 minutes. Season with salt and red pepper flakes.

4. Transfer bean mixture to a blender or food processor and purée until smooth (work in batches if necessary). Return the beans to the soup pot. Add more chicken stock or water if soup seems too thick.

5. Stir the bacon and sausage into the soup. Serve soup garnished with tomato and scallions.

Chicken and Rice Stew (*Galinhada Mineira*)

Galinhada is the Brazilian version of arroz con pollo. This is a delicious one-skillet meal that will satisfy a hungry crowd.

INGREDIENTS | SERVES 8

8 chicken thighs
2 tablespoons fresh lime juice
2 teaspoons kosher salt
1 teaspoon freshly ground black pepper
2 cloves garlic, minced
3 tablespoons olive oil
1 medium onion, peeled and diced
1 medium green bell pepper, seeded and diced
2 tablespoons tomato paste
1 teaspoon cumin
4 cups chicken stock
1 bay leaf
2 cups uncooked white rice
1 cup frozen peas and/or corn
½ cup chopped fresh parsley

Chicken Parts

Many Brazilians use a whole chicken, cut into pieces, when making this dish. If you prefer both white meat and dark meat, use the whole chicken or substitute the pieces that you like best. Boneless, skinless chicken breasts are less flavorful and can become tough if overcooked. If you prefer to use boneless chicken breasts, brown them lightly in the skillet, simmer them in the broth until just cooked through, remove them from the skillet, and add them back in just before serving.

1. Place the chicken thighs in a large bowl. Add lime juice, salt, pepper, and garlic and toss to mix. Cover and marinate for 30 minutes to 1 hour in the refrigerator.

2. Heat the olive oil in a large, deep skillet over low heat. Add the chicken thighs, turn the heat up to medium, and brown them on all sides, 3–4 minutes per side. Add onion, green pepper, tomato paste, and cumin and sauté the vegetables with the chicken until the vegetables are soft and fragrant, about 5–8 minutes.

3. Add the stock, bay leaf, and enough water to mostly cover the chicken. Reduce heat to medium-low and simmer for 20–30 minutes. Stir in the rice, cover, and cook for 10 minutes. Add the peas and/or corn and cook for 5 minutes longer, adding more water or chicken stock if needed.

4. Remove the bay leaf and stir in the parsley just before serving.

Coconut Butternut Squash Soup (*Sopa de Abóbora e Coco*)

You might not think that butternut squash would pair well with the tropical flavor of coconut, but the combination most certainly succeeds in this aromatic soup.

INGREDIENTS | SERVES 6

2 tablespoons olive oil

1 medium onion, peeled and diced

1 medium butternut squash, peeled and cut into 1" cubes

1 large sweet potato, peeled and cut into 1" cubes

1 teaspoon cumin

1 tablespoon brown sugar

1 teaspoon salt

¼ teaspoon red pepper flakes

4 cups vegetable or chicken stock

1 (13.5-ounce) can coconut milk

2 tablespoons fresh lime juice

1 small bunch kale, stems removed and cut into thin ribbons

Save the Seeds

The seeds from the butternut squash can be toasted, and have a delicious nutty flavor that is similar to larger pumpkin seeds. Rinse the seeds, removing any squash fibers, and pat them dry with paper towels. Toast the seeds in a skillet over low heat with 1 tablespoon butter and ½ teaspoon salt until browned and crisp. Use the toasted seeds to garnish the soup.

1. Heat the oil in a large soup pot over medium heat. Add the onion to the pot and cook until translucent, about 5–8 minutes. Add squash, sweet potato, cumin, brown sugar, salt, and red pepper flakes. Cook, stirring, until the squash starts to brown around the edges, about 10 minutes.

2. Add the stock, increase heat to high, and bring to a boil. Reduce heat to low, cover, and simmer until squash and sweet potatoes are tender, about 8–10 minutes.

3. Use a slotted spoon to remove the vegetables and place them in a blender. Add coconut milk and lime juice to the blender and process until mixture is smooth. Whisk the squash/coconut milk mixture back into the soup.

4. Add kale and simmer soup for 3–5 minutes more, then serve immediately.

Cream of Manioc Soup (*Creme de Mandioquinha*)

This creamy soup gets its unique flavor from manioc root. Look for frozen manioc (also known as yuca and cassava) in Latin grocery stores, which is conveniently peeled and ready to use.

INGREDIENTS | SERVES 6

2 tablespoons butter

1 small onion, peeled and diced

3 medium leeks (white and light green parts only), finely chopped

1 pound manioc root, peeled, cored, and cut into 2" pieces

4 cups vegetable stock

1 cup heavy cream

¼ cup grated Parmesan cheese

1 teaspoon salt

1 teaspoon freshly ground black pepper

1. Heat butter in a medium saucepan over medium-high heat. Sauté onion and leeks until tender, about 5 minutes. Add the manioc and stock. Bring to a boil, reduce heat to medium-low, cover, and simmer until manioc is tender, about 30 minutes.

2. Place the cooked manioc and half of the cooking liquid into a blender and blend until smooth.

3. Add puréed manioc back to the stew. Whisk in the cream, the Parmesan, and more stock if soup is too thick. Season with salt and pepper and serve warm.

Peeling Fresh Manioc

Cut the roots into 4" lengths. Remove the brown peel by trimming it off with a sharp knife. Cut each piece of manioc into quarters vertically, and remove the fibrous inner core. Do not eat the manioc when raw.

Cream of Corn Soup (*Creme de Milho Verde*)

This soup is super easy and fast to make, and delicious. Use fresh corn for best results.

INGREDIENTS | SERVES 4

3 ears sweet corn (or 2 cups frozen corn kernels, thawed), divided

2 cups milk

1 cup vegetable stock

2 tablespoons butter

½ cup diced onion

2 tablespoons cornstarch

⅓ cup grated Monterey jack cheese

1 teaspoon salt

1 teaspoon freshly ground black pepper

1. Place all but ¼ cup of the corn kernels, milk, and stock in a blender and process until smooth.

2. Heat the butter in a large saucepan over medium heat and sauté the onion until soft, about 5–8 minutes. Stir in the cornstarch and cook for 1 minute. Add the corn/milk mixture and cook, stirring, until soup thickens and turns creamy.

3. Add the cheese, salt, and pepper and stir over low heat until cheese is melted. Serve soup garnished with the reserved corn kernels.

Brazil Nut Soup (*Sopa de Castanha*)

A soup made from nuts may sound unusual, but Brazil nuts are exceptionally creamy in texture and they thicken and flavor this soup perfectly.

INGREDIENTS | SERVES 6

1½ cups (about 12 ounces) shelled Brazil nuts

2 tablespoons butter

1 medium onion, peeled and diced

1 leek (white and light green parts only), diced

2 stalks celery, diced

1 medium carrot, peeled and diced

1 teaspoon salt

½ teaspoon freshly ground black pepper

4 cups chicken stock

¼ cup chopped fresh parsley leaves

½ cup heavy cream

Brazil Nut Ecology

Brazil nuts grow on large, old-growth trees in the Amazon. These trees can live to be 500 years old, and their pollination (and nut production) depends on the presence of a particular species of orchid that attracts a particular bee. Brazil nuts can be harvested each year without damaging the trees and are one of the Amazon's potential sustainable resources, but the nut production requires a delicate environmental balance that is recently threatened by deforestation.

1. Preheat oven to 350°F. Place the nuts on a baking sheet and roast them for 10–15 minutes. Let cool, then rub off the skins.

2. Melt butter in a large soup pot over medium heat. Add onion, leek, celery, carrot, salt, and pepper and cook until the vegetables are soft, about 5–8 minutes. Add stock to the vegetables and bring to a simmer.

3. Place the nuts in a food processor or blender and process them until they are finely chopped. Add 1–2 cups of the vegetable mixture and process until smooth. Return nut/vegetable mixture to the pot and add the parsley.

4. Reduce heat to low and simmer soup for 10–15 minutes more. Whisk in the cream and remove from heat. Serve immediately.

Pork and Hominy Stew (*Canjiquinha Mineira*)

This nourishing stew has a unique ingredient called canjiquinha, *which is ground white hominy corn. You can find ground hominy corn in Latin food markets—it's often labeled "Mote" or "Maíz Blanco Trillado" (when ground) in Spanish.*

INGREDIENTS | SERVES 6

1 pound coarsely ground dried hominy corn

1 pound pork loin, cut into 1" cubes

4 cloves garlic, minced, divided

2 tablespoons minced fresh parsley

1½ teaspoons kosher salt

1 teaspoon freshly ground black pepper

4 cups beef or chicken stock

3 slices bacon

8 ounces smoked sausage, diced

1 medium onion, peeled and diced

1 small bunch kale, stems removed and chopped

Hominy Corn

Hominy corn is consumed throughout Latin America, and is especially important in Mexican cuisine. Hominy corn has been treated with a chemical process called nixtamalization, in which the corn is soaked in an alkaline solution to remove the hulls. This is done on an industrial scale today, but indigenous people used lime and ash to nixtamalize corn for hundreds of years. Nixtamalized corn is more nutritious and has a unique flavor that is especially appreciated in tortillas and tamales.

1. Place hominy corn in a large bowl and cover with water. Cover and leave to soak overnight.

2. Place the pork in a medium bowl with the half the garlic, parsley, salt, and pepper. Cover bowl and marinate overnight in the refrigerator.

3. Drain the corn and place in a large saucepan or soup pot. Add the stock and enough water to cover the corn with 1½" of liquid. Bring liquid to a boil over medium-high heat. Reduce heat to low, cover, and simmer for 40–60 minutes, or until corn is soft.

4. Add the bacon to a deep skillet and cook over medium heat until crispy. Remove bacon, crumble, and reserve. Sauté the pork, the diced sausage, and the onions in the bacon fat until the pork is well browned and cooked through, about 5–8 minutes. Add pork mixture to the corn.

5. Just before serving, sauté the kale in the same skillet with the remaining garlic and the crumbled bacon for 2–3 minutes over medium heat.

6. Add kale mixture to the corn and pork stew, or serve on the side.

Leão Veloso Seafood Stew (*Sopa Leão Veloso*)

This is a famous dish in Rio de Janeiro, named after a Brazilian diplomat (Paulo Leão Veloso) who became a fan of bouillabaisse while living in France.

INGREDIENTS | SERVES 8

1 pound firm white fish fillets

1½ teaspoons salt, divided

1 teaspoon freshly ground black pepper, divided

4 tablespoons olive oil, divided

1 medium onion, peeled and chopped

2 cloves garlic, minced

2 tomatoes, peeled and diced

1 small red chili pepper, seeded and minced

½ cup chopped fresh parsley, divided

½ cup chopped scallions

1 teaspoon ground coriander

1 pound mussels in shells, washed

1 cup white wine

6 cups seafood stock

1 pound small-medium shrimp

1 cup lobster meat

1 cup crabmeat

Small square toast croutons, for garnish

1. Sprinkle the fish fillets with ½ teaspoon salt and ½ teaspoon black pepper. Heat 2 tablespoons olive oil in a large stockpot over medium heat. Sauté the fish in the oil until lightly browned on both sides and cooked through, about 5 minutes per side. Remove fish from pot and set aside to cool.

2. Add the remaining 2 tablespoons of olive oil and the onion to the pot. Cook over medium heat until onion is soft, about 5 minutes. Add the garlic and cook for 1 minute. Add the tomatoes, chili pepper, ¼ cup parsley, scallions, coriander, and remaining salt and black pepper. Cook until tomatoes are soft, about 5 minutes.

3. Add the mussels and white wine to the pot. Cover and cook for 6–8 minutes, or until mussels open. Remove mussels from the pot and set aside. When cool enough to handle, remove mussels from shells. Set mussels aside and discard shells.

4. Add stock to the pot, increase heat to high, and bring to a boil. Reduce heat to low, add the shrimp, and cook until they just turn pink. Remove shrimp with a slotted spoon and set aside. Peel the shrimp once they are cool enough to handle.

5. Add the lobster to the pot and simmer for 5 minutes. Shred the sautéed fish and add it to the pot along with the crabmeat. Simmer for 5 minutes more.

6. Add the mussels, shrimp, and remaining parsley and simmer until heated through. Serve hot, with croutons.

Oxtail Stew (*Rabada*)

This European-style hearty oxtail stew is a favorite in Brazil, especially in the state of Minas Gerais.

INGREDIENTS | SERVES 8

4 pounds oxtail, cut into chunks

2 teaspoons kosher salt

2 teaspoons ground black pepper

6 tablespoons olive oil, divided

1 large onion, peeled and chopped

4 cloves garlic, minced

2 tablespoons tomato paste

2 large tomatoes, peeled and diced

2 medium carrots, peeled and cut into ½" pieces

½ cup chopped fresh cilantro

1 teaspoon cumin

1 tablespoon smoked paprika

1 bay leaf

6 cups beef stock

1 cup watercress leaves

½ cup chopped scallions

Accompaniments

Serve this stew with *angu* (polenta) or white rice and *farofa* (toasted manioc crumbs). Some people add potatoes or manioc to the stew during the last bit of cooking. Another option is to serve the stew with cooked potatoes that are seasoned with butter and salt, and tossed with chopped watercress.

1. Soak the oxtail in salted cold water for 30 minutes, then rinse well. Remove any excess fat. Season the meat with salt and pepper.

2. Add 4 tablespoons olive oil to a heavy stockpot over high heat. Add the oxtail and sauté until well browned on all sides, about 5 minutes (work in batches if necessary). Remove from pot and set aside on a plate.

3. Add the remaining olive oil to the stockpot. Lower heat to medium and sauté onion until soft and translucent, about 5 minutes. Add the garlic and cook for 1 minute more. Add the tomato paste, tomatoes, carrots, cilantro, cumin, and paprika and reduce heat to low. Simmer until all of the liquid has evaporated, about 5–8 minutes.

4. Increase heat to high and add the oxtail back to the pot, along with bay leaf and stock. Bring to a boil and then reduce heat to low. Cover and simmer until meat is very tender, about 2½ hours. Uncover and simmer stew until it thickens to desired consistency, about 20 minutes.

5. Stir in the watercress and scallions just before serving. Serve warm.

Simple Chicken Soup (*Canja de Galinha*)

Brazilians eat this nourishing soup to cure colds and other ailments. It's a basic chicken and vegetable soup, thickened with rice. Serve with thick slices of Portuguese-Style Corn Bread (Broa)—see recipe in Chapter 10.

INGREDIENTS | SERVES 6

2 tablespoons olive oil

2 stalks celery, diced

1 medium onion, peeled and diced

2 medium carrots, peeled and diced

2 cloves garlic, minced

2 tablespoons chopped fresh parsley

½ pound boneless, skinless chicken breasts

½ teaspoon salt

½ teaspoon freshly ground black pepper

4 cups chicken stock

½ cup uncooked white rice

Galinhas and Galos

Technically the name of this soup in Portuguese means "hen soup." People used to distinguish between hens (*galinhas*) and roosters (*galos*) when writing recipes. Roosters were thought to have tough but flavorful meat, excellent for stewing. The meat from mature hens and roosters has more muscle and cartilage than modern commercially raised chickens (which are butchered at a very young age) and must be cooked slowly at low temperatures. However, the results are said to be far superior in flavor.

1. Heat the oil in a medium soup pot over medium-high heat. Add the celery, onion, carrots, garlic, and parsley and sauté until the vegetables are soft and fragrant, about 5 minutes.

2. Season the chicken breasts with the salt and pepper and add them to the pot. Sauté for about 6 minutes on each side until lightly browned.

3. Add the chicken stock and bring just to a simmer. Cover the pot, reduce heat to low, and simmer for about 12–15 minutes, or until chicken is tender. Cut into the chicken breasts to make sure that they are cooked through, then remove them and set aside. Once they are cool enough to handle, coarsely shred the chicken. Reserve.

4. Add the rice to the pot and simmer for 15 minutes, or until rice is cooked. Remove soup from heat.

5. Add the shredded chicken to the soup and serve immediately.

Beef and Pork Stew with Chickpeas (*Puchero*)

This hearty stew is originally from Andalusia in Spain and is popular throughout Latin America. There are many different versions, but in Brazil it is usually prepared with chickpeas.

INGREDIENTS | SERVES 10

3 cups dried chickpeas

1 bay leaf

4 tablespoons olive oil

6 ounces thick-sliced bacon, cut into cubes

1½ pounds beef short ribs, cut into pieces

1½ pounds boneless pork roast, cut into 1" cubes

4 smoked sausages, such as *linguiça*, sliced into rounds

1 medium onion, peeled and finely chopped

4 cloves garlic, minced

2 medium carrots, peeled and finely diced

2 teaspoons turmeric

1 teaspoon smoked paprika

1½ teaspoons salt

1 large sweet potato, peeled and diced

1 large potato, peeled and diced, or 1 cup peeled and cubed manioc

1 cup tomato sauce

6–8 cups beef stock

2 cups halved green beans

1 cup whole pitted black olives

¼ cup chopped fresh parsley

1. Place the chickpeas in a large bowl, cover with water, and soak overnight.

2. Drain the chickpeas and place them in a large saucepan. Add the bay leaf and cover with 1–2" of water. Bring to a boil over high heat. Reduce heat to low, cover, and simmer until tender, about 1½ hours. Drain and set aside.

3. Heat the oil in a large stockpot over medium-high heat. Add the bacon and cook until crispy. Add the beef ribs and brown on all sides. Add the pork and brown on all sides. Add the sausages and brown lightly.

4. Add the onions, garlic, carrots, turmeric, paprika, and salt to the pot and cook, stirring, until onions are soft, about 5–8 minutes.

5. Add the sweet potato, potato, tomato sauce, and enough stock to cover everything by 1–2" of liquid. Bring to a boil, reduce heat to low, cover, and simmer stew for 1½ hours.

6. Add the chickpeas, green beans, and olives and simmer for 20–30 minutes.

7. Just before serving, stir in parsley.

Thickening Stews

Most Brazilian cooks use cornstarch to thicken stews during the last few minutes of cooking. To add the cornstarch without making clumps, place cornstarch in a small bowl (about 1 tablespoon per cup of stew). Stir an equal amount of cold water into the cornstarch until smooth. Stir the cornstarch mixture into the hot stew and simmer, stirring, until stew thickens.

CHAPTER 5

Main Courses (*Pratos Principais*): Beef, Chicken, and Pork (*Carne, Frango, e Porco*)

Steak with Fried Egg (*Bife à Cavalo*)

A cavalo means "horseback" in Portuguese, and this comfort-food dish is so named because the egg is "riding horseback" on the fried steak. To be very authentic, serve with rice, French fries, and salad, all on the same plate.

INGREDIENTS | SERVES 2

2 (6-ounce) steaks (about ½" thick) with visible marbling (strip steak, rib steak, or porterhouse)

1 clove garlic, minced

1 teaspoon kosher salt

1 teaspoon freshly ground black pepper

2 tablespoons olive oil

3 tablespoons butter

2 large eggs

Perfect Fried Eggs

Break each egg into a small bowl (one per bowl). Preheat a nonstick skillet containing 3 tablespoons of butter or oil over medium heat. Carefully pour eggs into the hot skillet, spaced 2" apart. Try to pour the egg white into the skillet before the yolk, to better center the yolk. Cook until the egg white sets and the edges begin to curl. Spoon some of the butter or oil over the top of the egg during cooking to help cook the yolk (for sunny-side up) or flip the egg over and cook briefly for a firmer yolk (over easy).

1. If needed, dry the steaks well with paper towels. Sprinkle both sides of the steaks with garlic, salt, and pepper and let rest for 15 minutes.

2. Heat the oil in a large heavy skillet (cast iron works well) over high heat until skillet is very hot (almost smoking). Add the steaks and cook for about 5 minutes without turning them. When you start to see the juices coming to the surface, turn the steaks.

3. Cook the steaks for 3–5 minutes on the other side, or until well browned (thinner cuts need less cooking time). Touch the center of the steaks to test for doneness. If it's very soft, the steak is rare. If it feels firm, the steak is well done. If it's somewhere in the middle, the steak is medium. When cooked to desired doneness, remove steaks from skillet, place them on a plate, and cover with foil.

4. Add the butter to the skillet and reduce heat to medium. Pour the eggs into the skillet, spacing them well. Cook until the whites are firm.

5. Top each steak with a fried egg and serve immediately.

Breaded Fried Steak (*Bife à Milanesa*)

This is a great way to enjoy thinner, less expensive cuts of steak. You can also make milanesas with chicken or pork using the same technique.

INGREDIENTS | SERVES 4

4 (5-ounce) thin-cut top round or sirloin steaks

1 clove garlic, minced

1 teaspoon kosher salt

1 teaspoon freshly ground black pepper

2 large eggs

1–2 tablespoons water

1 cup all-purpose flour

1 cup very fine bread crumbs

½ teaspoon salt

1 teaspoon dried oregano

2 tablespoons finely grated Parmesan cheese

⅓ cup vegetable oil

1. Pound the steaks to about ¼" thickness. Season with garlic, salt, and pepper and let rest for 15 minutes.

2. Place the eggs in a shallow bowl and whisk them together with 1–2 tablespoons of water. Place the flour on a plate. Mix the bread crumbs with the salt, oregano, and Parmesan, and place on a separate plate.

3. Dip each steak in the flour, coating both sides, then the egg (letting the excess drip off), and then in the bread crumb mixture to coat.

4. Heat the vegetable oil in a large skillet over medium-high heat. Once the oil is hot, cook the steaks, turning once, until they are dark golden brown, about 3–4 minutes.

5. Remove steaks to a plate lined with paper towels. Serve warm.

Stuffed Fried Steak (*Bife a Milanesa Recheado*)

One fun variation on this dish is to "stuff" the steaks with ham, cheese, and tomato before frying them. Pound each steak as thin as possible and cut it into two equal pieces. Top one piece with a slice of ham, a slice of cheese (such as mozzarella), and a thin slice of tomato. Top with the other piece of steak and secure with a toothpick. Bread and fry the stuffed steaks, following the original directions.

Braised Roulades of Beef in Tomato Sauce (*Bife à Role*)

Olives, vegetables, and bacon are common additions in the Brazilian version of this Italian dish.

INGREDIENTS | SERVES 4

4 (5-ounce) thin-cut top round or sirloin steaks

1 teaspoon kosher salt

1 teaspoon freshly ground black pepper

1 medium red bell pepper, seeded and cut into ½" strips

1 medium yellow bell pepper, seeded and cut into ½" strips

1 medium carrot, peeled and cut into ½" strips

½ cup sliced olives

4 slices bacon

2 tablespoons olive oil

1 medium onion, peeled and chopped

2 cloves garlic, minced

1 (32-ounce) can crushed tomatoes

1 teaspoon dried oregano

2 cups beef stock or water

2 tablespoons chopped fresh parsley

1. Pound the steaks to about ¼" thickness. Season with salt and pepper on both sides.

2. Place one steak on a cutting board. Place several strips of pepper and carrot crosswise on the steak, toward one of the short ends. Add 1 tablespoon sliced olives. Lay a piece of bacon down the middle of steak, letting some of the bacon extend past the opposite short end. Starting at the short end with the veggies, roll up the steak, enclosing the vegetables and wrapping any extra bacon around the roll. Secure roll with toothpicks. Repeat with the other three steaks.

3. Heat the olive oil in a deep skillet over medium-high heat. Brown the rolls well on all sides, about 5 minutes. Add the onion and sauté until lightly browned, about 5–8 minutes. Add garlic, tomatoes, oregano, remaining olives, and beef stock or water to the skillet. Bring to a boil, then reduce heat to low. Cover and simmer for 1–1½ hours, turning the rolls several times, or until the beef is very tender.

4. Serve the beef rolls with the tomato sauce, garnished with fresh parsley.

Beef Short Rib Casserole (*Vaca Atolada*)

This slow-cooked stew originally came from cow drovers who made it with beef jerky and manioc when they were stuck (atolada) crossing the mountains. Nowadays this delicious stew is often prepared with beef short ribs.

INGREDIENTS | SERVES 6

1½ pounds beef short ribs

1 teaspoon kosher salt

1 teaspoon freshly ground black pepper

3 slices bacon, chopped

2 medium onions, peeled and chopped

4 cloves garlic, minced

1 tablespoon tomato paste

4 large tomatoes, chopped

½ cup chopped scallions

½ cup chopped fresh parsley

4 cups beef stock

1 bay leaf

1½ pounds manioc

1. Preheat the oven to 350°F. Season the ribs with salt and pepper.

2. Place bacon in a heavy, ovenproof pot. Cook over medium heat until the bacon is crispy. Remove the bacon and reserve.

3. Add the beef ribs to the pot and cook over high heat until they are well browned on all sides, about 5 minutes per side. Remove ribs and set aside.

4. Add onions and garlic to the pot and cook over medium heat until onions are fragrant and translucent, about 5–8 minutes. Add tomato paste, tomatoes, scallions, and parsley and cook until the tomatoes are soft, about 10 minutes.

5. Add the ribs back to the pot, along with stock and bay leaf. The ribs should be just submerged in the liquid—add more stock or water if needed.

6. Cover the pot and place in the oven. Cook for 2 hours.

7. While the meat is cooking, peel the manioc and cut into 2" pieces, removing the fibrous core. Add the manioc to the pot and return to the oven for 45 minutes longer, until the manioc is tender and the meat is falling off the bone. Season to taste and remove bones before serving if desired.

Brazilian-Style Chicken Potpie (*Empadão de Frango*)

This exotic version of chicken potpie is a bit different. The pie has both a top and bottom crust, and is typically baked in a springform pan, which makes for an elegant presentation.

INGREDIENTS | SERVES 8

3½ cups plus 2 tablespoons all-purpose flour, divided
1½ teaspoons salt, divided
1 teaspoon baking powder
2 sticks butter
3 egg yolks, divided
1–3 tablespoons milk
1½ pounds bone-in chicken breasts and/or thighs
2 medium onions, peeled, divided
1 bay leaf

2 cups chicken stock
2 tablespoons olive oil
2 cloves garlic, minced
2 tablespoons tomato paste
1 cup fresh or frozen corn
1 cup frozen peas
½ cup chopped green olives
1 cup coarsely chopped hearts of palm
½ cup chopped scallions
½ teaspoon freshly ground black pepper

1. Place 3½ cups flour, 1 teaspoon salt, baking powder, and butter in a food processor. Pulse several times until crumbly. Add 2 egg yolks and 1 tablespoon milk, and pulse until mixture starts to come together. Add 1–2 tablespoons more milk if dough is too dry and crumbly. Wrap dough in plastic wrap and refrigerate for 30 minutes (or overnight).

2. Place chicken in a large stockpot. Quarter 1 onion and add it to the pot, with bay leaf and stock. Add water to cover and bring to a boil over high heat. Reduce heat to low, cover, and simmer for 25–30 minutes. Cool chicken, then remove skin and bones and finely shred the meat by hand. Set aside chicken and the cooking liquid.

3. Heat oil in a deep skillet over medium heat. Finely chop remaining onion and add it to the skillet with the garlic. Cook 5–8 minutes. Add tomato paste, corn, peas, olives, hearts of palm, and scallions and sauté for 5 minutes. Add 2 tablespoons flour and stir well.

4. Add chicken, 1 cup of the reserved broth and remaining salt and pepper. Cook for 5–8 minutes more until mixture thickens.

5. Preheat the oven to 350°F.

6. Remove dough from the refrigerator and divide it into two pieces, one about twice as big as the other one. On a floured surface, roll the larger piece of dough into a 13" circle. Use it to line a 10" tart pan, springform pan, or deep pie plate. Press dough into the sides of the pan. Prick the bottom of the dough with a fork.

7. Add the filling to the pan. Roll the remaining dough out into a 10" circle and place it on top of the filling. Crimp the edges to seal. Lightly beat remaining egg yolk. Brush dough with yolk.

8. Bake pie for 40–45 minutes, or until crust is golden brown. Remove from oven and let cool for 15 minutes before serving.

Ground Beef Kabob (*Espetinho de Carne Moída*)

These beef skewers can be browned on a stovetop in a cast-iron skillet or cooked on the grill. Serve the skewers with pita bread and a salad of lettuce, tomato, and onion with vinaigrette, and tahini sauce.

INGREDIENTS | SERVES 4

1½ pounds ground beef

2 tablespoons finely minced onion

2 cloves garlic, minced

1 tablespoon chopped fresh parsley

1 tablespoon minced scallions

1 teaspoon cumin

1 teaspoon paprika

1 teaspoon salt

1 teaspoon freshly ground black pepper

1–2 tablespoons mustard (optional)

2 tablespoons vegetable oil

¼ cup soy sauce

1. In a medium bowl, gently mix the ground beef, onion, garlic, parsley, scallons, cumin, paprika, salt, and pepper. Add a tablespoon of mustard if desired to help bind the ingredients together.

2. Take about ⅓ cup of the mixture (or more, depending on desired size) and shape it around a large wooden skewer into an oblong, hot dog–like shape. Repeat with remaining ground-beef mixture.

3. Heat the vegetable oil in a large skillet over medium-high heat. Brown the skewers on all sides, brushing them with the soy sauce as they cook. Cut into one of the skewers to test for doneness—cook until meat is browned all the way through—about 8–10 minutes.

Stewed Chicken with Okra (*Frango com Quiabo*)

This is a classic dish from Minas Gerais. The okra is fried until crispy and then set aside to be added at the very end of the cooking time, eliminating any possibility of sliminess.

INGREDIENTS | SERVES 6

1 pound fresh or frozen okra, trimmed and sliced into ½" rounds

3 teaspoons kosher salt, divided

1½ pounds chicken pieces (thighs and/ or breasts)

1 teaspoon freshly ground black pepper

4 tablespoons fresh lime juice

6 cloves garlic, minced, divided

4 tablespoons vegetable oil

2 medium onions, peeled and finely chopped

1 medium tomato, finely chopped

1 teaspoon paprika

¼ cup chopped fresh parsley

¼ cup chopped scallions

3–4 cups chicken stock

Quick *Angu*

This chicken and okra dish is typically served with a creamy, polenta-like dish called *angu*. To make a simple *angu*, sauté 1 teaspoon minced garlic in 2 tablespoons butter in a saucepan until fragrant. Whisk 1 cup of very fine cornmeal with 3 cups chicken stock and ½ teaspoon salt. Add the cornmeal mixture to the saucepan and cook for 5–10 minutes, stirring constantly, until thickened and creamy. Serve immediately.

1. Place okra in a colander and toss with 1 teaspoon salt. Set aside, stirring occasionally, for 45 minutes.

2. Place the chicken in a large bowl with 1 teaspoon salt, pepper, lime juice, and 1 tablespoon garlic. Toss to mix, cover, and marinate for 45 minutes in the refrigerator.

3. Heat oil in a deep skillet over medium heat. Cook the okra until very crispy and bright green, 3–5 minutes, carefully turning it once or twice. Toss okra with 1 teaspoon kosher salt, then remove okra from the oil with a slotted spoon and place on paper towels to drain.

4. Remove the chicken from the marinade and brown it on all sides in the same skillet used to cook the okra. Remove the chicken and set aside on a plate. Add onions, tomato, paprika, parsley, scallions, and the remaining garlic to the pan. Sauté vegetables over medium heat until the onions are translucent and the tomato is soft, about 5–8 minutes. Add the chicken back to the skillet, along with the stock. Bring liquid to a boil, then reduce heat to low.

5. Simmer the chicken until it is cooked through and tender, about 30 minutes. Add the okra and simmer for 5 minutes more, without stirring. Remove from heat and serve.

Brazilian-Style Shepherd's Pie (*Escondidinho de Frango*)

This tasty casserole has creamy chicken and vegetables topped with a thick layer of cheesy mashed potatoes.

INGREDIENTS | SERVES 8

1½ pounds medium potatoes or manioc root, peeled and cut into quarters

8 ounces cream cheese

2 tablespoons butter

2 teaspoons salt, divided

1 teaspoon freshly ground black pepper, divided

2 tablespoons olive oil

1 medium onion, peeled and finely chopped

2 cloves garlic, minced

1 tablespoon paprika

3 medium tomatoes, diced

¼ cup chopped fresh cilantro

½ cup chopped scallions

1 cup fresh or frozen corn kernels

2 tablespoons all-purpose flour

2–3 cups finely shredded cooked (poached or roasted) chicken breast

1 cup chicken stock

1 cup heavy cream

8 ounces grated mozzarella cheese

¼ cup grated Parmesan cheese

Poached Chicken Breasts

Place chicken breasts in a saucepan with 1 peeled and quartered onion, 2 peeled whole cloves garlic, and a bay leaf. Cover with chicken stock (or use bouillon cubes and water) and bring to a gentle boil over medium-high heat. Reduce heat to low, cover, and simmer for 10 minutes, then remove from heat and let rest, covered, for 10 minutes more. Check for doneness (return to a simmer if needed). Shred chicken with 2–4 tablespoons of the broth in a food processor using the plastic blade.

1. Boil the potatoes (or manioc) in salted water until tender when pierced with a fork. Mash potatoes or pass them through a potato ricer. Stir in cream cheese and butter while potatoes are still hot. Season with 1 teaspoon salt and ½ teaspoon pepper. Set aside.

2. Heat the olive oil in a deep skillet over medium heat. Add onion and garlic and cook until soft, about 5–8 minutes. Add paprika, tomatoes, cilantro, scallions, and corn and sauté until tomatoes are soft, about 10 minutes.

3. Add flour to the vegetables and sauté for 1–2 minutes. Add chicken and stock and simmer gently until mixture thickens. Remove from heat and stir in cream and remaining salt and pepper.

4. Preheat the oven to 350°F. Butter a 9" × 13" casserole dish.

5. Place the chicken mixture in the casserole dish and then spread the potato mixture evenly over the chicken. Sprinkle the mozzarella and the Parmesan cheese over the potatoes.

6. Cover with foil and bake for 20 minutes, until heated through, then remove the foil and place under the broiler for 2–3 minutes, or until the cheese is melted and lightly browned. Serve warm.

Quick Rice Casserole (*Arroz de Forno*)

This dish is a great way to use up leftover cooked rice. All kinds of leftovers could go into the casserole—assorted grated cheeses, vegetables, even other cooked grains like quinoa.

INGREDIENTS | SERVES 6

3 large eggs

¼ cup cream cheese, softened

½ cup milk or cream

¼ cup grated Parmesan cheese

1 teaspoon salt

2 tablespoons butter

1 small onion, peeled and diced

1 teaspoon dried oregano

1 cup frozen corn and peas

4 cups cooked rice

8 ounces deli-style smoked ham

1 cup grated cheese (mozzarella, Monterey jack, or Cheddar)

Perfect Rice

Mince 2 cloves of garlic. Place garlic in heavy saucepan with ¼ cup grated onion and 3 tablespoons vegetable oil. Sauté garlic and onion for 2 minutes. Add 2 cups rice (rinsed several times) and a teaspoon of salt. Add water to cover rice by almost an inch. Cover and cook over low heat for 15–20 minutes, or until liquid is absorbed, then turn off heat and let rest, covered, for 10 minutes. Uncover and fluff before serving.

1. Preheat oven to 350°F. Butter a 9" square casserole dish.

2. Place the eggs, cream cheese, milk or cream, Parmesan cheese, and salt in a blender and process until smooth.

3. In a small skillet, heat butter over medium heat. Sauté onion until soft, about 5 minutes. Add the oregano and the corn and peas and cook for 1 minute. Remove from heat.

4. Place 2 cups rice in the casserole dish. Top with the sautéed vegetables. Layer the ham slices over the rice and vegetables, and sprinkle ½ cup grated cheese over the ham. Cover everything with the remaining rice. Pour egg mixture over the rice. Sprinkle remaining cheese on top.

5. Bake for 30 minutes, or until heated through.

Chicken and Cashew Stir-Fry (*Frango Xadrez*)

The word xadrez means "chess" in Portuguese, and could refer to how these ingredients are cut into colorful squares (like the squares on a chess board). Serve this dish with rice and soy sauce on the side.

INGREDIENTS | SERVES 4

3 tablespoons vegetable oil

12 ounces boneless, skinless chicken breasts, cut into 1" cubes

½ teaspoon salt

½ teaspoon ground black pepper

2 cloves garlic, minced

1 teaspoon minced fresh ginger

1 small onion, peeled and diced

1 medium green bell pepper, cut into 1" squares

1 medium red bell pepper, cut into 1" squares

1 medium yellow bell pepper, cut into 1" squares

10 button mushrooms, washed and cut into 1" pieces

2 tablespoons cornstarch

¼ cup soy sauce, plus more for serving

½ cup chicken stock

¾ cup toasted peanuts or cashews

1. Heat oil over high heat in a deep skillet or wok. Season chicken with salt and pepper. Cook the chicken until well seared on all sides and almost cooked through, about 5–8 minutes. Remove chicken from skillet and set aside.

2. Add garlic, ginger, and onion to the skillet and cook for 2 minutes on high heat. Add the bell peppers and mushrooms and cook for 2–3 minutes more.

3. In a small bowl, whisk the cornstarch into the soy sauce and chicken stock. Add the mixture to the skillet along with the chicken. Cook for several minutes, stirring, until the sauce thickens and chicken is cooked through. Stir in the peanuts or cashews and remove from heat.

Roasted Pork Loin (*Lombo Assado*)

A citrus marinade adds lots of flavor, and the pan drippings are quickly transformed into a rich gravy. Brazilians serve roasted pork with farofa, a couscous-like dish made with toasted manioc meal (see Chapter 7 for farofa recipes).

INGREDIENTS | SERVES 6

1 small onion, peeled and coarsely chopped

2 cloves garlic, chopped

1 cup orange juice

¼ cup fresh parsley leaves

1½ teaspoons salt, divided

1½ teaspoons freshly ground black pepper, divided

1 teaspoon dried oregano

2 tablespoons olive oil

2–3 pounds pork tenderloin

½ cup water or chicken stock

½ cup heavy cream

1. Place onion, garlic, orange juice, parsley, 1 teaspoon salt, 1 teaspoon pepper, oregano, and olive oil in a blender or food processor. Blend until well mixed.

2. Pierce the top of the pork tenderloin with a fork in multiple places. Place the pork in a large zip-top plastic bag or baking dish and pour the marinade over it. Seal bag or cover dish and refrigerate for 2 hours or overnight.

3. Preheat oven to 350°F. Transfer the tenderloin and the marinade to roasting pan. Cover with foil and place in the oven.

4. Roast for 45 minutes, then remove pork from the oven. Remove foil, baste pork with the juices in the roasting pan, and return to the oven, uncovered, for 30 minutes more, or until the internal temperature reaches 140°F.

5. Remove pork from the oven and transfer to a serving platter. Place the roasting pan on the stove and add ½ cup of water or stock. Bring to a boil over medium-high heat and cook for 2–3 minutes, stirring and scraping the bottom of the pan. Strain the gravy into a saucepan and place over low heat. Whisk in cream and season with remaining salt and pepper.

6. Slice pork crosswise into thin slices and serve with the gravy.

Roast Leg of Lamb with *Cachaça*
(*Pernil de Cordeiro Assado na Cachaça*)

This celebratory dish feeds a crowd, but leftovers are delicious in sandwiches. The lamb is marinated in cachaça (a Brazilian white rum–like spirit) and seasoned with rosemary and thyme.

INGREDIENTS | SERVES 10

1 cup *cachaça*

¼ cup fresh lime juice

2 tablespoons honey

2 cloves garlic, minced

1 medium onion, peeled and chopped

2 tablespoons minced fresh rosemary, divided

1 teaspoon fresh thyme leaves

2 bay leaves

2 teaspoons kosher salt, divided

1 teaspoon freshly ground black pepper

1 (6-pound) leg of lamb

2 pounds small new potatoes

¼ cup olive oil

Cachaça

Cachaça is one of Brazil's most famous products—a white rum–like spirit made from fermented and distilled fresh (unprocessed) sugarcane juice. It is the key ingredient in a *caipirinha*, Brazil's national cocktail.

1. In a medium bowl, whisk together *cachaça*, lime juice, honey, garlic, onion, 1 tablespoon of rosemary, thyme, bay leaves, 1 teaspoon salt, and pepper. Place the leg of lamb in a large plastic bag, pour the marinade into the bag, and seal. Marinate for several hours in the refrigerator or overnight.

2. Preheat oven to 400°F. Place the leg of lamb and the marinade in a large roasting pan. Cover with foil and roast for 1 hour.

3. Cook the potatoes in boiling, salted water (skins on) until just tender with a fork, about 10–15 minutes. Drain potatoes, and toss them with olive oil, 1 teaspoon kosher salt, and remaining rosemary. Add the potatoes to the roasting pan, and return lamb to the oven, uncovered. Reduce oven temperature to 350°F.

4. Roast lamb for 30 minutes to an hour longer, or until the internal temperature reaches 145°F–150°F for medium rare. Remove lamb from oven and let rest for 15 minutes before slicing.

Bacon-Wrapped Stuffed Pork Loin
(*Rocambole de Lombo Recheado*)

This is a special occasion pork roast, perfect for a dinner party. The roast slices into elegant spirals of pork filled with sausage, olives, and dried fruit.

INGREDIENTS | SERVES 8

3 pound boneless pork loin
¼ cup fresh lime juice
1 cup white wine
2 teaspoons salt, divided
1 teaspoon freshly ground black pepper
2 cloves garlic, minced
2 tablespoons olive oil
8 slices bacon, divided

1 medium onion, peeled and chopped
1 cup diced smoked sausage
½ cup chopped green olives
½ cup raisins
3 tablespoons butter, divided
1 cup apple cider
1 tablespoon all-purpose flour
½ cup chicken stock

1. Butterfly the pork loin. Place in a large baking dish. Whisk together the lime juice, wine, 1 teaspoon salt, pepper, garlic, and olive oil. Pour over the pork. Cover and marinate in the refrigerator for 2 hours or overnight.

2. Dice one slice of bacon and place in a large skillet. Cook over medium-high heat until crispy. Add onion and cook about 5 minutes. Add sausage, olives, raisins, and ½ teaspoon salt, and sauté for 1–2 minutes. Remove from heat and let cool.

3. Spread filling over the pork. Roll up pork, starting at the short end, enclosing the filling. Wrap pork roll with remaining bacon slices and secure with twine in several places. Preheat oven to 400°F.

4. Heat 1 tablespoon butter over medium heat in the skillet. Brown pork on all sides, then place in a roasting pan. Add cider to the skillet and increase heat to medium-high. Bring to a low boil, scraping and stirring at the same time. Pour cider over the pork. Cover with foil.

5. Bake 30 minutes, then remove foil, baste, and bake for about 30–45 minutes more, or until the internal temperature reaches 140°F. Place pork roast on a platter.

6. Place the roasting pan on the stove over medium heat, add flour, and stir for 1 minute. Add stock, stirring and scraping the pan. Cook for 3 minutes, until slightly thickened. Season with remaining salt. Stir in remaining butter and strain into a serving dish.

7. Slice the pork roast into spirals to serve. Serve gravy on the side.

How to Butterfly a Pork Loin

Place the pork on a cutting board. With a sharp knife, make a lengthwise cut along one side, about ½" from the bottom, and "unroll" the pork away from the knife. Pound meat even thinner with a meat mallet.

Ham and Cheese Blender Casserole (*Torta de Liquidificador*)

Ham and cheese is one of the most popular fillings for this casserole, but cooked ground beef, shredded chicken, sausage and onions, or even sardines would also be great.

INGREDIENTS | SERVES 8

½ cup vegetable oil

½ cup melted butter

2 cups milk

1 cup low-fat plain yogurt

2 large eggs

1½ teaspoons salt, divided

1 teaspoon freshly ground black pepper, divided

4 tablespoons grated Parmesan cheese, divided

1 teaspoon dried oregano

1 tablespoon baking powder

1 cup cornstarch

2 cups all-purpose flour

10 ounces sliced smoked ham

2 tomatoes, peeled, seeded, and diced

5 ounces grated mozzarella cheese

5 ounces grated Monterey jack cheese

1. Preheat oven to 350°F. Butter a 10" round cake pan or springform pan, or a 9" square casserole dish.

2. Place oil, butter, milk, yogurt, eggs, 1 teaspoon salt, ½ teaspoon pepper, 2 tablespoons Parmesan cheese, oregano, baking powder, cornstarch, and flour in a blender. Pulse until smooth and well blended.

3. Pour half of the batter into the cake pan. Place the ham slices on top. Scatter tomato over the ham, and sprinkle the remaining salt and pepper over the tomato. Cover the tomato with mozzarella and Monterey jack. Pour the remaining batter over the cheese. Sprinkle remaining Parmesan over the top of the casserole.

4. Bake the casserole for 35–40 minutes, until puffed and golden brown. Let cool for 5–10 minutes before slicing into wedges to serve.

Bahian-Style Coconut Chicken (*Moqueca de Frango*)

Traditional Bahian moqueca is a colorful stew of fish and vegetables, seasoned with coconut milk, orange dendê (palm) oil, and cilantro. This version has all the same flavors but is made with chicken.

INGREDIENTS | SERVES 6

2 pounds boneless, skinless chicken breasts, cut diagonally into ½"thick slices

1 teaspoon salt

1 teaspoon ground black pepper

¼ cup fresh lime juice

2 tablespoons olive oil

2 tablespoons *dendê* (palm) oil or olive oil

1 medium onion, peeled and finely diced

3 cloves garlic, minced

1 medium onion, peeled and sliced into rings

1 medium red bell pepper, seeded and sliced into rings

1 medium green bell pepper, seeded and sliced into rings

1 cup chopped fresh cilantro, divided

1 cup chicken stock

1 (13.5-ounce) can coconut milk

Pirão

Traditional *moqueca* is often served with a side of *pirão*, a sauce/condiment made of fish broth mixed with ground manioc meal. To make a *pirão* to serve with this recipe, add a little extra chicken stock when cooking the chicken. Before adding the coconut milk, remove a cup of hot chicken broth and add it to a small saucepan. Gradually stir in ⅓ to ½ cup ground manioc meal, and stir until mixture thickens to desired texture. Season with salt to taste, garnish with chopped cilantro, and serve with the *moqueca*.

1. Place the chicken in a large bowl with the salt, pepper, and lime juice. Cover and set aside to marinate for 30 minutes in the refrigerator.

2. Heat olive oil in a large skillet over medium-high heat. Remove chicken from marinade (reserve marinade) and add chicken to the skillet. Brown on all sides. Remove chicken and set aside.

3. Add the *dendê* oil (or more olive oil) to the skillet and reduce heat to medium. Cook the diced onion until soft, about 5–8 minutes. Add the garlic and cook 1 minute. Stir in the onion rings, bell peppers, and ½ cup cilantro and cook until vegetables are soft, about 10 minutes.

4. Add the chicken, stock, and the reserved marinade to the skillet. Cook until chicken is just tender and cooked through, about 12–15 minutes.

5. Reduce heat to low and add coconut milk. Simmer until heated through, about 2 minutes. Remove from heat and garnish with the remaining cilantro.

Beef and Okra Bahian Stir-Fry (*Quiabada*)

It's difficult to find a substitute for carne seca, which is salted and dried (rather than smoked like beef jerky), outside of Brazil. This recipe substitutes bacon and sausage, which are tasty if not exactly the same.

INGREDIENTS | SERVES 6

2 pounds top sirloin, cut into bite-size pieces

2 cloves garlic, minced

2 teaspoons cumin

1½ teaspoons kosher salt, divided

1 teaspoon freshly ground black pepper

4 pieces bacon, chopped

1½ pounds fresh okra, cut into 1" pieces

8 ounces *linguiça* or *chouriço*, cut into 1" slices

2 tablespoons olive oil, divided

1 medium onion, peeled and finely chopped

1 cup beef stock

1 bay leaf

½ cup chopped fresh cilantro

½ cup chopped scallions

1. Place beef in a large bowl with garlic, cumin, 1 teaspoon salt, and pepper. Toss to mix well.

2. Cook bacon in a large skillet over medium-high heat until crispy. Remove the bacon and set aside, leaving rendered fat in the skillet. Sauté the okra in the same skillet until bright green and crisp, about 3–5 minutes. Remove from skillet and set aside.

3. Add the sausage to the same skillet and cook until browned on all sides. Remove sausage from skillet and set aside.

4. Add 1 tablespoon olive oil and beef to the skillet and cook until browned on all sides. Remove beef from skillet and set aside.

5. Add the remaining olive oil and onion to the skillet. Lower heat to medium and cook until onion is soft and translucent, about 5–8 minutes. Return beef, sausage, and bacon to the skillet. Add the beef stock and bay leaf and cook until beef is tender, about 10 minutes.

6. Stir in the okra, cilantro, and scallions and cook until everything is heated through, about 5 minutes more. Taste for seasoning and add remaining salt if needed.

CHAPTER 6

Main Courses (*Pratos Principais*): Seafood (*Frutos do Mar*)

Bahian Seafood Stew (*Moqueca de Peixe Baiana*)

Moqueca is traditionally cooked in a clay pot, and served with white rice, fried plantains, and farofa *toasted in bright orange* dendê *(palm) oil (see Chapter 7 for farofa recipes).*

INGREDIENTS | SERVES 6

1½ pounds fish fillets (sea bass, grouper, snapper, and mahi mahi are all good choices)

Juice of 2 limes

2 teaspoons salt, divided

1 teaspoon freshly ground black pepper

1 teaspoon ground coriander

3 tablespoons *dendê* (palm) oil

3 tablespoons olive oil

4 cloves garlic, minced

1–2 teaspoons minced red chili pepper

1 teaspoon paprika

2 tomatoes, diced (reserve 2 small slices for garnish, if desired)

1 large onion, thinly sliced

1 green bell pepper, seeded and thinly sliced crosswise

1 red bell pepper, seeded and thinly sliced crosswise

1 (13.5-ounce) can coconut milk

1½ cups seafood stock

1 small bunch fresh cilantro, finely chopped, divided

3 scallions, chopped

1. Cut fish into 2–3" pieces and place them in a zip-top plastic bag with lime juice, 1 teaspoon salt, pepper, and coriander. Refrigerate for 1 hour.

2. Add the *dendê* oil and olive oil to a deep skillet or stew pot. Add the garlic, chili pepper, and paprika, and cook over medium heat until garlic is soft, about 5 minutes. Add the fish fillets (reserve marinade) and cook for 1–2 minutes on each side. Remove fish and reserve.

3. Add the fish marinade to the skillet, along with tomatoes. Cook until tomatoes are soft, about 5 minutes. Add the onions and peppers and cook for 5 minutes more.

4. Add the coconut milk and seafood stock to the vegetables and simmer for 5 minutes. Taste for seasoning and add the remaining teaspoon of salt (or to taste). Carefully place the fish on top of the vegetables. Add the cilantro (reserve 1 tablespoon for garnish) and scallions. Cover and simmer over low heat for 10 minutes, or until fish is cooked through.

5. Serve warm over white rice garnished with tomato slices and cilantro.

Variations: Shrimp and Condiments (*Camarão e Pirão*)

Many people like to add shrimp to this stew. Simply add ½ pound peeled shrimp (previously marinated in lime juice and salt) during the last 5 minutes of cooking. *Moqueca* is often served with *pirão*, a condiment made with some of the cooking broth mixed with manioc flour. To make a simple *pirão*, remove ½ cup of the broth and heat it on the stove with an additional 1 cup of seafood stock. Stir in about ¾ cup coarse manioc meal (or more if needed) until desired texture is obtained.

Seafood Stew from Espírito Santo
(*Moqueca de Peixe Capixaba*)

Espírito Santo is a state on the southern coast of Brazil and is known for its seafood. Moqueca from Espírito Santo does not have coconut milk, and olive oil and annatto (colorau) take the place of the palm oil (dendê). This stew is often served with Pirão (see recipe in Chapter 7).

INGREDIENTS | SERVES 6

1½ pounds fish fillets (sea bass or other firm white fish)

Juice of 2 limes

1 teaspoon salt

1 teaspoon freshly ground black pepper

6 tablespoons olive oil, divided

3 cloves garlic, minced

2 teaspoons annatto powder, divided

1–2 teaspoons minced red chili pepper

4 tomatoes, seeded and chopped

2 onions, peeled and chopped

1 large bunch cilantro, stemmed and chopped

1 bunch scallions, chopped

2 cups seafood stock

Annatto Oil

If you can't find annatto powder, or you happen to have annatto seeds, you can make annatto oil and use that to cook the vegetables in this stew. Heat a teaspoon of crushed annatto seeds in a skillet with 1 cup of olive oil, and cook until olive oil turns slightly reddish. Strain.

1. Cut fish into 2–3" pieces and place them in a zip-top plastic bag with the lime juice, 1 teaspoon salt, and black pepper. Refrigerate for 1 hour.

2. Add 3 tablespoons olive oil to a deep skillet. Add the garlic, 1 teaspoon annatto, and chili pepper, and cook over medium heat until garlic is soft, about 5 minutes. Add the fish fillets and cook for 1–2 minutes on each side, then remove to a plate and set aside.

3. Add the tomatoes and onions to the pan and cook until onions are soft, about 5–8 minutes. Add the cilantro and scallions and cook, stirring, for 2 minutes.

4. Gently place the fish pieces in the pan, on top of the vegetables, spooning some of the vegetable mixture over the fish. Add the seafood stock. Sprinkle remaining annatto and olive oil over the vegetables and fish. Cover pan, reduce heat to low, and simmer for 15–20 minutes, or until fish is cooked.

5. Serve warm with white rice and *pirão*.

Baked Crab in Shells (*Casquinha de Siri*)

*This recipe makes enough to fill 10 real or ceramic scallop shells (available online)
for an appetizer, or 5 larger ramekins for a main course.*

**INGREDIENTS | SERVES 4 AS MAIN
COURSE, 10 AS APPETIZER**

1 pound fresh or frozen crab meat

Juice of 1 lime

3 slightly stale French bread rolls,
crumbled

1 cup coconut milk

2 tablespoons olive oil

2 tablespoons *dendê* (palm) oil, or
1 teaspoon annatto powder and 2
tablespoons olive oil

2 cloves garlic, minced

1 medium onion, peeled and diced

1 tablespoon tomato paste

1 teaspoon salt

½ teaspoon freshly ground black pepper

¼ cup finely chopped scallions

2 tablespoons minced fresh parsley

½ cup fine bread crumbs

2 tablespoons butter, melted

½ cup grated Parmesan cheese

Lime wedges, for garnish

1. Place the crab in a strainer and rinse with water. If using frozen crab, let thaw completely in strainer and press out excess water. Sprinkle crab with lime juice.

2. Place the bread in a medium bowl and pour the coconut milk over it. Set aside. Preheat the oven to 375°F.

3. Place the olive oil and *dendê* oil in a medium skillet. Add the garlic and onions and cook until onions are soft and fragrant, about 5–8 minutes.

4. Add the crab, tomato paste, salt and pepper (to taste) and cook for 2 minutes. Add the bread mixture and scallions, bring to a simmer, and cook for 2 minutes more.

5. Divide crab mixture between 10 shells (or 5 ramekins).

6. In a small bowl, stir together the parsley, bread crumbs, butter, and Parmesan and sprinkle some of the mixture over each shell.

7. Bake for 10–15 minutes, or until bread crumbs are golden brown and filling is bubbly. Serve warm, with lime wedges.

Shrimp and Cheese Fondue in a Pumpkin Shell
(*Camarão na Moranga*)

The city of Bertioga is famous for this fondue-like dish of seasoned shrimp in a cheesy tomato cream sauce, baked inside of a hollowed pumpkin. Serve with white rice.

INGREDIENTS | SERVES 8

1 small pumpkin (8" in diameter, about 5 pounds)

4 tablespoons olive oil, divided

1 pound medium shrimp, peeled, deveined, and coarsely chopped

6 whole shrimp, peeled except for tails, for garnish

Juice of 2 limes

1½ teaspoons salt

1 teaspoon freshly ground black pepper

2 tablespoons butter

2 cloves garlic, minced

½ cup minced onion

1 medium red bell pepper, seeded and chopped

1 medium tomato, seeded and chopped

1 tablespoon ketchup

2 tablespoons all-purpose flour

1 cup heavy cream

1 cup coconut milk

¼ cup chopped scallions

¼ cup chopped fresh parsley

8 ounces cream cheese

¼ cup grated Parmesan cheese

1. Cut a circle around the stem and remove the top of the pumpkin. Scoop out the inside of the pumpkin, scraping the sides to remove all the fibrous material and seeds. Brush the inside of the pumpkin with 2 tablespoons olive oil. Wrap the outside of the pumpkin in foil, leaving the top opening uncovered. Place on a baking sheet and set aside.

2. Preheat oven to 375°F.

3. Season the shrimp (including the whole shrimp) with lime juice, salt, and pepper. Place the butter in a medium skillet over medium heat. Sauté the shrimp with the garlic until they just turn pink. Remove shrimp and set aside.

4. Add remaining olive oil, onion, and bell pepper to the same skillet and cook until soft, about 5–8 minutes. Add the tomato and ketchup and cook until liquid has evaporated. Add the flour and cook for 1 minute.

5. Add the cream, coconut milk, scallions, and parsley and cook, stirring, until mixture simmers and thickens, about 3–5 minutes. Remove from heat and stir in the shrimp (except for the whole shrimp) and cream cheese.

6. Use a ladle to spoon mixture into the pumpkin. Replace the top of the pumpkin, and loosely cover top with foil. Bake pumpkin in the oven for 40–45 minutes. Carefully remove top of pumpkin, and sprinkle the top of the filling with the Parmesan. Return to the oven until Parmesan is browned.

7. Carefully unwrap foil from pumpkin, and gently transfer pumpkin to a platter (support the bottom of the pumpkin as it may be soft). Hang the whole shrimp decoratively around the opening in the pumpkin.

Salmon in Passion Fruit Sauce (*Salmão ao Molho de Maracujá*)

Frozen passion fruit pulp is available in many grocery stores. If you have access to fresh passion fruit, the seeds are edible and make a pretty garnish for this dish (see sidebar).

INGREDIENTS | SERVES 4

4 (6-ounce) salmon fillets

Juice of 2 limes

1½ teaspoons salt, divided

1 teaspoon freshly ground black pepper, divided

2 tablespoons butter

3 shallots, minced, or 1 small onion, peeled and grated

¼ cup capers

2 teaspoons cornstarch

1 cup passion fruit pulp

2 tablespoons olive oil

2 tablespoons minced fresh parsley

Passion Fruit (*Maracujá*)

Passion fruit is a slightly oblong fruit, green or dark red in color, with an inside pulp that is yellow, a bit gelatinous, and full of green seeds. Before it ripens, passion fruit is stringent and tart. As it ripens, the skin of the fruit becomes wrinkled and brownish, and the pulp becomes very fragrant and sweet. To extract the liquid pulp, scoop out all of the pulp and seeds from the inside of a ripe passion fruit, and heat the mixture over low heat in a small saucepan until it becomes more liquid and less gummy. Strain the pulp before using, reserving seeds if desired.

1. Place the salmon in a 9" square glass baking dish and sprinkle with lime juice, 1 teaspoon salt, and ½ teaspoon pepper. Chill in the refrigerator, covered, for 20 minutes.

2. Place the butter in a saucepan or small skillet and add the shallots and the capers. Cook over medium heat until shallots are soft, about 5 minutes. Add remaining salt and pepper (to taste) and cornstarch and cook for 1 minute. Add the passion fruit pulp and bring to a simmer, stirring frequently. Cook until mixture thickens slightly, about 3–5 minutes. Remove from heat and set aside.

3. Place the olive oil in a heavy skillet over medium heat. Add the salmon fillets and cook for about 4 minutes on each side, or until cooked through.

4. Place the salmon on a serving plate, and pour sauce over the salmon. Garnish with the parsley.

Fried Fish with Onions, Tomatoes, and Vinegar
(*Escabeche de Peixe*)

Before refrigeration, escabeche was used as a method of pickling fish to preserve it. The combination of fried fish in a vinegar-based onion and tomato sauce is so good, however, that the dish lives on.

INGREDIENTS | SERVES 6

Juice of 2 limes

2 teaspoons salt, divided

2 teaspoons freshly ground black pepper, divided

1½ pounds firm white fish fillets

2 tablespoons olive oil

2 medium onions, peeled and sliced into thin rings

2 medium tomatoes, seeded and diced

2 cloves garlic, minced

1 bay leaf

¾ cup red wine vinegar

Vegetable oil, for frying

1½ cups all-purpose flour, divided

½ cup cornmeal

2 large eggs

¼ cup chopped scallions

¼ cup chopped parsley

Escabeche Sandwich

This dish is great for sandwiches, too. Prepare the onion and tomato sauce and set aside. Batter and fry the fish, then drain on paper towels. Place some of the onions and tomatoes on 6 sliced French bread rolls, then divide the fried fish among the rolls and serve immediately.

1. Combine lime juice, 1 teaspoon salt, and 1 teaspoon pepper in a shallow dish. Add fish and marinate, covered, for 30 minutes in the refrigerator.

2. Heat olive oil in a large skillet over medium heat. Add the onions and cook until soft, about 5–8 minutes. Add the tomatoes, garlic, bay leaf, vinegar, ½ teaspoon salt, and ½ teaspoon pepper. Reduce heat to low and simmer 10 minutes. Remove bay leaf.

3. Heat 1 inch of vegetable oil in a deep skillet to 350°F.

4. In a shallow bowl, whisk together 1 cup flour, cornmeal, and remaining salt and pepper. Place remaining flour in another shallow bowl. Whisk eggs lightly in a third shallow bowl.

5. Dredge the fish fillets in the plain flour. Dip each fillet in the beaten egg (allow excess to drip off) and then in the cornmeal mixture. Fry the fish in the oil, in batches if necessary, until crispy and cooked through (about 2–3 minutes per side). Drain on paper towels.

6. Layer the fish with the tomatoes and onions in a serving dish, and sprinkle scallions and parsley on top. Serve warm.

Shrimp and Cassava Casserole (*Escondidinho de Camarão*)

Escondidinho means "hidden," and in this case the shrimp is hidden under a layer of mashed cassava or yuca (mandioca). This dish originated in northeastern Brazil, where it is traditionally prepared with dried beef. This is the coastal version, a sort of seafood shepherd's pie.

INGREDIENTS | SERVES 10

2 pounds medium shrimp, cleaned

Juice of 2 limes

2 teaspoons salt, divided

2 teaspoons freshly ground black pepper, divided

2 pounds manioc, peeled, inner fibers removed

2 tablespoons butter

4 tablespoons grated Parmesan cheese

½ cup heavy cream

4 tablespoons olive oil, divided

1 medium onion, peeled and chopped

2 large tomatoes, seeded and chopped

1 tablespoon cornstarch

1 (13.5-ounce) can coconut milk

2 tablespoons chopped fresh cilantro

2 cloves garlic, minced

¾ cup grated cheese (Cheddar, Monterey jack, or mozzarella)

1. Place the shrimp in a bowl and toss with the lime juice, 1 teaspoon salt, and 1 teaspoon pepper.

2. Cut the manioc into large chunks and place in a large pot. Cover with water, bring to a boil, cover, and simmer until manioc is very tender, about 25–30 minutes. Drain. Pass the manioc through a potato ricer, into the bowl of a standing mixer. Add the butter, ½ teaspoon salt, ½ teaspoon pepper, Parmesan, and cream, and beat until well mixed and fluffy. Set aside.

3. Place 2 tablespoons olive oil in a large skillet and add the onion. Cook over medium heat until onion is soft, about 5–7 minutes. Add the tomatoes and cook until tomatoes are soft and liquid has evaporated, about 5 minutes.

4. Add remaining salt and pepper and the cornstarch, and cook for 1 minute. Add the coconut milk and bring to a simmer, stirring until mixture thickens. Reduce heat to low.

5. Place remaining olive oil in a skillet over medium heat. Add the shrimp and sauté until pink. Transfer shrimp to the coconut milk mixture and mix well.

6. Preheat the oven to 350°F. Lightly grease a 9" × 13" casserole dish with butter.

7. Spread half of the mashed manioc to cover the bottom of the dish. Place the shrimp mixture on top, then cover with remaining manioc. Sprinkle grated cheese over the top.

8. Bake for 30–40 minutes, until cheese is melted and slightly browned and casserole is heated through.

Seafood Frittata from Espírito Santo (*Torta Capixaba*)

Torta capixaba is a Lenten dish, usually served on Good Friday. A rich seafood stew is topped with beaten eggs, decorated with sliced onions and olives, and baked in the traditional clay pot.

INGREDIENTS | SERVES 12

½ pound jumbo lump crab meat

½ pound salt cod, desalted and flaked (optional) (see sidebar in recipe for Baked Salt Cod in this chapter for how to prepare salt cod for cooking)

½ pound shrimp, peeled and deveined

Juice of 2 limes

6 tablespoons olive oil, divided

3 cloves garlic, minced

1 teaspoon annatto powder

1 large onion, peeled and finely chopped, plus 8 small round onion slices

2 medium tomatoes, seeded and chopped

2 (14-ounce) jars hearts of palm, drained and finely chopped

1 teaspoon salt

1 teaspoon freshly ground black pepper

¼ cup chopped scallions

¼ cup chopped fresh cilantro

½ cup chopped green olives, plus 6 whole olives

8 large eggs

2 large hard-cooked eggs, sliced

1. Season the crab, salt cod, and shrimp with the lime juice.

2. Place 3 tablespoons olive oil in a large skillet. Add the garlic and annatto and cook over medium heat for 1 minute. Add the crab meat and salt cod and cook for 2 minutes. Add the shrimp and cook until shrimp turns pink. Remove seafood from skillet and set aside.

3. Place the remaining olive oil in the same skillet and add the chopped onions. Cook until very soft, about 5–7 minutes. Add the tomatoes and cook until soft, about 5 more minutes. Add the hearts of palm, salt, and pepper and cook until all of the liquid has evaporated. Add the scallions, cilantro, and chopped olives.

4. Beat 2 of the eggs slightly and stir into the vegetables, along with the reserved seafood.

5. Preheat oven to 350°F. Place everything in a deep baking dish (such as a springform pan) or large pie pan. Press down with a spatula to make all the ingredients level. Bake for 15 minutes.

6. Beat the remaining eggs until very light and slightly stiff, like a meringue. Spread over the top of the casserole. Arrange the onion slices, egg slices, and whole olives decoratively on top of the eggs.

7. Return to oven and bake until beaten eggs are lightly browned and puffed, about 15–20 minutes.

Baked Salt Cod with Onions, Peppers, and Potatoes
(*Bacalhau ao Forno*)

Salt cod (bacalhau) is widely consumed in Brazil. The seasoning in this dish is very simple, allowing the flavor of the salt cod to really stand out.

INGREDIENTS | SERVES 8

1½ pounds salt cod, soaked (to remove salt) and dried (see sidebar)

4 large potatoes

¾ cup olive oil

3 medium onions, peeled and sliced

3 medium tomatoes, sliced

½ cup chopped scallions

½ cup chopped parsley

1 tablespoon minced garlic

1 teaspoon dried oregano

2 medium red peppers, seeded and thinly sliced

20 large black olives

Desalting Salt Cod (*Bacalhau*)

Salt cod is supposed to taste salty, but the excess salt must be removed before it is edible. To remove the salt, place the salt cod in a bowl and cover with water. Place the bowl in the refrigerator for 24 hours, changing the water every 4–6 hours. Drain salt cod and pat dry. Remove any skin and bones. Store well wrapped for up to 2 days in the refrigerator, or cook immediately.

1. Cut salt cod into 4" pieces, place them in large saucepan and cover with water. Bring to a boil and cook until just tender (not too soft), about 10–15 minutes. Remove the fish from the water, reserving water. Break the fish into bite-size chunks.

2. Peel the potatoes and cut them in half crosswise. Cook the potatoes in the same water until just tender. Drain. Let cool, then slice the potatoes into thin rounds.

3. Preheat the oven to 350°F. Use 2 tablespoons of the olive oil to grease the bottom of a 9" × 13" baking pan.

4. Place ⅓ of the sliced onions and tomatoes on the bottom of the pan. Top with a layer of half of the potatoes. Place the fish on top of the potatoes. Layer half of the scallions and parsley over the fish. Drizzle half of the remaining olive oil over everything.

5. Add another ⅓ of the onions and tomatoes, and sprinkle the garlic and oregano over the top. Add the remaining potatoes, topped with the rest of the parsley and scallions. Add the bell pepper slices, remaining ⅓ of onions and tomatoes, and olives on top. Drizzle the rest of the olive oil over the whole casserole.

6. Bake for 30–40 minutes, until the vegetables are soft and fragrant.

Savory Salt Cod and Vegetable Pie (*Empadão de Bacalhau*)

This flaky pie is filled with a creamy mixture of vegetables and salt cod. The salt cod must be soaked for 24 hours in water to remove the excess salt, so plan ahead.

INGREDIENTS | SERVES 10

2 tablespoons olive oil

1 medium onion, peeled and diced

2 cloves garlic, minced

1 large tomato, diced

1 medium red bell pepper, seeded and diced

1 pound salt cod, desalted and any bones or skin removed (see sidebar in Baked Salt Cod recipe in this chapter for how to prepare salt cod for cooking)

½ cup vegetable stock

1 cup chopped hearts of palm

½ cup frozen corn

½ cup chopped green olives

¼ cup chopped scallions

2 tablespoons chopped fresh parsley

¾ teaspoon salt

1 teaspoon ground black pepper

2 tablespoons cornstarch

½ cup heavy cream

½ cup mayonnaise

1 chilled Pastry Crust (see sidebar)

1 hard-cooked egg, peeled and sliced

1 egg yolk

Pastry Crust (*Massa para Empadão*)

Place 3½ cups flour, ¾ teaspoon salt, and 1 teaspoon baking powder in the bowl of a food processor. Cut 2 sticks of butter (8 ounces) into 1" pieces and add to the bowl. Pulse briefly several times until flour mixture is crumbly. Add 2 egg yolks and 1 tablespoon of milk, and pulse until mixture starts to come together as a dough. Add 1–2 tablespoons more milk if dough is too dry and crumbly. Wrap dough in plastic wrap and refrigerate for 30 minutes.

1. Place the oil in a large skillet. Cook the onion over medium heat until soft, about 5–8 minutes. Add the garlic, tomato, bell pepper, salt cod, and vegetable stock and cook until the liquid has evaporated, about 6–10 minutes.

2. Add hearts of palm, corn, olives, scallions, parsley, salt (to taste), and pepper and cook for 2 minutes. Add the cornstarch and mix well. Add the cream and mayonnaise and simmer, stirring, until mixture thickens, about 3–5 minutes. Remove from heat and set aside.

3. Preheat the oven to 350°F. Divide the dough into 2 pieces, one about twice as big as the other one. On a floured surface, roll the larger piece of dough into a 13" circle. Use it to line a 10" springform pan or deep pie pan, letting the dough come up the sides. Press dough into the sides of the pan with your fingers. Prick the bottom of the dough with a fork.

4. Add the filling to the crust-lined pan. Top with slices of hard-boiled egg. Roll the remaining dough out into a 10" circle and place it on top of the filling (or cut dough into strips and make a lattice top). Crimp the edges to seal, and brush dough with egg yolk.

5. Bake for 40–45 minutes, or until crust is golden brown. Remove from oven and let cool for 15 minutes before serving. Serve warm or at room temperature.

Shrimp Bobo (*Bobó de Camarão*)

*This shrimp and manioc stew is essentially a West African dish that made its way to Brazil.
Look for reddish palm oil (dendê) in Brazilian groceries or online.*

INGREDIENTS | SERVES 6

1 pound medium shrimp, peeled and deveined

Juice of 2 limes

1½ teaspoons salt, divided

1 teaspoon ground black pepper

1 pound fresh or frozen manioc (also called yuca or cassava), peeled

1 (13.5-ounce) can coconut milk, divided

6 tablespoons *dendê* oil, or 6 tablespoons olive oil mixed with 1 teaspoon annatto powder, divided

2 cloves garlic, minced

1 medium onion, peeled and finely chopped

1 medium red bell pepper, seeded and finely chopped

1 medium green bell pepper, seeded and finely chopped

1 medium tomato, seeded and chopped

¼ cup chopped scallion

¼ cup chopped parsley

1. Place the shrimp in a bowl and toss with lime juice, 1 teaspoon salt, and pepper. Set aside.

2. Cut the manioc into large chunks, removing inner fibrous core, and place in a large pot. Cover with water and simmer until manioc is very tender, about 25–30 minutes. Drain. Place the manioc in a food processor while still hot with ½ cup of the coconut milk and remaining salt, and process until smooth. Set aside.

3. Place 2 tablespoons of the *dendê* oil in a stockpot. Sauté the shrimp with the garlic over medium heat until they just start to turn pink. Remove shrimp and set aside.

4. Add 2 tablespoons of the *dendê* to the same pot and add the onion and bell peppers. Cook over medium heat until soft, about 5–8 minutes. Add the tomatoes and cook until liquid has evaporated.

5. Add the manioc and coconut milk mixture with the remaining coconut milk to the pan. Cook, stirring, until mixture thickens slightly, about 5 minutes.

6. Add the shrimp, scallions, and parsley to the pot. Drizzle with remaining *dendê* oil.

7. Serve warm with white rice.

Fish Baked in Banana Leaves (*Peixe na Folha de Bananeira*)

The banana leaves protect the fish and steam it at the same time, with the seasonings sealed into the packet with the fish. Frozen banana leaves are available at many Latin grocery stores and some supermarkets.

INGREDIENTS | SERVES 4

Juice of 2 limes
1 teaspoon salt
1 teaspoon ground black pepper
¼ cup chopped fresh cilantro
¼ cup coconut milk
1 small red chili pepper, seeded
4 large fish fillets
4 large banana leaves

1. Place the lime juice, salt, black pepper, cilantro, coconut milk, and chili pepper in a blender or food processor and process until just mixed.

2. Place the fish in a glass baking dish and cover with the marinade. Chill for 30 minutes.

3. Preheat oven to 375°F. Place a banana leaf on the counter. Place a fish fillet in the center. Spoon 1–2 tablespoons of marinade over the fish. Wrap the fish tightly in the banana leaf, securing with twine if needed. Repeat with remaining fish fillets. Place wrapped fish on a baking sheet.

4. Bake for 20–25 minutes, depending on thickness of the fillets. (Check after 15 minutes to see if fish is cooked through.)

5. Unwrap fillets and serve with white rice and fried plantains. The banana packets can also be cooked on a grill. (Place on grill for 5 minutes per side, then test for doneness.)

Salmon Burgers (*Hambúrguer de Salmão*)

Hamburgers are very popular in Brazil, especially loaded with all kinds of crazy toppings. But Brazilians also love seafood, and are becoming increasingly health conscious. So it's easy to see why salmon burgers are a natural fit.

INGREDIENTS | SERVES 4

Juice of 1 lime
¼ cup fresh cilantro
¼ cup chopped scallions
2 cloves garlic
¼ cup mayonnaise
1 tablespoon teriyaki sauce
1 teaspoon salt
1 teaspoon ground black pepper
1 pound salmon, cut into large chunks
1 large egg
½ cup very fine bread crumbs
2 tablespoons olive oil
4 hamburger buns

Quick Hollandaise (*Molho Holandês*)

These "burgers" are also delicious served with hollandaise sauce in place of a bun (or on the bun in place of the mayonnaise). To make a quick hollandaise sauce, place 3 egg yolks in a blender with ¼ teaspoon salt, and 1 tablespoon lime juice. Melt ¾ stick butter in a small saucepan (do not boil). Add the hot butter to the eggs in a steady stream, running the blender at the same time, blending until thickened. If sauce gets too thick, thin it with 1–2 tablespoons hot water.

1. Place the lime juice, cilantro, scallions, and garlic in the bowl of a food processor and process in short pulses until everything is finely minced. Remove 2 tablespoons of the mixture and mix with the mayonnaise. Set aside.

2. Add the teriyaki sauce, salt, pepper, and salmon to the food processor and pulse 2 or 3 times briefly, just until salmon is shredded. Transfer mixture to a medium bowl.

3. Stir the egg and the bread crumbs into the salmon mixture. Shape into 4 round patties. Heat the olive oil in a skillet over medium heat, and cook the salmon patties for 4–5 minutes on each side, or until cooked through.

4. Spread the buns with the prepared mayonnaise, place the salmon burgers on the buns, garnish with lettuce and tomato or other garnishes, if desired, and serve.

Shrimp with Chayote Squash (*Camarão com Chuchu*)

This is a famous dish from Rio de Janeiro, even memorialized in a famous song by Carmen Miranda. Serve this dish with white rice.

INGREDIENTS | SERVES 6

1 pound medium shrimp, peeled

2 cloves garlic, minced

Juice of 2 limes

1½ teaspoons kosher salt, divided

1 teaspoon freshly ground black pepper

4 tablespoons olive oil, divided

1 large onion, peeled and finely chopped

1 medium tomato, seeded and finely diced

4 chayote squash, peeled and cubed

1 cup water

¼ cup chopped fresh parsley

¼ cup chopped scallions

1. Place the shrimp in a bowl with the garlic, lime juice, 1 teaspoon salt, and pepper. Toss to mix well and chill for 30 minutes.

2. Add 2 tablespoons of oil to a large skillet and sauté the shrimp over medium-high heat until they just turn pink. Remove shrimp from skillet and set aside.

3. Add the remaining 2 tablespoons oil to the skillet. Cook the onion until soft and translucent, about 5–8 minutes. Add the tomato and cook until all the liquid has evaporated, about 5 minutes.

4. Add the chayote and the water. Cover and simmer until squash is just tender, about 10 minutes.

5. Add the shrimp back to the skillet, along with the parsley and scallions. Stir until everything is heated through.

6. Season with remaining salt to taste and serve.

CHAPTER 7

Side Dishes (*Acompanhamentos*)

Cornmeal "Couscous" with Bacon
(*Cuscuz Nordestino com Bacon*)

In Brazil you can buy a form of precooked, coarsely flaked cornmeal called milharina *that has a texture like couscous when steamed. You can order* milharina *online from Brazilian food vendors.*

INGREDIENTS | SERVES 4

2 cups milharina, or very coarsely ground cornmeal

1 teaspoon salt

1 cup water, plus more for steaming

3 slices bacon, chopped

½ cup minced onion

6 sun-dried tomatoes (jarred in oil), chopped

½ cup sliced black olives

3 tablespoons capers

1 teaspoon dried oregano

Molded *Cuscuz*

Cuscuz is sometimes molded into shapes by packing it into greased bowls or other molds, steaming it for several minutes (the microwave works well for this), then inverting it onto the plate. Molded *cuscuz* makes a pretty side dish for a plate of beans. *Cuscuz* can also be shaped with a larger mold and then sliced into serving-size pieces. A *cuscuzeira* (couscous steamer) can act as a mold—it is designed so that you can lift out the *cuscuz* in the shape of a tall wheel.

1. Place the cornmeal in a medium bowl and add the salt. Mix the water into the cornmeal with a fork until the cornmeal has small, even clumps. Line a steamer basket or colander with cheesecloth (or a thin dishtowel) and place the cornmeal on top of the cheesecloth. Set the colander over a pot of boiling water (the water should not touch the colander), and cover tightly. Steam for 30 minutes. Drizzle ⅓ cup of water over the cornmeal several times during cooking.

2. While the cornmeal is steaming, place bacon in a medium skillet and cook over medium heat until crispy. Remove bacon, chop, and set aside. Add onion and cook until translucent and fragrant, about 5–8 minutes. Add sun-dried tomatoes, olives, capers, and oregano. Cook for 2–3 minutes more.

3. The cornmeal should be soft and fluffy after 30 minutes of steaming. If it seems too crunchy, drizzle it with another ⅓ cup of water and steam for 5–10 more minutes. Once it's ready, turn the cornmeal out of the colander and into the skillet with the onion mixture. Add the chopped bacon and fluff with a fork to mix well.

4. Keep covered until ready to serve. Serve warm.

Savory Toasted Manioc (*Farofa à Brasileira*)

This is a standard recipe for farofa, which is enjoyed as a side dish and also used as a condiment. Brazilians like to get creative with this dish and add tropical fruit, seafood, vegetables, etc.

INGREDIENTS | SERVES 4

4 slices bacon, chopped

6 ounces smoked sausage (such as *linguiça* or *chouriço*), diced

1 small onion, peeled and chopped

1 clove garlic, minced

4 tablespoons butter

2½ cups manioc meal, toasted or plain (*farinha de mandioca*)

2 tablespoons chopped fresh parsley

1 teaspoon salt

½ teaspoon freshly ground black pepper

2 large hard-cooked eggs, peeled and chopped into ½" pieces

1. Place the bacon in a medium skillet and cook over medium heat until fat begins to render. Add sausage and cook until both the bacon and sausage are browned and crispy. Add onion and cook until it is soft and slightly browned, anout 5–8 minutes. Add garlic and cook for 1 minute more.

2. Melt the butter in the skillet. Add the manioc meal and cook, stirring, until manioc is brown and well toasted.

3. Stir in the parsley and salt and pepper to taste, and mix well. Stir in the hard-cooked eggs and remove from heat. Serve warm.

Farofa with Scrambled Eggs

Add a couple of tablespoons of oil to a skillet, pour in 2 whisked eggs, and cook them over medium heat until they are scrambled. Season with salt and pepper and set them aside on a plate. Prepare the *farofa* as usual in same skillet, adding the eggs back in at the end.

Simple Bread Crumb "Farofa" (*Farofa de Pão*)

*This popular version of farofa calls for dry bread crumbs in place of the manioc.
It's a great way to try farofa if you can't find manioc meal in your local grocery store.*

INGREDIENTS | SERVES 4

1 (12") stale French baguette (1–2 days old), cut into 1" cubes
2 tablespoons olive oil or vegetable oil
1 small onion, peeled and minced
1 clove garlic, minced
4 tablespoons butter
2 tablespoons minced fresh parsley
1 teaspoon salt
½ teaspoon freshly ground black pepper

1. Place the cubes of bread in a food processor and process until you have coarse crumbs (work in batches if necessary). Set aside.

2. Heat oil in a medium skillet over medium-low heat. Add onion and cook until soft and lightly browned, about 5–8 minutes. Add the garlic and cook for 1 minute.

3. Add butter to the skillet. Once butter is melted, add the bread crumbs and sauté until they are toasted and brown. Stir in parsley and salt and pepper to taste, and remove from heat. Serve warm.

Brazilian-Style Greens (*Couve à Mineira*)

Couve is the general term for vegetables in the cabbage family, but the word usually refers to collard greens. This dish is traditionally prepared with collard greens, but kale (couve-galega) works well, too.

INGREDIENTS | SERVES 4

1 large bunch collard greens or kale
2 slices bacon, diced
2 tablespoons olive oil
4 cloves garlic, peeled and crushed
1 tablespoon cider vinegar
1 teaspoon kosher salt

Tips

Wash the greens very well, as they can be sandy. If you don't like the slightly bitter taste of collard greens and kale, blanch the greens in boiling salted water for several minutes before chopping them. Chop the greens into very thin strips, and cook them in a large skillet. Add finely chopped smoked sausage (in addition to the bacon) for extra flavor.

1. Wash the collard greens or kale well. Remove the stems. Take a handful of the leaves and roll them up into a cylinder. With a sharp knife, slice the cylinder crosswise into very thin strips.

2. Place bacon in a large skillet and cook over medium-high heat until browned and crispy. Add olive oil and garlic and sauté for 1 minute.

3. Add vinegar and sliced greens to the skillet. Sprinkle the salt over the greens, cover, and cook for 2–3 minutes. Remove cover and cook, stirring, until liquid has evaporated. Serve immediately.

Pineapple Raisin Farofa (*Farofa de Abacaxi*)

Tropical fruits are often added to farofas. This pineapple raisin version makes an excellent accompaniment for grilled chicken or fish.

INGREDIENTS | SERVES 4

4 tablespoons butter, divided

1 cup cubed fresh pineapple

2 tablespoons brown sugar

¼ cup raisins

1 teaspoon minced fresh ginger

¼ cup minced onion

2 cups manioc meal (*farinha de mandioca*), toasted or plain

1 teaspoon salt

2 tablespoons minced fresh cilantro, divided

1. Melt 2 tablespoons butter in a medium skillet over medium heat. Add pineapple and brown sugar and sauté until pineapple starts to caramelize, about 5 minutes. Stir in raisins and cook for 1 minute. Remove pineapple and raisins from skillet and set aside.

2. Add the remaining butter, ginger, and onion to the skillet and cook until the onion is translucent and soft, about 5–8 minutes. Add manioc meal and sauté until it is toasted and golden brown. Season with salt to taste.

3. Stir the pineapple, raisins, and 1 tablespoon of cilantro into the *farofa*. Sprinkle the remaining cilantro over the *farofa* and serve.

Manioc Fries (*Mandioca Frita*)

When properly cooked, manioc is crispy on the outside but soft on the inside. It's best to use fresh manioc root instead of frozen when making these fries.

INGREDIENTS | SERVES 4

3 cups vegetable stock

2 pounds fresh manioc root, peeled and cut into wedges, inside fibers removed

1 tablespoon butter

2 teaspoons kosher salt, divided

2–3 cups vegetable oil, for frying

1. Place the vegetable stock in a large saucepan and bring to a simmer over medium heat. Add the manioc wedges, adding water if needed to cover. Boil manioc for about 30 minutes, or until tender when pierced with a fork.

2. Drain the manioc and place in a bowl. Toss with butter and 1 teaspoon salt.

3. In a deep skillet or pot, heat vegetable oil over medium-high heat to 350°F.

4. Working in batches, fry the manioc until golden brown on all sides. Remove with a slotted spoon and drain on paper towels.

5. Season fries with remaining salt and serve hot.

Creamed Cornmeal (*Angu*)

This polenta-like dish can be prepared with cornmeal (fubá) or with fresh corn, though cornmeal is most common. Serve with stews or grilled meats, or as a vegetarian main dish (omitting the bacon).

INGREDIENTS | SERVES 4

6 ounces thick-cut bacon, cubed

4 cups vegetable or chicken stock

2 cups finely ground cornmeal

1 teaspoon salt

2 tablespoons butter

1 tablespoon chopped fresh parsley

Fresh Corn *Angu*

To prepare *angu* using fresh corn, remove the kernels from about 6 ears of corn. Place them in a blender with 1 cup vegetable stock and blend until smooth. Place mixture in a saucepan and cook over medium-low heat, stirring, until thickened to desired texture. Stir in 2 tablespoons of butter and 1 teaspoon salt.

1. Place bacon in a medium saucepan and sauté over medium heat until browned and crispy. Remove bacon and reserve.

2. Add stock to the same saucepan and bring to a simmer. Gradually whisk in cornmeal and salt. Cook over low heat, stirring constantly, until mixture thickens enough to see the bottom of the pan for several seconds after stirring, about 20–30 minutes.

3. Remove from heat and stir in the butter and the parsley. Serve warm, garnished with the bacon pieces.

Butternut Squash Purée (*Quebebe*)

This simple and delicious side dish comes from northeastern Brazil. Usually the squash is cooked and then stirred until it has the texture of mashed potatoes, but it can also be served as a stew.

INGREDIENTS | SERVES 4

3 tablespoons butter

1 small onion, peeled and finely diced

4 cloves garlic, minced

1 medium butternut squash, peeled and cut into 1" cubes

2 tablespoons brown sugar

1–2 cups water

1 teaspoon salt

½ teaspoon freshly ground black pepper

2 tablespoons chopped fresh parsley, divided

1. Melt butter in a large skillet over medium heat. Add onion and sauté until soft and fragrant, about 5–8 minutes. Add garlic and sauté for 1 minute.

2. Add squash and brown sugar and sauté, stirring, until the squash is lightly browned. Add 1 cup of water, salt, and pepper. Reduce heat to low and cover. Cook until squash is tender, adding more water if needed.

3. Remove from heat and stir 1 tablespoon parsley into the squash, breaking up and mashing the squash while stirring, until it has the texture of lumpy mashed potatoes. Sprinkle with remaining parsley and serve.

Roasted Eggplant and Tomatoes (*Assado de Berinjela e Tomate*)

This pretty stack of roasted eggplant, roasted tomato, and cheese goes with almost any meal, and can even stand alone as a main course.

INGREDIENTS | SERVES 6

1 medium eggplant, stemmed and sliced crosswise into ½" rounds

1½ teaspoons kosher salt, divided

4 tablespoons olive oil

12 fresh basil leaves

2 large tomatoes, sliced crosswise into ¼" rounds

2 teaspoons dried oregano

6 ounces grated mozzarella cheese

6 tablespoons grated Parmesan cheese

1. Place the sliced eggplant in a colander and sprinkle with 1 teaspoon salt. Set aside for 30 minutes.

2. Preheat oven to 375°F. Line a baking sheet with parchment paper. Brush the eggplant slices with olive oil on both sides.

3. Place eggplant slices on the baking sheet 1" apart. Top each one with 2 basil leaves. Add a tomato slice on top of each piece of eggplant. Mix oregano with remaining salt and sprinkle evenly over tomatoes. Sprinkle about 1 tablespoon mozzarella on top of each vegetable stack, and top each with 1 tablespoon Parmesan.

4. Bake for 25 minutes, or until vegetables are soft and cheese is browned. Serve immediately.

Sweet Corn Bread (*Pamonha Assada*)

This moist corn bread version is simple to make, and is a great accompaniment for soups and stews.

INGREDIENTS | SERVES 8

4 cups fresh corn kernels (from about 6 cobs)

1 (14-ounce) can condensed milk

½ cup buttermilk

6 tablespoons butter, melted

4 large eggs

1 teaspoon salt

6 tablespoons cornstarch

2 teaspoons baking powder

1. Preheat oven to 350°F. Generously butter a 9" cake pan.

2. Place the corn, condensed milk, and buttermilk in a blender and pulse until well mixed.

3. Add butter, eggs, salt, cornstarch, and baking powder and blend until well mixed. Pour mixture into prepared pan.

4. Bake until cake springs back to the touch and is golden brown.

5. Serve warm.

Creamed Manioc with Seafood (*Pirão*)

Pirão is an essential accompaniment to many seafood dishes.
It's a thick and creamy gravy of seafood stock thickened with manioc meal.

INGREDIENTS | SERVES 6

12 ounces fish fillets of choice

2 teaspoons salt, divided

Juice of 2 limes

3 tablespoons olive oil

1 large onion, peeled and diced

2 cloves garlic, minced

2 large tomatoes, seeded and diced

½ cup chopped scallions

¼ cup chopped fresh cilantro, divided

1 teaspoon freshly ground black pepper

3 cups water or vegetable stock

1 cup coarse manioc meal (*farinha de mandioca*)

1. Place fish in a shallow dish and sprinkle with 1 teaspoon salt and lime juice. Cover and chill in the refrigerator for 30 minutes.

2. Heat olive oil in a stockpot over medium heat. Add onion and sauté until translucent, about 5–8 minutes. Add garlic, tomatoes, scallions, ⅛ cup cilantro, pepper, and remaining salt. Cook until vegetables are soft and most of the liquid has evaporated, about 3–5 minutes.

3. Add the fish to the pot and cover with the water (or stock). Cover and simmer gently for 10 minutes, or until fish is cooked through. Remove fish from the pot and set aside. When cool enough to handle, flake fish into small pieces.

4. Simmer broth uncovered for 5–10 minutes. Reduce heat to low and whisk the manioc meal into the broth very gradually, stirring constantly to prevent clumps. Stir in the fish. Continue to stir over low heat for 5–10 minutes. Add more manioc meal if needed to thicken to desired consistency.

5. Garnish with remaining cilantro before serving.

Pork Cracklings (*Torresmo*)

Fried pork rinds are an essential accompaniment to certain Brazilian dishes, such as the national dish feijoada. Torresmo are also a popular bar snack.

INGREDIENTS | SERVES 10

2 pounds pork belly
Juice of 1 lime
3 teaspoons salt, divided

1. Cut the meat from the fat and reserve for another use. Cut the fat into 1" × 2" pieces. Toss the pieces with the lime juice and 2 teaspoons salt.

2. Add the pork fat to a heavy pot and cook over high heat. Stir to ensure even cooking. As the fat melts, the cracklings will cook in the rendered fat. Cook until well browned and crispy.

3. Use a slotted spoon to transfer the cracklings to a plate lined with paper towels.

4. Season with remaining teaspoon of salt, if desired.

Fried Bananas (*Banana à Milanesa*)

Breaded and fried bananas are a traditional accompaniment for certain dishes from Minas Gerais, especially refried beans (Tutu de Feijão)—see recipe in Chapter 8.

INGREDIENTS | SERVES 4

4 firm bananas, not perfectly ripe but not green
1 cup all-purpose flour
1 large egg
½ teaspoon salt
1½ cups bread crumbs
Vegetable oil, for frying

1. Peel the bananas and cut in half lengthwise. Place the flour in a shallow dish. Whisk the egg in a separate shallow dish. In a third shallow dish, stir the salt into the bread crumbs.

2. Dip the bananas into the flour, and then into the egg, letting the excess drip off. Dip the bananas into the bread crumbs to coat.

3. Heat several inches of oil in a deep skillet or pot to 350°F (or until a piece of banana sizzles when it touches the oil). Fry the bananas until golden brown.

4. Remove bananas from the oil with a slotted spoon and drain on paper towels. Serve warm.

Marinated Zucchini (*Abobrinha Marinada*)

This garlicky zucchini makes a nice accompaniment to grilled meats. It keeps well in the refrigerator, and is delicious on sandwiches or with pasta.

INGREDIENTS | SERVES 6

¾ cup olive oil, divided

4 large zucchinis, sliced crosswise and diagonally into thin slices

4 cloves garlic, minced

2 tablespoons vinegar

¼ teaspoon red pepper flakes

1 tablespoon chopped fresh parsley

1 tablespoon chopped fresh basil

1 teaspoon dried oregano

1 teaspoon salt, or to taste

1 teaspoon freshly ground black pepper

1. Heat 4 tablespoons of the olive oil in a large skillet. Add the zucchini slices and the garlic and cook until zucchini is lightly browned about 3–4 minutes. Remove from heat.

2. Place zucchini slices in a bowl, add remaining ingredients, and mix well.

3. Store zucchini in a small enough container so that it is completely covered in olive oil. Refrigerate overnight before serving.

Sautéed Okra and Tomatoes (*Quiabo com Tomates*)

Okra is a beloved vegetable in Brazil. When fresh okra is sautéed whole, it stays nice and crisp.

INGREDIENTS | SERVES 4

3 slices bacon, diced

1 pound fresh okra, ends trimmed

1 teaspoon salt, divided

1 teaspoon freshly ground black pepper, divided

1 small onion, peeled and finely chopped

1 medium red bell pepper, seeded and diced

1 teaspoon smoked paprika

3 medium tomatoes, seeded and cut into strips

1. Place the bacon in a large skillet and cook over medium heat until crispy. Remove bacon and set aside on a plate lined with paper towels.

2. Add the okra to the same skillet with ½ teaspoon salt and ½ teaspoon pepper. Sauté over medium-high heat until bright green and crisp, and just lightly browned around the edges, about 5 minutes. Remove okra to the plate with the bacon.

3. Add the onion, bell pepper, remaining salt and pepper, and paprika to the same skillet and cook until vegetables are soft, about 5–8 minutes. Add the tomatoes and cook until tomatoes are soft and liquid has evaporated, about 5 minutes.

4. Add okra and bacon back to the skillet and stir just to warm the okra. Serve warm or at room temperature.

Manioc Soufflé (*Suflê de Mandioca*)

Manioc has a creamy texture and unique flavor that lends itself to this elegant cheesy soufflé.

INGREDIENTS | SERVES 6

1 pound manioc root, peeled, and cut into 3" pieces
5 tablespoons butter, divided
4 tablespoons very fine bread crumbs
3 large eggs, separated
3 tablespoons grated Parmesan cheese
1 teaspoon salt
1 teaspoon freshly ground black pepper
6 ounces provolone cheese, cubed

1. Boil the manioc in salted water until tender when pierced with a fork. Drain and pass cooked manioc through a potato ricer into the bowl of a standing mixer. (If you don't have a potato ricer, you can process the manioc in a food processor.)

2. Preheat the oven to 350°F. Melt 1 tablespoon of butter and brush it onto the insides of 6 (6-ounce) ramekins. Sprinkle the insides of the ramekins with the bread crumbs.

3. Stir remaining butter, egg yolks, Parmesan, salt, and pepper into the manioc and mix well.

4. Beat the egg whites until stiff. Gently fold the egg whites into the manioc mixture.

5. Fill each ramekin halfway with the manioc mixture. Add a few cubes of cheese to each ramekin, and then top with remaining manioc mixture.

6. Bake soufflés for 20 minutes until puffed and golden.

CHAPTER 8

Rice and Beans (*Arroz e Feijão*)

Everyday Black Beans (*Feijão Preto*)

These flavorful basic black beans are a side dish on every plate, especially in Rio de Janeiro, where black beans reign. Everyone cooks their beans their own personal way, but this is a basic Brazilian-style recipe to get you started.

INGREDIENTS | SERVES 6

2 cups dried black beans

6 cups water

3 tablespoons olive oil, divided

2 scallions, chopped

1 bay leaf

1 onion, chopped

2 cloves garlic, minced

1 teaspoon cumin (optional)

1 teaspoon smoked paprika (optional)

8 ounces smoked sausage (such as *linguiça* or *chouriço*), chopped or sliced

½ teaspoon salt

½ teaspoon freshly ground black pepper

1. Place the beans in a bowl and cover with the water. Soak beans overnight.

2. The next day, place the beans and their soaking liquid in a large pot with a tablespoon of olive oil, the scallions, and the bay leaf. Bring beans to a simmer over medium heat, then reduce heat to low, cover, and simmer the beans until they are just tender, about 1 hour.

3. While the beans are simmering, place the remaining olive oil in a skillet with the chopped onion and cook onion over low heat until it is soft and translucent, about 5–8 minutes. Add the garlic, cumin, and paprika. Add the sausage and cook over medium heat until browned.

4. When the beans are tender, transfer about a cup of beans with their liquid to the skillet and mash the beans with a potato masher while combining them with the sausage and onions.

5. Add the sausage/onion mixture to the pot of beans. Season beans with salt and pepper to taste. Simmer for 15–20 minutes longer, to allow flavors to blend. Remove bay leaf before serving.

Brazilian-Style Refried Beans (*Tutu de Feijão*)

These refried beans from Minas Gerais are similar to Mexican refried beans, with the addition of toasted manioc meal to thicken the texture. Other important additions include bacon (or sausage) and a garnish of sliced hard-cooked eggs.

INGREDIENTS | SERVES 6

2 cups dried red beans

6 cups water

1 bay leaf

8 ounces bacon or pork belly, diced into ½" pieces

1 medium onion, peeled and chopped

3 cloves garlic, minced

2 scallions, chopped

½ cup chopped fresh parsley

1 teaspoon salt

½ teaspoon freshly ground black pepper

2 large hard-cooked eggs, peeled and sliced

1. Place the beans in a bowl and cover with the water. Soak beans overnight.

2. The next day, place the beans and their soaking liquid in a large pot with the bay leaf. Bring beans to a simmer over medium heat, then reduce heat to low, cover, and cook the beans until they are just tender, about 1–1½ hours.

3. Drain beans, reserving 2 cups of the cooking liquid, and place them in a blender. Purée the beans until smooth, adding the reserved cooking liquid as needed.

4. Place the bacon in a large skillet and cook over medium heat until crispy. Remove bacon and drain on paper towels, leaving the rendered fat in the pan.

5. Cook the onion in the bacon fat over medium-low heat until it is soft and translucent, about 5–8 minutes. Add the garlic, scallions, and parsley and cook for 1 minute more.

6. Add the puréed beans to the skillet and cook until bubbling, stirring often. Add salt and pepper.

7. Place beans in a serving dish and garnish with egg slices and bacon.

Cowboy Beans (*Feijão Tropeiro Mineiro*)

Cattle drivers (tropeiros) used to carry supplies to miners working in Minas Gerais, including certain food staples, such as salted dried beef, manioc meal, and dried beans. This region features many dishes made from those ingredients, such as this nourishing one pot meal.

INGREDIENTS | SERVES 10

2 cups dried pinto or carioca beans

6 cups water

1 bay leaf

8 ounces bacon or pork belly, diced into ½" pieces

8 ounces smoke cured sausage (such as *linguiça*), chopped or sliced

4 large eggs

2 tablespoons butter or lard

4 cloves garlic, minced

1 cup manioc flour

1 cup very finely sliced collard greens

1 teaspoon salt

1 teaspoon freshly ground black pepper

4 scallions, chopped

½ cup chopped fresh parsley

Fried pork rinds (*torresmo*), for garnish (optional)

1. Place the beans in a bowl and cover with the water. Soak beans overnight.

2. The next day, place the beans and their soaking liquid in a large pot with the bay leaf. Bring beans to a simmer over medium heat, then reduce heat to low, cover, and simmer the beans until they are tender, about 1–1½ hours. Drain the beans and set aside.

3. Place the bacon in a large soup pot and cook over medium heat until fat starts to render. Add the sausage and cook until browned. Remove bacon and sausage and set aside.

4. Whisk the eggs together briefly and add to the pot, scrambling them lightly to form larger clumps. Remove and set aside.

5. Add 2 tablespoons butter or lard to the pot. Add the garlic and cook until softened, about 2–3 minutes. Add the manioc flour and cook until lightly toasted.

6. Add the sausage and bacon back to the pot, along with the beans and the collard greens, and stir well. Cook until everything is heated through. Taste for seasoning and add salt and pepper to taste.

7. Stir in the eggs, scallions, and parsley and serve. Garnish each serving with 1 or 2 pork rinds.

Coconut Beans (*Feijão de Coco*)

The combination of beans and coconut may sound unusual, but it works beautifully in this dish from Pernambuco, a state in northeastern Brazil.

INGREDIENTS | SERVES 8

2 cups dried pinto or carioca beans
6 cups water
1 bay leaf
2 cloves garlic
1 small onion, peeled and quartered
½ cup chopped fresh cilantro
4 scallions, chopped
1 teaspoon cumin
1 teaspoon paprika
1 (13.5-ounce) can coconut milk
1 teaspoon salt
2 tablespoons chopped green onions

1. Place the beans in a bowl and cover with the water. Soak beans overnight.

2. The next day, place the beans and their soaking liquid in a large pot with the bay leaf. Bring beans to a simmer over medium heat, then reduce heat to low, cover, and simmer the beans until they are tender, about 1–1½ hours. Drain the beans, reserving 2 cups of cooking liquid, and set aside.

3. Place the garlic, onion, cilantro, and scallions in a blender or food processor and process until smooth. Add the beans and process, adding some of the cooking liquid, to make a smooth paste.

4. Transfer the bean mixture to a large saucepan. Add the cumin, paprika, coconut milk, and salt. Simmer, stirring constantly, until mixture thickens (10–15 minutes). Mixture should have the consistency of a thick soup.

5. Serve warm, garnished with chopped green onions.

Basic Brazilian-Style Rice (*Arroz Brasileiro*)

The formula for this basic but flavorful white rice is based on the Portuguese tradition of making a refogado—a mixture of onions and garlic cooked in oil until soft and fragrant.

INGREDIENTS | SERVES 4

1 cup long-grain white rice

4 tablespoons vegetable oil

⅓ cup finely chopped onion

2 cloves garlic, crushed or minced

⅓ cup finely diced tomato (optional)

1 teaspoon salt

2 cups water

1. Rinse the rice several times with water and set aside.

2. Place the vegetable oil in a medium saucepan over medium heat. Add the onion and cook until soft and fragrant, about 5 minutes.

3. Add the garlic, tomato (if using), and salt and cook, stirring often, until tomato is very soft and liquid has evaporated, about 3–5 minutes.

4. Add the rice and cook for 2–3 minutes, stirring constantly.

5. Add the water. Cover the pot and reduce the heat to low. Cook for 15 minutes, then turn off the heat, leaving the pot on the burner, and keep covered for 10 minutes longer.

6. Remove cover, fluff rice with a fork, and serve.

Orange Rice (*Arroz com Laranja*)

This savory orange rice goes well with roasted meats or BBQ. Sometimes this pretty rice is served in molded form: The cooked rice is packed into a small greased bowl, then turned out onto the plate, which makes for a very attractive presentation.

INGREDIENTS | SERVES 4

1½ cups long-grain white rice
2 tablespoons vegetable oil
⅓ cup finely chopped onion
¼ cup cashew pieces
½ teaspoon salt
1½ cups orange juice
1½ cups vegetable broth or water
½ cup golden raisins
1 tablespoon orange zest

1. Rinse the rice several times with water and set aside.

2. Place the vegetable oil in a medium saucepan over medium heat. Add the onion and cook until soft and fragrant, about 5–8 minutes.

3. Add the rice, cashew pieces, and salt and cook for 2–3 minutes, stirring constantly.

4. Add the orange juice and vegetable broth. Cover the pot and reduce the heat to low. Cook for 10 minutes. Stir in the raisins and cook for 5 minutes more. Turn off heat and let rice rest, covered, for 10 minutes.

5. Remove cover. Add orange zest and fluff rice with a fork before serving.

Colorful Rice (*Arroz Colorido*)

Carrots, peas, corn, and scallions brighten up ordinary rice for special occasions.

INGREDIENTS | SERVES 6

3 tablespoons vegetable oil
6 ounces ham, cut into small cubes (optional)
¼ cup finely diced onion
2 cloves garlic, minced
1 large carrot, peeled and cut into small (¼") cubes
1 cup frozen peas
1 cup fresh or frozen corn kernels
1½ cups white rice
3 cups water
2 cubes chicken bouillon or vegetable bouillon
½ cup chopped scallions
½ teaspoon salt

1. Place the vegetable oil in a large saucepan over medium heat. Add the ham (if using) and cook until lightly browned. Remove ham and reserve.

2. Add the onion to the same pot and sauté until translucent, abut 5–8 minutes. Add the garlic and carrots and sauté for 2–3 minutes.

3. Add the peas, corn, and rice and sauté for 1–2 minutes, stirring. Add the water and bouillon and bring to a simmer. Cover pan, reduce heat to low, and cook for 10–15 minutes, until and water is absorbed. Turn off heat and leave rice covered for 10 minutes more.

4. Fluff rice, stir in the scallions and ham, and season with salt to taste. Serve warm.

Oxcart Driver's Rice (*Arroz Carreteiro*)

Carreteiros drove oxen-pulled carts accompanying the tropeiros, or famous cattle drivers of Minas Gerais. The carts carried food supplies, including sun-dried beef jerky, rice, and other nonperishables, and the drivers were responsible for cooking the meals. The drivers made this stew of rice and salted dried beef, and it has become one of the most iconic dishes of gaúcho cuisine.

INGREDIENTS | SERVES 6

2 cups long-grain white rice
4 slices bacon, diced
1 cup shredded beef barbecue (already cooked)
1 large onion, peeled and chopped
2 cloves garlic, minced
1 teaspoon salt
4 cups beef broth
⅓ cup chopped scallions
⅓ cup chopped fresh parsley

1. Rinse the rice several times with water and set aside.

2. Place the bacon in a large skillet over medium heat. Cook until bacon is crispy and fat has rendered.

3. Add the shredded beef and sauté until lightly browned, about 2–3 minutes.

4. Add the onion and sauté until soft and fragrant, about 5 minutes. Add the garlic and the salt and stir well.

5. Add the rice and cook for 2–3 minutes, then add the beef broth. Reduce the heat to low, cover, and simmer for 15–20 minutes or until rice is cooked and liquid is absorbed.

6. Uncover and stir in the scallions and parsley. Serve warm.

Crazy Rice (*Arroz Louco*)

This fried rice lives up to its name, as it has a seemingly crazy combination of ingredients.

INGREDIENTS | SERVES 6

4 slices bacon, diced

4 large eggs

½ teaspoon salt

½ teaspoon freshly ground black pepper

2 tablespoons vegetable oil

2 smoke-cured sausages, such as *linguiça*, cut into small cubes

½ cup chopped onion

2 cloves garlic, minced

¼ cup sliced green olives

½ cup frozen yellow corn

¼ cup raisins

3 cups cooked white rice

2 tablespoons chopped parsley

½ cup potato sticks

1. Place the bacon in a large skillet and cook over medium heat until crispy. Remove bacon to a paper towel, reserving the bacon grease.

2. In a small bowl, whisk the eggs together and season with salt and pepper. Cook the eggs in the bacon fat, stirring occasionally, until eggs are scrambled. Remove from heat and set aside.

3. Add the oil and the sausage to the skillet and cook until sausage is slightly browned.

4. Add the onions and sauté until soft and fragrant, about 5 minutes. Add the garlic, olives, corn, and raisins and sauté for 2–3 minutes. Add the rice, scrambled eggs, and parsley and mix well.

5. Transfer rice to a serving dish and garnish with the potato sticks just before serving.

Coconut Rice (*Arroz com Coco*)

Coconut rice has a bit of tropical flair, and goes well with both seafood and chicken.

INGREDIENTS | SERVES 4

1½ cups long-grain white rice

2 tablespoons butter

¼ cup finely chopped onion

½ cup dried shredded unsweetened coconut

½ teaspoon salt

1 (13.5-ounce) can coconut milk

1½ cups water

1. Rinse the rice several times with water and set aside.

2. Place the butter in a medium saucepan over medium heat. Add the onion and cook until soft and fragrant, about 5–8 minutes.

3. Add the shredded coconut and cook for 1–2 minutes. Add the rice and salt and cook for 2–3 minutes, stirring constantly.

4. Add the coconut milk and water. Cover the pot and reduce the heat to low. Cook for 15 minutes. Remove from heat and set aside, covered, for 10 minutes.

5. Remove cover. Fluff rice with a fork before serving.

Baked Rice (*Arroz de Forno*)

This cheesy casserole is a great way to use up leftover cooked rice.

INGREDIENTS | SERVES 6

2 tablespoons butter

1 medium onion, peeled and chopped

2 cloves garlic, minced

2 medium tomatoes, peeled, seeded, and diced

½ cup chopped green olives

½ teaspoon salt

4 cups cooked white rice

½ cup grated Parmesan cheese, divided

2 large eggs

1 cup heavy cream

1½ cups shredded mozzarella cheese, divided

1 teaspoon dried oregano, divided

1. Place the butter in a large skillet over medium heat. Add the onion and cook until soft and translucent, about 5–8 minutes. Add the garlic, tomatoes, green olives, and salt and cook until tomatoes are soft and most of their liquid has evaporated, about 5 minutes. Stir in the cooked rice and remove from heat.

2. In a small bowl, whisk together ¼ cup Parmesan cheese, the eggs, and the cream. Set aside.

3. Preheat oven to 350°F. Place half of the rice mixture in the bottom of a 9" square casserole. Top with 1 cup of the mozzarella cheese. Sprinkle ½ teaspoon oregano over the cheese.

4. Add the remaining rice mixture on top of the cheese. Pour the egg/cream mixture over the entire casserole. Top with the remaining Parmesan, mozzarella, and oregano.

5. Cover casserole with foil and bake for 30 minutes. Remove foil and bake for 10 minutes more, or until cheeses have melted and are lightly browned.

Black Beans and Rice (*Arroz de Feijão Preto*)

In Brazil, this dish is often served with grilled meats.

INGREDIENTS | SERVES 4

2 tablespoons butter

1 medium onion, peeled and chopped

2 cloves garlic, minced

1 bay leaf

½ teaspoon hot pepper sauce

½ teaspoon salt

1 tablespoon tomato paste

1½ cups cooked black beans, in their cooking liquid

1½ cups white rice

1 cup water or chicken stock

Juice of 1 lime

2 tablespoons minced fresh cilantro

1. Place the butter in a large saucepan over medium heat. Add the onion and cook until soft and translucent, about 5–8 minutes. Add the garlic, bay leaf, hot pepper sauce, salt, and tomato paste and cook until well mixed and fragrant, about 2–3 minutes.

2. Stir in the black beans and the rice and 1 cup water or chicken stock, and cook over low heat until they are well mixed and most of the liquid has evaporated, about 15 minutes.

3. Remove from heat and stir in the lime juice and cilantro just before serving.

White Beans with Sausage (*Feijão Branco com Linguiça*)

Brazilians often cook white beans the Italian way, with sausage, tomatoes, oregano, and bay leaves.

INGREDIENTS | SERVES 6

2 cups dried white beans

4 slices bacon, diced

4 Italian-style sausages or similar

1 large onion, peeled and diced

4 cloves garlic, minced

1 large tomato, peeled, seeded, and diced

1 teaspoon smoked paprika

2 teaspoons dried oregano

1 bay leaf

6 cups water or vegetable stock

1 teaspoon salt

1 teaspoon freshly ground black pepper

¼ cup chopped fresh parsley

1. Place the beans in a bowl, cover with water, and leave to soak overnight.

2. The next day, drain the beans and set aside. Add the bacon to a stockpot and cook over medium heat until crispy. Add the sausage and cook until browned.

3. Add the onion to the stockpot and cook until translucent, about 5–8 minutes. Add the garlic, tomato, paprika, oregano, and bay leaf, and cook until tomato is soft, about 5 minutes.

4. Add the beans and the water or vegetable stock and bring to a simmer over medium heat. Reduce heat to low, cover, and cook for 1 hour, or until beans are just tender. Season with salt and pepper to taste and simmer, uncovered, for another 30–40 minutes.

5. Garnish with parsley and serve.

Black-Eyed Peas and Rice (*Baião de Dois*)

Baião is the name of a particular folk dance and type of music from northeastern Brazil, and this dish is called "baião for two," since the black-eyed peas and the rice make such great dance partners. Use fresh black-eyed peas for this dish when you can find them; otherwise, frozen ones work well.

INGREDIENTS | SERVES 4

4 slices bacon, diced

1 medium onion, peeled and chopped

2 cloves garlic, minced

¼ cup chopped fresh cilantro

¼ cup diced scallions

½ teaspoon hot pepper sauce

¾ teaspoon salt

2 cups fresh black-eyed peas

3 cups chicken stock or water, divided

1¼ cups white rice

8 ounces smoked mozzarella cheese, cubed

Cowpeas (*Feijão-verde, Feijão-fradinho, Feijão-de-corda*)

There are many names for this beloved bean in Brazil and South America, including *feijão-carita*, or "bean with a little face." These nutritious beans were first cultivated in Africa but have spread to other regions, thanks to their drought and heat tolerance. In Brazil, black-eyed peas are associated with Afro-Brazilian cuisine, especially with the famous Bahian specialty *acarajé*, a fritter made with black-eyed peas and dried shrimp.

1. Place the bacon in a large saucepan over medium heat. Cook until bacon is crispy. Remove bacon with a slotted spoon and set aside.

2. Add the onion to the skillet and cook the onion in the bacon grease until it is soft and translucent, about 5–8 minutes.

3. Add the garlic, cilantro, scallions, hot pepper sauce, and salt, and cook until well mixed and fragrant, about 2–3 minutes.

4. Add the black-eyed peas and 2 cups of the chicken stock. Cover the pan, reduce the heat to low, and simmer until the beans are tender, about 40 minutes. Add the rice and remaining chicken stock. Cover and cook for 15 minutes more, checking occasionally to see if more liquid is needed.

5. Remove from heat and stir in the mozzarella just before serving.

CHAPTER 9

Sauces and Condiments (*Molhos*)

Brazil Nut Pesto (*Molho Pesto de Castanha-do-Pará*)

In Portuguese, the name of this large nut, castanha-do-pará, translates to "chestnut from Pará" (a state in the northern Amazonian region of Brazil). This pesto recipe is similar to traditional Italian pesto made with pine nuts but takes advantage of the creamy, rich flavor of this local nut.

INGREDIENTS | SERVES 4

1 cup coarsely chopped Brazil nuts

2 cloves garlic, peeled

½ cup fresh parsley leaves

2 tablespoons grated Parmesan cheese

1 teaspoon lemon zest

1 teaspoon salt

½ teaspoon freshly ground black pepper

⅓ cup olive oil

1. Place the Brazil nuts in the bowl of a food processor with the garlic. Process until finely chopped.

2. Add the parsley and the Parmesan and process in short pulses until finely chopped.

3. Add the lemon zest, salt (to taste), and pepper. Add the olive oil slowly, processing mixture until you have a relatively smooth paste.

4. Refrigerate pesto in a jar or other glass container, completely covered with a thin layer of olive oil, for up to 5 days. To serve with pasta, thin pesto slightly with pasta cooking water, then toss with cooked pasta and extra Parmesan cheese.

Brazil Nut Facts

Brazil nut trees are dependent on a complex and fragile ecological system. Certain orchids must be present around the base of the trees. These orchids attract the specific species of bee that can pollinate the tree's flowers. Rodents must bury the seeds in order for new trees to grow. The fruit that falls from these huge trees is heavy, and can be dangerous to people standing below. On a more positive note, Brazil nuts are high in the mineral selenium, which is thought to have some protective effects against cancer. Brazil nuts are very high in fat, and quickly turn rancid if not stored properly.

Red Pepper Sauce (*Molho de Pimenta*)

This basic spicy pepper sauce goes with just about anything, and it will keep for a couple of weeks in the refrigerator (stored in a glass jar).

INGREDIENTS | SERVES 10

½ cup vinegar
½ cup good-quality olive oil
1 (2") hot red chili pepper
3 medium red bell peppers
1 teaspoon salt
1 teaspoon sugar
2 cloves garlic, peeled
1 small onion, peeled and chopped
1 bay leaf

1. Place the vinegar and olive oil in a blender.

2. Remove the stems and seeds from the peppers and add them to the blender, along with the salt, sugar, garlic, and onion.

3. Process mixture until smooth. Transfer mixture to a saucepan and add the bay leaf. Simmer sauce over low heat for 5–8 minutes, until it thickens slightly.

4. Remove from heat and let cool. Remove the bay leaf. Place the sauce in a glass jar and store in the refrigerator for up to 2 weeks.

Brazilian Chili Peppers

Brazilians cook with many different chili peppers, ranging from very hot to mild and sweet. Two of the most common (often used to make pepper sauce) are the *malagueta* pepper and the *dedo-de-moça* (girl's finger) pepper. The *malagueta* pepper (which is named after a different West African plant) is used frequently in Bahian cuisine. *Pimenta-dedo-de-moça* is a 3"-long, finger-like red pepper that is native to Brazil. It's slightly milder than the *malagueta* variety, but a bit hotter than a jalapeño.

Tomato Onion Vinaigrette for Grilled Meats
(*Molho à Companha*)

This condiment/salsa of tomatoes and bell peppers is served at churrascarias (Brazilian barbecue restaurants) to accompany grilled meats. This sauce is best on the day that it is made.

INGREDIENTS | SERVES 10

2 tomatoes, peeled, seeded, and finely chopped

1 medium red bell pepper, seeded and finely chopped

1 medium green bell pepper, seeded and finely chopped

1 large onion, peeled and finely chopped

2 tablespoons chopped fresh parsley

1 tablespoon chopped fresh cilantro

4 tablespoons vinegar

4 tablespoons olive oil

1 teaspoon salt

½ teaspoon freshly ground black pepper

1. Place the tomatoes, bell peppers, onion, parsley, and cilantro in a medium bowl and toss together to mix.

2. In a small bowl, whisk together the vinegar, olive oil, salt, and black pepper. Add to the vegetables and mix well.

3. Store salsa in the refrigerator until ready to use. Serve on the same day that sauce is prepared for best flavor, but sauce will keep refrigerated for up to 3 days.

Chili Pepper Sauce with Lime (*Molho de Pimenta e Limão*)

This brightly flavored pepper sauce has the added tang of lime juice, which is excellent with grilled fish. Stir a bit of this sauce into some mayonnaise for a delicious sandwich spread, or use it as a marinade.

INGREDIENTS | SERVES 8

4 or 5 pickled chili peppers
1 clove garlic, peeled
½ cup chopped onion
1 tablespoon chopped fresh parsley
1 teaspoon salt
½ teaspoon ground black pepper
⅓ cup fresh lime juice
¼ cup olive oil

1. Place the chili peppers, garlic, onion, parsley, salt, and black pepper in a food processor or blender and pulse briefly several times, until ingredients are finely minced.

2. Add the lime juice and pulse briefly to mix. Add the olive oil in a steady stream and pulse to mix.

3. Transfer mixture to a glass jar and store in the refrigerator until ready to use, or up to 1 week.

Green Mayonnaise Dressing (*Molho de Maionese Verde*)

This dressing is delicious with sausages, with fried potatoes or manioc, and on sandwiches. You can add other herbs to the mayonnaise, like basil, oregano, or chives.

INGREDIENTS | SERVES 6

1 egg yolk
2 tablespoons fresh lime juice
½ teaspoon salt
1 teaspoon yellow mustard
½ cup plain yogurt or heavy cream
1½ cups vegetable oil
1 clove garlic, chopped
½ cup chopped fresh parsley
½ cup chopped scallions

1. Combine the egg yolk, lime juice, salt, mustard, and yogurt or cream in a blender or food processor and blend until smooth.

2. Add the vegetable oil in a steady stream while the blender or processor is running, and blend until mixture is emulsified, creamy, and thickened.

3. Add garlic, parsley, and scallions and pulse briefly until well mixed.

4. Use immediately or store in the refrigerator for 2–3 days.

Smell Green (*Cheiro Verde*)

Chopped fresh parsley and chopped scallions are so commonly used in Brazilian cooking that they are often packaged together in the supermarket and labeled *cheiro verde*, which translates literally to "smell green." They do add a nice burst of fresh, spring-like flavor when added to your favorite dish in combination.

Creamy Garlic Sauce (*Molho de Maionese para Churrasco*)

This aioli-style garlic mayonnaise is delicious with all kinds of grilled meats, but it is also good on sandwiches or as a dipping sauce for vegetables.

INGREDIENTS | SERVES 10

2 cloves garlic, peeled

¼ cup chopped onion

2 tablespoons fresh lime juice

1 teaspoon smoked paprika

½ teaspoon cumin

½ teaspoon hot pepper sauce

1½ cups mayonnaise

1. Place the garlic and onion in the bowl of a food processor. Process with several brief pulses until finely chopped.

2. Add the lime juice, smoked paprika, cumin, hot pepper sauce, and mayonnaise and process briefly until well mixed and smooth.

3. Store in refrigerator until ready to use, for up to 5 days.

Homemade Mayonnaise (*Maionese Caseira*)

Mayonnaise is quick and easy to make with a blender or food processor. Add 1 whole egg and 1 egg yolk (use very fresh eggs, as they will not be cooked) to a blender or food processor with 1 teaspoon Dijon mustard. Process until well mixed. While the blender or processor is running, gradually add 1 cup vegetable oil (or olive oil) until mixture is smooth and emulsified. Add 1 tablespoon fresh lime juice and salt and pepper to taste. Store mayonnaise for up to 4 days in the refrigerator.

Chimichurri Sauce (*Molho Chimichurri para Churrasco*)

*This garlicky herb sauce is associated with Argentinian grilling, but Brazilians enjoy it as well.
It is the perfect accompaniment for grilled steak.*

INGREDIENTS | SERVES 10

4 cloves garlic, peeled and coarsely chopped

1½ cups packed fresh parsley leaves

½ cup packed fresh cilantro leaves

1 tablespoon dried oregano

1 teaspoon kosher salt

½ teaspoon red pepper flakes

½–1 cup olive oil

1. Place the garlic in a food processor and pulse until finely chopped. Add the parsley and cilantro and pulse briefly until finely chopped.

2. Transfer chopped herbs and garlic to a small bowl, and stir in the oregano, salt (to taste), and red pepper flakes. Add enough olive oil to completely cover the herbs.

3. Store in refrigerator until ready to serve, or up to 3 days. Serve at room temperature.

Rosé Sauce (*Molho Rosé*)

*Brazilians enjoy this tasty tomato-mayo sauce with French fries and other fried foods.
One popular bar snack is a plate of hard-cooked quail eggs, served with toothpicks and
this sauce for dipping (Ovos de Codorna com Molho Rosé).*

INGREDIENTS | SERVES 10

1 cup mayonnaise

½ cup ketchup

2 cloves garlic, peeled

1 teaspoon Dijon mustard

¼ teaspoon red pepper flakes

1 teaspoon paprika

1 tablespoon olive oil

1 tablespoon fresh lime juice

Place all of the ingredients in a food processor or blender and process until smooth. Store in the refrigerator for up to a week.

Sun-Dried Tomato Sauce (*Molho de Tomate Seco*)

Dried plum tomatoes give the sauce its rich, sweet flavor.

INGREDIENTS | SERVES 4

1 cup sun-dried tomatoes
2 cloves garlic, peeled
½ cup olive oil
¼ cup fresh basil leaves
1 teaspoon salt
½ teaspoon freshly ground black pepper
2 tablespoons grated Parmesan cheese

Jarred Sun-Dried Tomatoes in Oil (*Conserva de Tomate Seco*)

If you happen to have sun-dried tomatoes that are packed in oil instead of dried tomatoes, skip the soak in boiling water and add 1 cup of the jarred tomatoes with their oil directly to the food processor. Add the garlic and process until smooth, adding extra olive oil if needed. Add the basil, salt, black pepper, and Parmesan and process briefly to mix.

1. Place the sun-dried tomatoes in a heatproof bowl and cover them with boiling water. Set aside for 30 minutes.

2. Drain tomatoes and place them in the bowl of a food processor with the garlic. While the processor is running, add the olive oil in a steady stream until you have a smooth paste.

3. Add the basil leaves, salt, pepper, and Parmesan and pulse briefly to mix.

4. Store in an airtight container in the refrigerator until ready to serve, or up to 4 days. Serve sauce warm on pasta (thin with water or vegetable broth, if desired) or at room temperature with toasted bread slices.

Passion Fruit Dressing (*Molho de Maracujá para Salada*)

This sweet yet tangy dressing is excellent on salads and can also be used as a marinade for chicken or fish. If fresh passion fruit is unavailable, frozen passion fruit pulp is often available in the frozen-food section.

INGREDIENTS | SERVES 6

¼ cup passion fruit purée
2 tablespoons sugar
1 tablespoon fresh lime juice
1 tablespoon orange juice
1 tablespoon white vinegar
¼ teaspoon salt
½ cup vegetable oil

1. Place the passion fruit purée, sugar, lime juice, and orange juice in a saucepan and heat over medium-low heat, stirring constantly, until sugar is dissolved, about 2–3 minutes.

2. Remove from heat and whisk in the vinegar and salt (to taste).

3. Add the vegetable oil in a steady stream, whisking continuously.

4. Refrigerate until ready to use, or for up to 1 week.

Yogurt Tahini Dressing (*Molho de Iogurte para Salada*)

*Brazilians enjoy this yogurt dressing on salads, and it makes a great dip for the popular
Middle Eastern snack Kibe (see recipe in Chapter 2).*

INGREDIENTS | SERVES 6

1 cup plain Greek yogurt

Juice of 1 lime

¼ cup fresh mint leaves, finely chopped

2 tablespoons minced fresh parsley

1 clove garlic, minced

⅓ cup tahini

½ teaspoon salt

½ teaspoon freshly ground black pepper

2–3 tablespoons olive oil

1. In a small bowl, whisk the yogurt and lime juice together.

2. Add the mint, parsley, garlic, tahini, salt (to taste), and pepper and mix well.

3. Whisk in the olive oil to desired consistency.

4. Refrigerate until ready to use, or for up to 5 days.

Savory Açaí Sauce (*Molho de Açaí*)

*Açaí berries are the fruit of the açaí palm. These intensely colored purple berries taste
a little bit like blackberries, and some people also detect a note of chocolate.
Açaí pulp is available in the frozen-food section of most grocery stores.*

INGREDIENTS | SERVES 4

¼ cup minced onion

2 tablespoons butter

2 teaspoons cornstarch dissolved in ¼ cup water

¼ cup port wine

1 tablespoon sugar

½ cup açaí pulp

½ teaspoon salt

1. In a small saucepan, sauté the onion in the butter over medium heat until soft and fragrant, about 5–8 minutes.

2. Add the cornstarch/water mixture and sauté for 1 minute more, stirring constantly.

3. Add the port and the sugar and simmer until mixture thickens. Whisk in the açai pulp and the salt and cook for 2–3 minutes more. Remove from heat and let cool.

4. Refrigerate until ready to use, or for up to 3 days.

Pão de Queijo (Chapter 10)

Creme de Papaya (Chapter 12)

Escabeche de Peixe (Chapter 6)

Assado de Berinjela e Tomate (Chapter 7)

Moqueca de Peixe Baiana (Chapter 6)

Sopa de Abóbora e Coco (Chapter 4)

Frango Xadrez (Chapter 5)

Sagu de Vinho (Chapter 12)

Molho Chimichurri Para Churrasco (Chapter 9)

Feijoada Completa (Chapter 4)

Chocolate Quente Cremoso (Chapter 18)

Quindim (Chapter 12)

Maionese de Batata (Chapter 3)

Arroz com Laranja (Chapter 8)

Brigadeiros (Chapter 14)

Galinhada Mineira (Chapter 4)

Salada de Couve com Manga (Chapter 3)

Salada de Fruta com Molho de Maracujá (Chapter 3)

Bolinho de Fubá com Goiabada (Chapter 17)

Salada de Berinjela (Chapter 3)

Cachorro-Quente (Chapter 11)

Caipirinha (Chapter 18)

Mandioca Frita (Chapter 7)

Couve à Mineira (Chapter 7)
with smoked sausage

Creamy Coconut Shrimp (*Vatapá*)

Vatapá is a shrimp stew with ground nuts, coconut milk, and dendê oil (palm oil) that is thickened with bread crumbs. Vatapá is served as a side dish, and it is also cooked into a thick paste and used as a condiment for the black-eyed pea fritters called acarajé, a popular street-food snack in Bahia.

INGREDIENTS | SERVES 6

3 slightly stale French bread rolls

1 (13.5-ounce) can coconut milk

½ cup roasted peanuts, skins removed

½ cup roasted cashews

4 ounces dried shrimp

¼ cup fresh parsley leaves

¼ cup fresh cilantro leaves

1 medium onion, peeled and chopped

1 clove garlic, peeled

1 medium tomato, seeded and chopped

¾ teaspoon salt

2 tablespoons *dendê* oil

Dendê Oil

Dendê oil comes from an African palm tree with bright red fruit (brought to Brazil with the West African slaves). *Dendê* oil is obtained from the fruit, and is orange/red in color with a high saturated fat content, making it semi-solid at room temperature. It's a key ingredient in Bahian cooking, and its distinctive flavor and color are one of the identifying features of that unique Afro-Brazilian cuisine.

1. Crumble the bread and place it in a small bowl. Pour the coconut milk over the bread and set aside.

2. Place the nuts and the dried shrimp in a food processor and process until finely ground.

3. Add the parsley, cilantro, onion, garlic, tomato, and salt to the food processor and pulse several times until vegetables are finely chopped. Add the coconut milk and bread in 3 parts, mixing after each addition, until you have a smooth liquid paste. If the mixture is very thick, add some water or fish stock.

4. Transfer mixture to a medium saucepan and add the *dendê* oil. Simmer mixture over low heat, stirring constantly, until it is thick and fragrant.

5. Serve warm as a condiment for *acarajé*, or over rice. *Vatapá* will keep, refrigerated, for up to 3 days.

Shrimp and Okra Sauce (*Caruru*)

Caruru, *like* vatapá, *is served as both a side dish and a condiment for* acarajé *(deep-fried black-eyed pea fritters). The texture is more like a sauce—not as creamy and paste-like as* vatapá.

INGREDIENTS | SERVES 6

½ cup roasted peanuts, skins removed

½ cup roasted cashews

4 ounces dried shrimp

1 pound fresh okra

¼ cup *dendê* oil

½ teaspoon salt

1 small onion, peeled and finely chopped

2 teaspoons minced fresh ginger

2 cloves garlic, minced

1 small red chili pepper, seeded and minced

1 cup fish stock or water

1. Place the nuts and the dried shrimp in a food processor and process until they are finely ground.

2. Slice the okra crosswise into ½" pieces, reserving 2 or 3 whole okra for garnish if desired.

3. Place *dendê* oil in a large skillet over medium heat. Add the okra and salt and fry until crispy and lightly browned, about 3–5 minutes. Remove okra with a slotted spoon and set aside on a plate lined with paper towels.

4. Add onion to the skillet and sauté until fragrant and translucent, about 5–8 minutes. Add the ginger, garlic, and chili pepper and cook for 2–3 minutes more. Add the ground nuts and shrimp and cook, stirring frequently, for 4–6 minutes.

5. Add the okra and fish stock and simmer for 10–15 minutes over low heat, stirring constantly, until mixture is very fragrant and slightly thickened.

6. Serve warm either over rice or as a dipping sauce.

CHAPTER 10

Breads (*Pães*)

Gluten-Free Cheese Rolls (*Pão de Queijo*)

These unusual rolls are basically large cheese puffs. Pão de queijo is made with queijo minas, a firm salty cheese, but farmer cheese, Monterey jack, mozzarella, or Parmesan are all good substitutes. These are best when enjoyed straight from the oven.

INGREDIENTS | MAKES 18

2 cups milk or buttermilk

4 tablespoons butter

4 tablespoons vegetable oil

1 teaspoon salt

4½ cups manioc (tapioca) starch

4 large eggs

2 cups grated farmer cheese (or a combination of Monterey jack and mozzarella)

½ cup grated Parmesan cheese

Manioc Starch (*Polvilho*)

Manioc starch (also called tapioca starch) comes in two varieties: sweet (*polvilho doce*) and sour (*polvilho azedo*). Manioc starch is obtained from liquid that has been pressed from manioc root. When this liquid is fermented before it is processed, the starch has a tangy flavor (sour starch). Either starch can be used for these rolls. Some people prefer the distinctive buttermilk-like taste of the sour starch, while others prefer the sweeter unfermented starch. Most manioc starch available in the United States is fermented, but you can find *polvilho doce* (sweet tapioca starch) in Brazilian markets and online.

1. Preheat oven to 375°F. Line a large baking sheet with parchment paper.

2. Place the milk, butter, vegetable oil, and salt in a medium saucepan over medium-low heat. Bring to a simmer, stirring constantly.

3. Place the manioc starch in a large bowl. Pour the hot milk mixture into the bowl and mix well with a wooden spoon.

4. Stir in the eggs and the cheeses and mix well. Knead mixture briefly, just until it forms a smooth dough.

5. Use the palms of your hands to roll the dough into 2" balls. Place the balls on the baking sheet, spacing them about 2" apart.

6. Bake rolls for 25–30 minutes, or until rolls are puffed and round, and lightly browned. Rolls should have a nice crust and sound hollow when tapped. Remove from oven and serve immediately.

Portuguese-Style Corn Bread (*Broa*)

Broa *is a yeasted country-style cornmeal bread from Portugal.*
Broa *has a distinctive round shape and decorative crisscross pattern of slashes.*

INGREDIENTS | MAKES 1 LARGE LOAF

½ cup milk

½ cup water

2 tablespoons sugar

½ teaspoon fennel or anise seeds

2 teaspoons active dry yeast

1⅓ cups finely ground cornmeal

1⅔ cups bread flour

1 teaspoon salt

3 tablespoons olive oil

1. Place the milk, water, sugar, and fennel seeds in a medium saucepan and bring to a simmer over medium-low heat. Remove from heat and let cool.

2. Once the mixture has cooled until just warm to the touch, sprinkle the yeast over the mixture and set aside for 5 minutes.

3. Place the cornmeal, bread flour, salt, and olive oil in a large bowl (or the bowl of a standing mixer). Add the yeast mixture and knead until you have a smooth, stretchy dough, adding more flour as needed if dough is too sticky.

4. Place the dough in an oiled bowl and loosely cover with a dishcloth. Place in a warm spot and let rise for 1–2 hours, or until doubled in bulk.

5. Preheat the oven to 400°F. Punch down the dough and turn it out on a floured surface. Press or roll the dough into an 8" disk. Place the loaf on a baking sheet lined with parchment paper, and set aside in a warm place to rise for 45 minutes. Dust the loaf with flour and use a sharp knife to make decorative crisscross slashes on top of the loaf.

6. Bake loaf until it is lightly browned and sounds hollow when tapped, about 30–40 minutes. Let cool before slicing.

"Husband Keeping" Bread (*Pão Segura Marido*)

*This delicious and filling calzone-like bread should keep
any hungry man (or woman or teenager) safely at home for dinner.*

INGREDIENTS | MAKES 2 LOAVES

1 cup warm milk
1 teaspoon sugar
1 tablespoon quick-rising yeast
4¼ cups all-purpose flour, divided
1½ teaspoons salt
4 tablespoons butter, softened
¼ cup vegetable oil

4 tablespoons pizza sauce
1 tablespoon dried oregano, divided
6 ounces sliced deli ham
6 ounces sliced mozzarella cheese
8 ounces cream cheese, softened
1 beaten egg yolk
1 tablespoon grated Parmesan cheese

1. In a small bowl, stir together the milk and sugar and sprinkle the yeast over the milk. Set aside for 5 minutes.

2. Add 4 cups of the flour and the salt to the bowl of a standing mixer. Use the dough hook attachment to mix briefly.

3. Add the butter and oil to the flour and mix briefly. Add the milk mixture gradually, mixing at low speed.

4. Knead dough for 3–5 minutes, or until dough is very smooth and elastic, adding more flour if dough is too wet, or 1–2 tablespoons milk if dough is too dry.

5. Place dough in an oiled bowl, loosely cover, and let rise in a warm place until doubled in bulk, about 1 hour.

6. Preheat oven to 375°F. Divide dough into 2 halves. On a floured surface, roll out each half into an 8" × 10" rectangle.

7. Spread 2 tablespoons pizza sauce on each half, leaving 1" of dough free of sauce at the top of one long side. Sprinkle ½ tablespoon of oregano over the sauce. Layer the ham and mozzarella cheese on top of the tomato sauce, diving it equally between the 2 pieces of dough. Spread the cream cheese over the ham and mozzarella cheese, dividing it equally between the 2 halves.

8. Roll up each piece of dough, starting with a long side that is opposite of the side that is not covered with sauce. Place the loaves seam side down on a large baking sheet lined with parchment paper. Brush each loaf with egg yolk, and sprinkle with remaining oregano and Parmesan.

9. Bake loaves until they have risen, are golden brown, and sound slightly hollow when tapped, about 30–40 minutes. Remove from oven and let cool before slicing.

Cornmeal Popovers (*Broinhas de Fubá*)

These rolls are a tasty cross between the corn bread loaf Broa and the popover-like rolls Pão de Queijo (see both recipes in this chapter).

INGREDIENTS | MAKES 16

1 cup milk

1 cup water

¼ cup butter

1 teaspoon fennel or anise seeds

1 cup finely ground cornmeal

1 cup all-purpose flour

2 tablespoons sugar

1 teaspoon salt

5 large eggs

1. Place the milk, water, butter, and fennel seeds in a large saucepan and bring to a simmer over medium low heat.

2. Whisk in the cornmeal, flour, sugar, and salt, and mix well. Cook over low heat, stirring constantly, until mixture comes together as a dough.

3. Remove from heat and stir the eggs into the dough one at a time.

4. Preheat the oven to 400°F. Line a baking sheet with parchment paper and dust with flour.

5. Use an ice cream scoop or deep spoon dusted with flour to scoop up mounds of dough and place them 1" apart on the prepared baking sheet.

6. Bake rolls for 20–30 minutes, or until they are lightly browned and puffed. Rolls should sound hollow when tapped. Remove from heat and serve immediately (rolls may deflate slightly as they cool).

Sweet "Armadillo" Bread (*Pão Sovado*)

Pão sovado (also called pão tatu because its shape resembles an armadillo) has a rich and uniformly light texture, very similar to Portuguese sweet bread. It is excellent for breakfast, for sandwiches, or for making sweet rolls.

INGREDIENTS | MAKES 2 LOAVES

1 cup milk
½ cup butter
5 tablespoons sugar, divided
1 tablespoon active dry yeast
5 cups all-purpose flour
1½ teaspoons salt
3 large eggs, plus 3 egg yolks, divided
1 teaspoon brewed coffee

1. Place the milk, butter, and 1 tablespoon of the sugar in a small saucepan and heat over low heat until butter is melted. Remove from heat. Mixture should be just warm to the touch. Sprinkle yeast over the mixture and set aside for 5 minutes.

2. Add the flour, remaining sugar, salt, 3 eggs, and 2 egg yolks to the bowl of a standing mixer. Use the dough hook attachment to mix briefly.

3. Add the milk/yeast mixture to the mixer gradually, mixing at low speed at the same time.

4. Knead dough for 5–8 minutes, or until dough is very smooth and elastic.

5. Place dough in an oiled bowl, loosely cover, and let rise in a warm place until doubled in bulk, about 1½ hours.

6. Divide dough into 2 halves, and shape each half into a short oblong loaf. Place the loaves on a large baking sheet lined with parchment paper.

7. Whisk together the remaining egg yolk with the coffee and brush the mixture lightly onto the rolls. Set dough aside, loosely covered, and let rise.

8. Preheat oven to 350°F. Use a sharp knife to make several crosswise slashes in the top of each loaf, as well as one deeper slash down the length of each loaf. Brush loaves with egg/coffee wash one more time.

9. Bake loaves until they have risen, are golden brown, and sound slightly hollow when tapped, about 30–40 minutes. Remove from oven and let cool before slicing.

Onion Rolls (*Pão de Cebola*)

*Have you ever made bread with your blender? That's practically all you will need
to make these super easy savory onion rolls.*

INGREDIENTS | MAKES 20

¾ cup warm milk

¼ cup olive oil

2 large eggs, plus 1 egg yolk

1 teaspoon sugar

1 teaspoon salt

3 tablespoons dried minced onions, divided

2 tablespoons grated Parmesan cheese

4 cups all-purpose flour

2 teaspoons quick-rising yeast

1 teaspoon brewed coffee

1 tablespoon dried oregano

1 teaspoon poppy seeds

½ teaspoon kosher salt

1. Place the milk, olive oil, 2 eggs, sugar, salt, 2 tablespoons dried onion, and Parmesan in a blender. Blend just until smooth.

2. Whisk the flour and yeast together in a large bowl. Gradually add the liquid mixture, stirring until dough starts to form. Then knead dough until very smooth and elastic, adding more flour if dough is too sticky to handle.

3. Place dough in an oiled bowl, loosely cover, and let rise in a warm place until doubled in bulk, about 1 hour.

4. Divide dough into 20 pieces, and roll each piece into a smooth ball. Place rolls about 1" apart on a large baking sheet lined with parchment paper, or in a rectangular baking pan lined with parchment.

5. Mix the egg yolk with the coffee and brush rolls lightly with the mixture. Let rolls rise in a warm place until doubled in size, about 1 hour.

6. Preheat oven to 350°F. Brush rolls with egg/coffee wash one more time. Stir together the remaining dried onion, oregano, poppy seeds, and kosher salt and sprinkle mixture evenly onto the top of the rolls.

7. Bake rolls until they have risen and are golden brown, about 25–30 minutes.

Portuguese Bread Rolls (*Pão Português*)

These crusty rolls are similar to French bread, but they have a distinctive shape. The rolls are oblong with pointed ends, and there is a deep slash down the center of each roll that widens in the oven.

INGREDIENTS | MAKES 12

2 cups water, divided
5¼ cups bread flour, divided
2 teaspoons active dry yeast, divided
1½ teaspoons salt
3 tablespoons olive oil
1 cup ice

1. The night before baking the rolls, make the sponge: Place 1 cup water, 1¼ cups flour, and ½ teaspoon yeast in a small bowl and stir to mix. Cover with plastic wrap and set aside until the following day.

2. Place the remaining flour, the remaining yeast, the salt, and the sponge in the bowl of a standing mixer. Knead the mixture with the dough hook attachment until dough is smooth and elastic, adding a bit more flour if dough is too sticky or a bit more water if dough is too dry.

3. Place dough in an oiled bowl, loosely cover, and let rise in a warm place until doubled in bulk, about 1½ hours.

4. Divide the dough into 12 pieces and roll each piece into a ball. Let rest for 5 minutes. On a lightly floured surface, roll each ball into an oblong roll, and pinch the ends into points. Place rolls on a floured baguette pan or floured baking sheet. If using a baking sheet, separate the rolls with a floured dishtowel to prevent them from spreading. Let rolls rise in a warm place for 30 minutes.

5. Preheat the oven to 400°F. Remove dishtowel, if using. With a sharp knife, make a lengthwise cut in each roll, about ½" deep. Drizzle some olive oil into each cut.

6. Place rolls in the oven, and add shallow pan containing 1 cup of ice to the floor of the oven to create steam. Bake rolls until they are well browned and sound hollow when tapped, about 25–30 minutes.

Potato Bread Rolls (*Pão de Batata*)

Mashed potatoes make these rolls soft and slightly sweet, and help them keep much longer than regular bread. Use these rolls for sandwiches, or have one for breakfast with cheese.

INGREDIENTS | MAKES 20

⅓ cup warm milk

2 tablespoons sugar, divided

2 teaspoons active dry yeast

4 cups all-purpose flour

1 teaspoon salt

2 tablespoons butter, softened

2 tablespoons vegetable oil

2 large eggs

2 medium potatoes, peeled, boiled, and mashed

1 egg yolk

1. Place the milk in a small bowl with 1 teaspoon of sugar and sprinkle the yeast over the milk. Set aside for 5 minutes.

2. Place 4 cups of flour, remaining sugar, salt, butter, vegetable oil, eggs, and potatoes in the bowl of a standing mixer. Add the milk/yeast mixture and knead with the dough hook attachment until dough is smooth and elastic, adding a bit more flour if dough is too sticky or a bit more milk if dough is too dry.

3. Place the dough in an oiled bowl. Cover loosely and let rise in a warm place until doubled in bulk, about 1 hour.

4. Divide the dough into 20 pieces and roll each piece into a smooth ball. Place rolls 2" apart on a lightly floured baking sheet, and set aside in a warm place to rise for 30 minutes.

5. Preheat the oven to 375°F. Brush the rolls lightly with egg yolk. Bake for 25–30 minutes, or until rolls are lightly browned.

Sweet Bread Ring with Cream Filling (*Pão Doce com Creme*)

This sweet bread ring is filled with vanilla pastry cream. Though it might seem tricky to fill the dough with pastry cream and braid it, it's actually fun, and the dough is very forgiving.

INGREDIENTS | SERVES 10

2 cups warm milk, divided

4½ cups all-purpose flour, divided

1 cup sugar, divided

2 teaspoons quick-rising yeast

¼ cup butter, melted

¼ cup vegetable oil

2 large eggs, plus 3 egg yolks

1 teaspoon salt

2 teaspoons vanilla, divided

2 tablespoons cornstarch

1 tablespoon butter

1 teaspoon brewed coffee

1. Place 1 cup milk, 1 cup flour, ½ cup sugar, yeast, melted butter, oil, 2 eggs, salt, and 1 teaspoon vanilla in the bowl of a standing mixer. Mix with the dough hook attachment until smooth.

2. Add remaining flour gradually, kneading until dough is smooth and elastic, adding a bit more flour if dough is too sticky or 1–2 tablespoons of milk if dough is too dry.

3. Place the dough in an oiled bowl. Cover loosely and let rise until doubled in bulk, about 1 hour. Dough can rise in the refrigerator overnight. (Bring to room temperature before rolling out dough.)

4. While dough is rising, prepare pastry cream: In a medium heatproof bowl, whisk together the remaining sugar and cornstarch. Add 2 egg yolks and beat until pale yellow. Heat remaining milk in a small saucepan until almost boiling. Gradually whisk hot milk into egg/sugar mixture. Transfer mixture back to the saucepan, and cook over low heat, stirring constantly, until mixture thickens, about 5 minutes. Remove from heat and stir in 1 tablespoon butter and 1 teaspoon vanilla. Cover with plastic wrap and chill until ready to use.

5. Divide dough into 3 equal parts. Roll each part into a long, thin log and flatten into a rectangle (14" × 5"). Spread the pastry cream evenly over the 3 rectangles, leaving a ½" border. Roll each rectangle up, starting with a long side. Braid the 3 rectangles of dough together and shape the braid into a ring, uniting the ends. Place dough ring on a baking sheet lined with parchment paper.

6. Preheat the oven to 350°F. Whisk remaining egg yolk with coffee and brush over dough. Set dough aside to rise for 30 minutes.

7. Bake for 35–40 minutes, or until golden brown.

Italian Bread Loaf (*Pão Panhoca*)

This is a basic Italian bread loaf, great for sandwiches. Another popular way to enjoy these big, round loaves is to hollow them out and fill them with cheese fondue (see sidebar).

INGREDIENTS | MAKES 3 LOAVES

4½ cups all-purpose flour

1 teaspoon salt

1 teaspoon sugar

1 tablespoon quick-rising yeast

½ cup warm water

½ cup buttermilk

3 tablespoons melted butter

1 cup ice

Bread Pot Fondue (*Panhoca Recheado*)

Cut a circle in the top of a (6") round loaf of bread, and remove crust. Scoop out bread from inside loaf and reserve, leaving about ½" of crust all around. Brush inside of bread loaf with a mixture of 2 tablespoons melted butter, ½ teaspoon salt, and 1 teaspoons minced garlic. Toast loaf in the oven at 300°F for 5–10 minutes. In a saucepan, sauté 1 tablespoon minced garlic in 2 tablespoons of butter. Add 1½ tablespoons of flour and cook for 1 minute. Add 1½ cups of cream and cook, stirring, until mixture thickens slightly. Add ½ cup cream cheese, 8 ounces Gorgonzola cheese, and ¼ cup grated Parmesan cheese and stir until melted. Season with salt to taste and pour cheese mixture into the bread bowl, and serve with cubes of the reserved bread (plus more as needed) for dipping.

1. Place all ingredients in the bowl of a standing mixer fitted with the dough hook attachment and mix until well blended. Dough should be fairly stiff. Add more flour if needed. Continue to knead the dough until it is smooth and elastic.

2. Place the dough in an oiled bowl. Cover loosely and let rise in a warm place until doubled in bulk, about 1 hour.

3. Divide dough into 3 equal pieces, and shape each piece into a smooth ball. Place balls of dough on a large baking sheet lined with parchment and dusted with flour. Set aside in a warm place to rise until doubled, about 1 hour.

4. Preheat oven to 400°F. With a sharp knife, make 4 slashes in a crosshatch pattern on the top of each ball of dough. Lightly dust the loaves with flour.

5. Place loaves in the oven. Add a shallow pan containing 1 cup of ice to the floor of the oven to create steam. Bake loaves for 30–40 minutes, or until they are lightly browned and sound hollow when tapped.

Traditional Sweet Rolls (*Pão Doce Tradicional*)

Buttery, egg-rich sweet breads came to Brazil with the Portuguese. These round rolls coated with a sugar glaze and sprinkled with coconut are the most traditional form of this bread.

INGREDIENTS | MAKES 24

7 cups all-purpose flour, divided

1 tablespoon quick-rising yeast, divided

1¾ cups sugar, divided

1½ cups warm milk

1 cup butter, softened

5 large eggs

1 ½ teaspoons salt

1 cup water

1 teaspoon vanilla

⅓ cup shredded, dried, unsweetened coconut

1. Make the sponge: In a large bowl, combine 1 cup of the flour, 1 teaspoon yeast, 1 tablespoon of the sugar, and the milk. Stir until well mixed. Cover and set aside for 2–3 hours or overnight.

2. In the bowl of a standing mixer, beat the butter with 1 cup of sugar until smooth. Add the eggs and mix well. Add 1 cup of flour and the salt and mix until smooth.

3. Add the sponge to the mixer and mix well, using the dough hook attachment. Add the remaining flour, 1 cup at a time, mixing after each addition, as needed until dough is smooth and stretchy. Place in an oiled bowl and cover with a towel. Set aside to rise until doubled in size, about 1 hour.

4. Turn out dough onto a floured surface. Shape dough into a log. Cut log crosswise into 6 equal pieces, then cut each of those pieces into 4. Roll each piece into a ball.

5. Place rolls on a baking sheet lightly dusted with flour and set aside to rise in a warm place for 45 minutes. Preheat oven to 375°F.

6. Bake rolls for 30–40 minutes until dark golden brown.

7. While rolls are baking, prepare glaze: Place 1 cup water, remaining sugar, and a pinch of salt in a small saucepan over medium heat. Bring to a simmer and cook until sugar dissolves and syrup thickens slightly. Remove from heat and stir in the vanilla.

8. Brush tops of warm rolls with the glaze, then sprinkle with coconut.

Stuffed Cheese Rolls (*Pão de Queijo Recheado*)

There are many variations on these famous Brazilian cheese rolls made with tapioca starch. They are similar to cheese puffs, so adding a filling is a natural next step.

INGREDIENTS | MAKES 18

1 cup milk

½ cup vegetable oil

1 teaspoon salt

3 cups sweet manioc (tapioca) starch (*polvilho doce*)

3 large eggs

1½ cups grated Colby and Cheddar cheeses (mixed)

2 tablespoons grated Parmesan cheese

½ cup minced olives

18 (1") cubes mozzarella cheese

1 teaspoon dried oregano

Other Fillings

Use a 1" square of guava paste in place of the mozzarella and olives. Another technique is to fill the cheese breads after they come out of the oven using a pastry bag fitted with a small (¼") tip. Use the pastry tip to make a small hole in the bottom of each roll and pipe in something like warm Cheddar cheese sauce, or even softened dulce de leche.

1. Place the milk, vegetable oil, and salt in a small saucepan and bring just to a simmer over medium heat.

2. Place the tapioca starch in a large bowl and stir in the hot milk mixture. Add the eggs, one at a time. Add the grated cheeses and mix well. Mixture should come together as a dough. Add more tapioca starch if mixture is too wet to shape into balls, and more milk if it is too crumbly.

3. Preheat oven to 350°F. In a small bowl, mix the olives, mozzarella, and oregano together.

4. Divide the dough into 18 pieces. With buttered hands, shape each piece of dough into a ball. Make a hole in the middle of each ball. Place 1 piece of mozzarella cheese and some of the olive pieces in the middle of each roll, then close the dough over the filling. Roll into a smooth ball and place on ungreased baking sheet. Repeat with remaining pieces of dough.

5. Bake rolls for 20–25 minutes, until they are puffed and starting to brown in spots. Serve warm.

Coconut Sweet Rolls (*Rosca de Coco*)

These rolls are similar to American-style cinnamon rolls, except that they are filled with sugar and coconut. The rolls are typically arranged in the shape of a ring (rosca), but you can also bake them in a rectangular baking pan if you like fewer crispy edges.

INGREDIENTS | MAKES 12

¾ cup warm milk

1¼ cups sugar, divided

1 tablespoon active dry yeast

1¼ cups shredded, sweetened coconut, divided

4½ cups all-purpose flour

8 tablespoons softened butter, divided

¼ cup vegetable oil

2 large eggs

3 tablespoons plus ½ cup heavy cream, divided

½ cup condensed milk

Pinch salt

1 teaspoon vanilla

1. Preheat oven to 300°F. Place the milk in a small bowl with 1 tablespoon of sugar and sprinkle the yeast over the milk. Set aside for 5 minutes. Lightly toast ¼ cup of the coconut and set aside.

2. Add flour, ¾ cup sugar, 4 tablespoons butter, vegetable oil, and eggs to the bowl of a standing mixer. Add the milk/yeast mixture and knead with the dough hook attachment until dough is smooth and elastic, adding a bit more flour if dough is too sticky or 1–2 tablespoons of milk if dough is too dry.

3. Place the dough in an oiled bowl. Cover loosely and let rise until doubled in bulk, about 1 hour. Dough can rise in the refrigerator overnight. (Bring to room temperature before rolling out dough.)

4. On a floured surface, roll out dough into a large rectangle. Place 3 tablespoons of butter and 3 tablespoons of cream in a small saucepan over low heat until butter melts. Brush half of this mixture over the dough.

Sprinkle ¼ cup sugar and 1 cup coconut over the dough. Roll up dough starting with one of the long sides. Cut dough log crosswise into 12 spiral pieces.

5. Arrange rolls in a circle on a large baking sheet lined with parchment paper, with edges barely touching. Brush rolls with remaining butter/cream mixture. Let rise for 30 minutes.

6. Preheat the oven to 350°F. Bake for 25–30 minutes, or until rolls have risen and lightly browned. While they are baking, prepare the frosting: Heat condensed milk, ½ cup cream, remaining sugar, pinch of salt, and 1 tablespoon butter in a small saucepan over medium-low heat. Cook, stirring constantly, until mixture thickens slightly. Remove from heat and stir in vanilla.

7. Drizzle the warm frosting over the rolls immediately after taking them out of the oven, and sprinkle with toasted coconut.

Bahian Sweet Cheese Rolls (*Pãozinho Delícia da Bahia*)

These sweet, puffy, melt-in-your-mouth rolls are a specialty of Salvador, in the state of Bahia.

INGREDIENTS | MAKES 24

5 cups all-purpose flour, divided
½ cup sugar
1 tablespoon instant yeast
1½ cups warm milk
2 tablespoons vegetable oil
4 tablespoons melted butter, divided
2 large eggs
1 teaspoon salt
½ cup grated Parmesan cheese

Creamy Cheese Spread (*Recheio Cremoso*)

These rolls are often split in half and spread with a creamy cheese filling. To make the filling, place 1 cup milk, 2 tablespoons flour, 1 tablespoon butter, 1 egg yolk, and a pinch of salt in a small saucepan. Cook over low heat, stirring constantly, until thick and shiny. Remove from heat and stir in 2 tablespoons grated Parmesan cheese. Chill. When ready to use, whip cheese mixture with ⅓ cup of cream.

1. Place 3 cups flour in a large bowl or in the bowl of a standing mixer fitted with the dough hook attachment. Add the sugar and yeast and mix briefly.

2. Add milk and mix well. Add the oil, 2 tablespoons melted butter, eggs, and salt and mix well.

3. Add remaining flour ⅓ cup at a time, mixing well after each addition, stopping when dough is smooth and soft. Knead for 4–6 minutes, until dough is very smooth and shiny.

4. Cover dough loosely with a towel and set aside in a warm place to rise for 1–2 hours.

5. Preheat oven to 375°F. Lightly grease a large baking pan. Divide dough into 24 pieces and shape each piece into a smooth ball. Place the rolls on the baking sheet, spacing them 1½" apart. Let rolls rise until doubled in size, about 45 minutes.

6. Place rolls in the oven and reduce oven temperature to 325°F. Bake rolls for 15–25 minutes or until they are puffy but not browned.

7. Immediately brush tops of rolls with remaining melted butter and sprinkle with Parmesan.

Sweet Bread with Guava (*Pão Doce Tijolinho*)

Small pieces of sweet dough are filled with guava paste, rolled in coconut, and placed in a ring pan. Once baked, the rolls resemble cobblestones or bricks (tijolinhos).

INGREDIENTS | YIELDS 12 SERVINGS

1 cup warm milk

5 tablespoons sugar, divided

1 tablespoon active dry yeast

4¾ cups all-purpose flour, divided

1 teaspoon salt

8 tablespoons butter, divided

2 large eggs

½ cup shredded, sweetened coconut, lightly toasted

¼ cup brown sugar

8 ounces guava paste

1. Place the milk in a small bowl with 1 tablespoon of sugar and sprinkle the yeast over the milk. Set aside for 5 minutes.

2. Add 4½ cups of flour, 4 tablespoons sugar, salt, 4 tablespoons butter, and eggs to the bowl of a standing mixer. Add the milk/yeast mixture and knead with the dough hook attachment until dough is smooth and elastic, adding a bit more flour if dough is too sticky or 1–2 tablespoons of water if dough is too dry.

3. Place the dough in an oiled bowl. Cover loosely and let rise until doubled in bulk, about 1 hour. Dough can rise in the refrigerator overnight. Take it out of the refrigerator 30 mintues before shaping the rolls.

4. Butter and lightly flour a tube pan, bundt pan, or angel food cake pan.

5. In a small bowl, mix the toasted coconut, remaining flour, and brown sugar. Cut 4 tablespoons of butter into ½" pieces and add them to the bowl. Use a pastry cutter or your fingers to blend in the butter until the mixture resembles large crumbs.

6. Cut the guava paste into ½" squares. Take small pieces of dough (about the size of a Ping-Pong ball) and press 1 or 2 pieces of guava paste into the middle of each. Shape the dough into a ball around the guava paste. Roll each ball in the coconut crumb mixture and place it in the tube pan. Loosely stack the balls of dough as you go, evenly filling the pan. Place tube pan in a warm place and allow rolls to rise for 45 minutes.

7. Preheat the oven to 375°F. Bake rolls for 30–40 minutes, or until rolls have risen and are lightly browned.

8. Let cool for 10 minutes. Loosen sides of bread ring with a knife before turning it out of the pan. Enjoy warm or at room temperature.

Chocolate Sweet Bread (*Pão Doce de Brigadeiro*)

Chocolate truffles called *brigadeiros* are a favorite filling for this bread. Make marble-size truffles using the recipe for Brigadeiros in Chapter 14 and use them in place of the guava paste to fill the rolls. (Omit coconut mixture.)

Brazilian Pita Bread (*Pão Sírio*)

Brazilians enjoy Middle Eastern food, and pita bread is especially popular for sandwiches.

INGREDIENTS | MAKES 8

1¼ cups warm water
4 teaspoons sugar
1 tablespoon active dry yeast
4 cups all-purpose flour
3 tablespoons olive oil
1 teaspoon salt

1. Place the water and sugar in a large bowl and sprinkle the yeast over the water. Set aside for 5 minutes.

2. Add the flour, olive oil, and salt to the bowl and mix well, kneading until it becomes a smooth dough.

3. Divide the dough into 8 pieces and roll each piece into a smooth ball. Place balls on a floured surface. Allow dough to rest for 10–15 minutes.

4. Preheat oven to 425°F. Lightly oil a large baking sheet.

5. Working on a lightly floured surface, roll out each piece of dough into a 6" circle. Set aside.

6. Place baking sheet in the hot oven for 5 minutes. Remove from oven and place rounds of dough onto the baking sheet (bake in batches, if necessary). Bake until puffed and lightly browned, about 10–15 minutes. Remove from oven and let cool.

7. If saving breads for later use, place them in a plastic bag while they are still fairly warm, which will help to keep them soft and pliable.

Fast Blender Cheese Rolls (*Pão de Queijo de Liquidificador*)

These super quick Brazilian cheese rolls are perfect for breakfast or when you're in a rush to get dinner on the table.

INGREDIENTS | MAKES 12

1 cup whole milk

½ cup vegetable oil

1 teaspoon salt

3 large eggs

3 cups sweet tapioca starch (*polvilho doce*)

½ cup grated Cheddar cheese

½ cup grated Parmesan cheese

1. Brush 12 muffin tins with melted butter. Preheat oven to 350°F.

2. Place the milk, oil, salt, and eggs in a blender and pulse briefly to mix.

3. Place the tapioca starch in a large bowl, and add the liquid mixture. Stir well to mix. Add the cheeses and mix well.

4. Divide batter among muffin tins. Bake for 20–25 minutes or until puffed and lightly browned. Rolls should have a nice crust and sound hollow when tapped.

Paraguayan Corn Bread (*Sopa Paraguaia*)

The name of this cheesy, pudding-like corn bread is Spanish and translates to "Paraguayan Soup."

INGREDIENTS | SERVES 8

4 tablespoons butter

1 medium onion, peeled and chopped

3 cups fresh or frozen corn

5 large eggs

1 teaspoon salt

4 tablespoons vegetable oil

1¼ cups milk or buttermilk

1 cup shredded Monterey jack cheese

1 cup shredded mozzarella cheese

2 teaspoons baking powder

2 cups finely ground cornmeal

1. Preheat the oven to 350°F. Melt the butter in a medium skillet and sauté the onion over medium-low heat until soft. Add the corn and cook for 1 minute. Remove from heat and let cool slightly.

2. Add the corn/onion mixture, eggs, salt, vegetable oil, and milk or buttermilk in a blender and process until smooth.

3. Transfer the mixture to a large bowl and stir in the cheeses, baking powder, and cornmeal.

4. Place batter in a buttered bread pan, cake pan, or tube pan.

5. Bake for 45–55 minutes, or until bread just springs back when touched. Serve warm.

CHAPTER 11

Street Food (*Comida de Rua*)

Black-Eyed Pea Fritters (*Acarajé de Bahia*)

Acarajé are probably the most iconic street food in Brazil. Once fried, they are split almost in half and stuffed with dried shrimp, onions, hot sauce, and certain traditional fillings, such as vatapá *(creamy coconut shrimp) and* caruru *(shrimp and okra sauce).*

INGREDIENTS | MAKES 15

2 cups dried black-eyed peas

2 medium onions, peeled, divided

1½ teaspoons salt, divided

1½ teaspoons freshly ground black pepper

1 cup *dendê* oil or vegetable oil, divided

2 small red chili peppers

½ cup peeled dried shrimp

½ cup water

1 cup vegetable oil

1 cup Creamy Coconut Shrimp (*Vatapá*) or Shrimp and Okra Sauce (*Caruru*) (see recipes in Chapter 9) (optional)

1. Soak the black-eyed peas overnight and remove skins and "eyes" (see sidebar).

2. Place the beans in a food processor. Coarsely chop 1 onion and add it to the food processor, along with 1 teaspoon salt and 1 teaspoon black pepper. Process until very smooth, adding a very small amount water if needed—mixture should come together as a thick paste. Transfer to a bowl and refrigerate, covered, for 1 hour.

3. While the black-eyed pea mixture is chilling, make the hot sauce: Place 2 tablespoons of the *dendê* (or vegetable) oil in a small skillet. Slice the remaining onion and cook over medium-low until soft and fragrant, about 5–8 minutes. Seed the chili peppers and place them in the blender with half of the dried shrimp and ½ cup of water. Process until smooth, and add mixture to the onions. Add remaining shrimp and cook for several minutes, until sauce thickens. Season with remaining salt and pepper to taste.

4. Heat the remaining *dendê* oil and vegetable oil in a heavy saucepan to 350°F. While the

oil is heating, remove black-eyed pea mixture from the refrigerator and beat vigorously with a wooden spoon for 1–2 minutes.

5. When oil is hot, use 2 soup spoons to scoop portions of the black-eyed pea mixture. Try to shape the dough into an oblong (football) shape, and drop it into the hot oil. Cook in batches until *acarajé* are deep golden brown and cooked all the way through, about 5 minutes. Remove with a slotted spoon and place on paper towels to drain.

6. Cut the *acarajé* lengthwise almost in half and fill with some of the hot sauce and dried shrimp, and add some *vatapá* or *caruru*, if desired. Serve warm.

Black-Eyed Peas (*Feijão-Fradinho*)

To make *acarajé*, the skins and "eyes" of the black-eyed peas must be removed. This is a bit labor intensive, but there are some tricks to make it easier. First place the dried beans in a food processor and pulse a couple of times, just to break them up a bit (do not pulverize them). Soak the beans in water overnight. The next day, rub the beans between your hands before pouring off the water with any skins that floated to the top. Add more water to the bowl and repeat until skins and eyes have been removed.

Fried Beef Pastries (*Pastel de Carne*)

Brazilian pastéis *are typically rectangular, deep-fried pastries with a thin, crispy crust. Popular fillings include ground beef, cheese, chicken and creamy Catupiry cheese, shrimp, and hearts of palm.*

INGREDIENTS | MAKES 9

2 tablespoons vegetable oil

1 medium onion, peeled and chopped

2 cloves garlic, minced

1 pound ground beef

1 teaspoon cumin (optional)

1 teaspoon paprika

1 teaspoon salt

½ teaspoon freshly ground black pepper

2 tablespoons minced fresh parsley

2 scallions, chopped

¼ cup chopped green olives

1 large hard-cooked egg, peeled and chopped

1 recipe Pastel Dough (see sidebar)

Vegetable oil, for frying

Pastel Dough (*Massa de Pastel*)

Place 3¼ cups flour in a large bowl. Add 4 tablespoons softened vegetable shortening, 1 teaspoon salt, 2 tablespoons cachaça or rum, 1 teaspoon vinegar, 1 egg, and 10 tablespoons warm water. Mix everything together, kneading mixture with your hands until you have smooth dough. Add 1–2 tablespoons of water if dough is too dry, or more flour if dough is too sticky. Wrap in plastic wrap and refrigerate until ready to use, up to 1 day ahead.

1. Heat 2 tablespoons oil in a medium skillet over medium heat. Add the onion and cook until soft and fragrant, about 5–8 minutes.

2. Add the garlic and cook for 1 minute. Add the ground beef, cumin (if using), paprika, salt, and pepper and cook, stirring, until meat is well browned and most of the liquid has evaporated.

3. Add the parsley, scallions, olives, and egg and stir until heated through. Remove from heat and let cool.

4. On a floured surface, roll out the dough (see sidebar for recipe) into a large (21") square about ¼" thick. Let dough rest for 5 minutes.

5. Cut 7" squares of dough (a pizza cutter works well for this). Place 2 tablespoons of filling on each. Brush a little water on the edges of the dough and fold dough in half, pressing the seal closed with a fork.

6. Heat vegetable oil to 350°F in a deep skillet. Fry *pastéis* in batches, letting one side brown before flipping (about 2 minutes per side). Remove *pastéis* with a slotted spoon and drain on paper towels. Serve warm.

Fried Chicken Pastries (*Pastel de Frango com Catupiry*)

The key ingredient here is requeijão *cheese (often called* Catupiry, *a popular brand). It's a soft, spreadable white cheese. American-style cream cheese makes a reasonable substitute, but you can find* requeijão *at Brazilian grocery stores.*

INGREDIENTS | MAKES 9

2 tablespoons plus 2 cups vegetable oil, divided

1 medium onion, peeled and chopped

2 cloves garlic, minced

1½ cups shredded, cooked chicken breast

1 teaspoon paprika

1 teaspoon tomato paste

1 tablespoon all-purpose flour

½ cup chicken broth

½ cup fresh or frozen corn

¾ teaspoon salt

½ teaspoon freshly ground black pepper

2 tablespoons minced fresh parsley

1 scallion, chopped

4 ounces *requeijão* cheese (or cream cheese)

1 recipe Pastel Dough (see sidebar in Fried Beef Pastries recipe in this chapter)

1. Heat 2 tablespoons oil in a medium skillet over medium heat. Add the onion and cook until soft and fragrant, about 5 minutes.

2. Add the garlic and cook for 1 minute. Add the shredded chicken, paprika, and tomato paste and stir until well mixed.

3. Add flour and cook for 1–2 minutes. Add chicken broth and corn and cook, stirring, until mixture thickens. Season with salt and pepper. Stir in the parsley, scallions, and cheese. Remove from heat and let cool.

4. On a floured surface, roll out the dough into a large (21") square about ¼" thick. Let dough rest for 5 minutes.

5. Cut 7" squares of dough (a pizza cutter works well for this). Place 2 tablespoons of filling on each. Brush a little water on the edges of the dough and fold dough in half, pressing the seal closed with a fork.

6. Heat 2 cups oil to 350°F in a deep skillet. Fry *pastéis* in batches, letting one side brown before flipping (about 2 minutes per side). Remove *pastéis* with a slotted spoon and drain on paper towels. Serve warm.

Breaded Potato and Cheese Skewers
(*Espetinho Crocante de Batata com Queijo*)

These unusual treats are amazingly good, and fun to make.
Look for very small baby potatoes, about 1" in diameter.

INGREDIENTS | SERVES 8

16 baby potatoes

16 ounces mozzarella or Monterey jack cheese, cut into 16 cubes

1 cup very fine bread crumbs

1 teaspoon garlic powder

1 teaspoon salt

1 teaspoon dried oregano

1 teaspoon paprika

1 large egg

1 tablespoon water

Vegetable oil for frying

1 cup mayonnaise

1 teaspoon minced fresh garlic

1 teaspoon fresh lime juice

2 tablespoons minced green olives

1. Cook the potatoes in salted water until tender. Drain and cool.

2. Place 2 potatoes and 2 cubes of cheese on a skewer, alternating the potatoes with the cheese. Repeat with remaining potatoes and cheese.

3. In a shallow dish, stir together the bread crumbs, garlic powder, salt, oregano, and paprika. In a small bowl, whisk the egg with 1 tablespoon of water.

4. Use a pastry brush to brush the potatoes and cheese with the egg, then dip the skewers in the bread crumbs to coat.

5. Heat 1–2" of oil in a deep skillet to 350°F (or use a deep-fat fryer). Lower the skewers into the oil and cook, turning once, until golden brown, about 3–4 minutes per skewer. Remove from oil and cool on paper towels.

6. In a small bowl, combine the mayonnaise, garlic, lime juice, and olives. Place in a small serving dish.

7. Serve skewers warm with the mayonnaise sauce.

Brazilian Corn "Tamales" (*Pamonhas*)

Unlike Mexican tamales, which are made with masa harina (ground cornmeal dough), Brazilian pamonhas are made with fresh sweet corn (milho verde) and are wrapped in fresh (not dried) cornhusks. They are typically sold from the back of trucks fitted with megaphones, blaring music to lure customers.

INGREDIENTS | SERVES 12

12 large ears fresh sweet corn, not shucked

1 cup milk

1 teaspoon salt

1½ cups sugar

3 tablespoons melted butter

String for tying the *pamonhas*

1. Slice off the stem of the corn, then carefully remove the husks, trying to keep them in large pieces. Reserve husks.

2. Use a sharp knife to remove the corn from the cob. Place the corn in a food processor or blender with the milk. Process until very smooth.

3. Add the salt, sugar, and melted butter to the corn and stir well.

4. Take 1 or 2 husks and shape them into a hollow cylinder. Fold them in half lengthwise, bringing the pointed end up to the top to make a sort of cup. Fill the cylinder with the corn mixture. Wrap another 1 or 2 husks around the top half of the filled "cup," and fold it down to seal that end. Tie *pamonha* closed with a piece of string (it helps to have 2 people—one to hold the *pamonha* and one to tie the string).

5. Bring a large pot of water to strong boil. Place the *pamonhas* in the boiling water, lower heat, and simmer for 45 minutes to 1 hour. *Pamonhas* will become firm when ready, and the corn husks will be a bright yellow green.

6. Serve warm. Reheat *pamonhas* by steaming them or heating them in the microwave.

Crazy Beef Sandwich (*Sanduíche de Carne Louca*)

These sandwiches of shredded savory braised beef are Brazil's version of Sloppy Joes.

INGREDIENTS | SERVES 8

2 pounds beef chuck, cut into 1–2" cubes

¼ cup vegetable oil

¼ cup red wine vinegar

1 tablespoon soy sauce

1 tablespoon Dijon mustard

1 teaspoon Worcestershire sauce

2 medium onions, peeled and chopped

1 large tomato, seeded and diced

1 medium green bell pepper, seeded and diced

1 teaspoon dried oregano

3 cups beef stock

¼ cup chopped scallions

½ teaspoon salt

½ teaspoon freshly ground black pepper

8 large French bread rolls or 24 small rolls

1. Place beef in a nonreactive bowl or plastic zip-top bag with oil, vinegar, soy sauce, mustard, and Worcestershire sauce. Marinate for several hours or overnight.

2. Heat a large, heavy skillet over medium-high heat. Remove beef from marinade, reserving marinade. Sear beef until brown on all sides, working in batches if necessary. Remove beef to a plate and set aside.

3. Add marinade to the skillet, along with onions. Cook until onions are soft, about 5–8 minutes. Add tomato, green pepper, and oregano and cook for several minutes. Add beef to skillet, and add just enough beef stock to cover the meat. Cover skillet and reduce heat to low. Simmer until beef is very tender, 2–3 hours.

4. Transfer beef mixture to a bowl and shred the beef with 2 forks. Add the scallions, and season with salt and pepper to taste.

5. Serve beef in sandwich rolls.

Brazilian-Style Hot Dogs (*Cachorro-Quente*)

Brazilian hot dogs come loaded with garnishes that might sound unusual, such as quail eggs, mayonnaise, mashed potatoes, corn, peas, and potato sticks. Many Brazilians cook their hot dogs in tomato sauce before placing them in the bun.

INGREDIENTS | SERVES 4

2 tablespoons oil

1 small onion, peeled and chopped

1 clove garlic, minced

1 medium green bell pepper, seeded and diced

½ cup fresh or frozen corn

2 tablespoons chopped fresh parsley

2 scallions, chopped

½ teaspoon salt

1 cup tomato sauce

4 large hot dogs

4 large hot dog buns

2 tablespoon butter, melted

4 tablespoons mayonnaise

½ cup grated cheese (Parmesan, mozzarella, or both)

Mashed Potato Dog (*Cachorro-Quente Completo*)

Lightly butter and toast 4 hot dog buns. Make a slit down the length of each of 4 hot dogs about ¼" deep. Place hot dogs in a saucepan, cover with water, and simmer over medium-low heat for 5 minutes. Chop 4 slices of bacon into small pieces and fry until crispy. Spread ⅓ cup mashed potatoes inside each bun. Place the hot dogs in the middle of the potatoes, and top with Cheddar cheese, fried bacon, mayonnaise, grated carrots, peas, and shoestring potatoes.

1. Heat the oil in a medium skillet over medium-low heat and add the onion. Cook until onion is softened and fragrant, about 5–8 minutes. Add the garlic and green pepper and cook for 2–3 minutes. Add the corn, parsley, scallions, and salt to taste, and cook for 1 minute more.

2. Add the tomato sauce and bring to a simmer. Make a slit down the length of each hot dog, about ¼" deep. Place the hot dogs in the sauce and turn heat down to low. Simmer for 10 minutes.

3. While the hot dogs are cooking, brush the buns with the butter and lightly toast them in the oven or on the stove. Spread each bun with a tablespoon of mayonnaise.

4. Place the hot dogs in the buns with some of the sauce, top with the grated cheese, and serve immediately.

Grilled Ham and Cheese Sandwich (*Misto-Quente*)

Misto-quente means "hot mix," and it is the name for a very popular sandwich in Brazil—typically a simple grilled ham and cheese sandwich.

INGREDIENTS | SERVES 4

⅓ cup mayonnaise

2 tablespoons finely minced olives

1 teaspoon dried oregano

1 teaspoon smoked paprika

¼ cup sun-dried tomatoes (jarred in oil), diced

8 slices good-quality sandwich bread

8 slices smoked deli ham

8 slices Edam or mozzarella cheese (or cheese of choice)

4 tomato slices

2 tablespoons butter

1. In a small bowl, mix the mayonnaise, olives, oregano, paprika, and sun-dried tomatoes.

2. Spread 4 slices of the bread with the mayonnaise mixture. Top with 2 slices ham, 2 slices cheese, a slice of tomato, and another slice of bread.

3. Melt 1 tablespoon of butter in a large skillet over medium heat. Toast 2 of the sandwiches until well browned on both sides. Repeat with remaining 2 sandwiches. Serve warm.

Roast Beef Pita Sandwich (*Beirute*)

This sandwich is named for the city of Beirut, but it is native to São Paulo, where many Lebanese immigrants settled in the early twentieth century.

INGREDIENTS | SERVES 4

1 tablespoon olive oil

1 clove garlic, minced

12 ounces thinly sliced roast beef or smoked deli ham

4 large pita breads

12 ounces grated cheese of choice

8 lettuce leaves

1 tomato, sliced

4 large fried eggs (optional)

1 teaspoon dried oregano

4 tablespoons cream cheese (or *requeijão*)

1. Place the olive oil in a medium skillet. Add the garlic and sauté over medium heat for 1 minute, until garlic is sizzling and fragrant. Add the sliced roast beef or ham and cook until well heated.

2. Split the pitas in half to make 2 circles of bread. Place the meat on 4 pita halves, dividing it equally. Immediately top with the grated cheese, dividing it equally as well. Add 2 lettuce leaves and some tomato slices to each. Top with a fried egg if desired.

3. In a small bowl, mix the oregano with the cream cheese. Spread 1 tablespoon on each of the other halves of the pita breads and place them, spread side down, on top of the tomato slices (or fried egg).

4. Serve warm.

Ground Beef Pocket (*Buraco-Quente*)

This sandwich from São Paulo consists of a hollowed-out crusty French bread roll filled with a mixture of ground beef, onions, tomatoes, and cheese.

INGREDIENTS | SERVES 4

2 tablespoons vegetable oil
½ pound ground beef
1 small onion, peeled and chopped
2 cloves garlic, minced
1 cup tomato sauce
2 tablespoons chopped fresh parsley
1 teaspoon salt
½ teaspoon freshly ground black pepper
8 olives, chopped
½ cup grated mozzarella cheese
½ cup grated Monterey jack cheese
4 French bread sandwich rolls

1. Heat the oil in a medium skillet over medium heat. Add the ground beef and cook, stirring frequently, until beef is well browned. Add the onion and garlic and cook until softened and fragrant, about 5–8 minutes. Add the tomato sauce and simmer for 10 minutes over low heat until mixture thickens.

2. Add the parsley, and salt and pepper to taste. Stir in the olives and remove from heat. Let cool for 5 minutes, then stir in the cheeses.

3. Cut the end off of each roll, and use your fingers to hollow out the rolls, leaving about ½" of crust. Fill the rolls with the meat mixture. Place the ends back on the rolls, and heat them in a 350°F oven for 5 minutes to toast the bread.

4. Place sandwiches upright in a serving dish, with bread ends removed.

Coconut Tapioca Squares (*Cuscuz de Tapioca*)

This sweet treat comes from northeastern Brazil and is a popular snack to enjoy at the beach. The vendor drizzles cold condensed milk or coconut milk over it just before handing it over.

INGREDIENTS | MAKES 16

2 cups quick-cooking tapioca
1½ cups sweetened, flaked coconut, divided
½ teaspoon salt
1 cup milk
2 cups coconut milk, divided
⅓ cup sugar

Optional Chocolate Topping (*Molho de Chocolate*)

Place 1 (14-ounce) can of condensed milk in a medium saucepan. Add 2 tablespoons cocoa powder, 1 tablespoon butter, and a pinch of salt. Cook, stirring constantly, over medium-low heat until mixture thickens, about 10–15 minutes. Remove from heat and stir in ½ teaspoon vanilla. Pour chocolate over *cuscuz de tapioca* just after it has been placed in the baking pan, while it is still warm. Chill for 2 hours before cutting into squares.

1. In a medium heatproof bowl, mix together the tapioca, 1 cup coconut, and salt.

2. In a small saucepan, bring the milk, 1 cup of coconut milk, and sugar to a boil. Reserve remaining 1 cup of coconut milk in the refrigerator.

3. Remove milk mixture from heat and pour over tapioca mixture. Stir to mix, and set aside in the refrigerator to chill for 30 minutes.

4. Press mixture into an 8" square pan and chill for 2 hours. Cut into 16 squares, and roll squares in remaining coconut (toast coconut in oven first, if desired).

5. Drizzle each square with some of the chilled coconut milk just before serving.

Filled Doughnut Sticks (*Churros*)

Churros are popular throughout Brazil, where they are filled with things like dulce de leche (doce de leite), chocolate ganache, and guava paste.

INGREDIENTS | MAKES 20

1½ cups semisweet chocolate chips
¾ cup heavy cream
1 teaspoon instant espresso powder
¾ teaspoon salt, divided
2 teaspoons vanilla, divided
1 cup milk

1 tablespoon plus 1 cup sugar, divided
8 tablespoons butter
1¼ cups all-purpose flour
3 large eggs
2 teaspoons cinnamon
3–4 cups vegetable oil for frying
1 cup dulce de leche

1. Prepare the chocolate filling: Place the chocolate chips in a heatproof bowl. Place the cream and the espresso powder in a small saucepan with a ¼ teaspoon salt and bring to a boil. Pour hot mixture over the chocolate chips, stirring gently, and set aside for 5 minutes. Gently stir in 1 teaspoon vanilla until well mixed. Set aside.

2. Place the milk, 1 tablespoon sugar, remaining salt, and butter in a large saucepan and bring to a boil. Add the flour all at once, and stir with a spatula until mixture comes together into a ball. Cook, stirring constantly for 2–3 minutes more. Remove from heat.

3. Add the eggs one at a time, stirring well. Add remaining vanilla. Mixture should be shiny and smooth.

4. Place dough in a pastry bag fitted with a wide star piping tip. Pipe long lengths of dough onto wax-paper-lined baking sheet. Cut the dough into 4" pieces. Place the baking sheet in the freezer for 10 minutes.

5. Mix cinnamon and 1 cup sugar together in a shallow dish.

6. Heat vegetable oil in a heavy saucepan to 350°F. Fry *churros* in batches until golden brown. Drain *churros* briefly on paper towels, and immediately roll them in the cinnamon/sugar mixture to coat.

7. Place the chocolate filling in a pastry bag fitted with a round (#4) icing tip, or small enough to poke into the end of the churros. Place the dulce de leche (softened briefly in microwave, if needed) in second pastry bag with a similar tip. Place a wooden skewer through the middle of each *churro* to make an opening for the filling.

8. Fill half of the *churros* with chocolate and half with dulce de leche, and serve warm.

Tapioca Crepes with Cheese (*Tapioca*)

Tapioca are thin white crepes made entirely of manioc starch, a specialty of northeastern Brazil. They are typically filled with a variety of sweet and savory fillings and served as a snack or dessert.

INGREDIENTS | SERVES 6

1½ cups manioc (tapioca) starch (*polvilho*)

½ teaspoon salt

¾ cup water

1½ cups grated cheese (mozzarella, Cheddar, Monterey jack, or a combination)

Manioc (Tapioca) Starch (*Polvilho*)

Manioc starch is extracted from the starchy liquid that is pressed from the manioc tuber. Sometimes this liquid is fermented for a period of time before the starch is extracted, which produces a slightly sour-tasting starch called *polvilho azedo*. Unfermented tapioca starch, which is less commonly available in the United States, is called *polvilho doce*. Either kind can be used in this recipe, but the *polvilho azedo* has a stronger, more distinctive flavor.

1. Place the tapioca starch and salt in a medium bowl and stir to mix.

2. Add the water a few tablespoons at a time, mixing well with your hands and crumbling the tapioca. Continue to add water until all of the starch resembles coarse crumbs. If you add too much water, the starch will start to flow together—if this happens, just add some more starch.

3. Sift the dampened starch through a fine-mesh sieve into a clean bowl, using a wooden spoon to help push it through the sieve.

4. Heat a nonstick skillet over medium heat. Sprinkle about ¼ cup of the sifted starch onto the skillet in an even layer (you can use a sifter to do this step). Cook for 1 minute, and as soon as crepe will move and slide in the skillet, flip the crepe to the other side and cook for 1 minute more. Remove from skillet, sprinkle with ¼ cup grated cheese, then fold crepe in half.

5. Repeat with remaining starch and cheese. Serve warm.

Beach Cookies (*Biscoito de Polvinho*)

*If you visit the beaches of Rio de Janeiro, you will hear vendors calling out
"Olha o Globo" or "Look! Globo!" They are selling a commercial brand of these
gluten-free, melt-in-your-mouth cookies, a beach tradition.*

INGREDIENTS | MAKES 20

1 cup milk
1 cup vegetable oil
½ teaspoon salt
2 cups tapioca starch
2 large eggs
1 cup water

1. Preheat oven to 325°F. Place the milk, vegetable oil, and salt in a saucepan and bring to a boil.

2. Place the tapioca starch in the bowl of a standing mixer and mix briefly. While the mixer is running, gradually add the hot milk/oil mixture to the starch.

3. Add in the eggs one at a time and mix well.

4. Add the water slowly, mixing constantly, until the dough is soft, stretchy, and smooth, and thin enough to be just barely pourable.

5. Place the dough in a pastry bag with a ½" piping tip. Pipe circles 3" in diameter onto a greased baking sheet.

6. Bake until cookies are puffed and golden, 15–20 minutes.

CHAPTER 12

Desserts (*Sobremesas*)

Passion Fruit Mousse (*Mousse de Maracujá*)

This creamy mousse is easy to make and has an intense flavor that will transport you to the tropics. Fresh passion fruit can be difficult to find, but frozen passion fruit pulp is readily available and works well in this recipe.

INGREDIENTS | SERVES 4

¾ cup passion fruit pulp

1 tablespoon fresh lime juice

1 package powdered unflavored gelatin (about 2½ teaspoons)

1 (14-ounce) can sweetened condensed milk

1 teaspoon vanilla, divided

¼ teaspoon salt

1½ cups heavy cream, divided

1 tablespoon powdered sugar

Built-In Garnish

Passion fruit seeds are edible, and many people enjoy their crunchiness. Frozen passion fruit pulp is usually seedless, but if you have access to fresh passion fruit, you can reserve the seeds to sprinkle over the mousse as a garnish. Passion fruit are ripe when their skin becomes very wrinkled and slightly mottled.

1. Combine the passion fruit pulp and lime juice in a saucepan and sprinkle the gelatin on top. Set aside for about 5 minutes to let the gelatin dissolve.

2. Gently heat the mixture over low heat, stirring constantly, until mixture is hot (do not bring to a boil) and gelatin is completely dissolved.

3. Remove mixture from heat. Whisk in the condensed milk, ½ teaspoon vanilla, and the salt.

4. Place 1 cup of the cream and the powdered sugar in a separate bowl and beat until soft peaks form. Gently fold the cream into the passion fruit mixture.

5. Pour the mouse into a serving dish (or into 4 individual serving dishes). Place mousse in the refrigerator to chill for at least 8 hours, or until the gelatin is set.

6. When ready to serve, beat the remaining ½ cup of cream until soft peaks form. Fold in remaining ½ teaspoon vanilla. Top the mousse with the whipped cream, garnish with extra passion fruit pulp and seeds (if desired), and serve cold.

Brazilian Tropical Fruit Trifle (*Pavê de Frutas*)

This dessert is something of a cross between tiramisu and a trifle.
Layers of pastry cream, ladyfingers, fruit, and meringue make this a dessert to remember.

INGREDIENTS | SERVES 4

2 cups milk

1 tablespoon cornstarch

3 egg yolks

1 (14-ounce) can sweetened condensed milk

¼ teaspoon salt

1½ teaspoons vanilla, divided

1 (20-ounce) can pineapple chunks

1 cup fresh mango chunks

1 tablespoon fresh lime juice

1 (7-ounce) package ladyfingers, or 1 medium butter pound cake, sliced

¾ cup heavy cream

1 tablespoon powdered sugar

2 or 3 maraschino cherries, for garnish

Chocolate Pavê

Pavê de chocolate is a popular variation of this dessert. To make chocolate *pavê*, add 2 tablespoons cocoa powder to the milk along with the cornstarch. Omit the pineapple, mango, and lime juice, and use fresh strawberries and/or raspberries instead. Drizzle the ladyfinger layer with chocolate sauce. Top with chocolate shavings or chocolate sprinkles.

1. To prepare the custard, place the milk in a medium saucepan. Whisk the cornstarch into the milk. Add the egg yolks, condensed milk, and salt. Whisk well to mix.

2. Gently heat the mixture over medium-low heat, stirring constantly, until mixture thickens and just comes to the boil. Remove from heat and stir in 1 teaspoon of vanilla.

3. Drain the canned pineapple and reserve the syrup in a bowl. Add the mango to the pineapple chunks. Toss the fruit with the lime juice.

4. Dip half of the ladyfingers or slices of pound cake into the pineapple syrup, then place them in the bottom of a glass loaf pan, covering the bottom. Spread half of the custard over the ladyfingers. Repeat layers with remaining ladyfingers and custard.

5. Spoon the pineapple and mango chunks over the top custard layer.

6. Place the cream and powdered sugar in the bowl of a standing mixer. Beat the cream until soft peaks form. Fold in remaining ½ teaspoon vanilla. Spread the whipped cream over the fruit. Chill *pavê* for at least 4 hours before serving.

7. When ready to serve, garnish the *pavê* with maraschino cherries and serve cold.

Individual Coconut Custards (*Quindim*)

The coconut rises to the top of the custard as this dessert bakes and becomes the bottom crust when the custards are flipped from the molds. When prepared in a ring mold and served in slices, this dessert is called quindão.

INGREDIENTS | SERVES 12

7 tablespoons butter, divided

2 cups sugar, divided

12 egg yolks

1½ cups finely grated fresh or frozen coconut

½ teaspoon salt

1 teaspoon fresh lime juice

1 teaspoon vanilla or coconut flavoring

1. Melt 2 tablespoons of the butter and use it to generously brush the insides of the molds in a mini muffin pan. Sprinkle ¼ cup of the sugar over the buttered molds, and then turn the pan upside down to shake out the excess. Place the muffin pan inside of a baking pan with 2"-high sides (such as a roasting pan).

2. Preheat the oven to 350°F. Heat a kettle of water on the stove to almost boiling.

3. Melt the remaining butter and place it in a large mixing bowl. Whisk the remaining sugar into the butter until well mixed. Add the egg yolks and whisk until smooth. Add the coconut, salt, lime juice, and vanilla and mix well.

4. Divide the batter between the molds. Place the muffin pan (inside the roasting pan) into the oven. Pour the hot water into the roasting pan, until the water comes halfway up the outside of the molds.

5. Bake for about 15 minutes, or until the tops start to turn golden brown.

6. Remove *quindim* from the oven and from the water bath and let cool for 10 minutes. Gently run a knife around the edges of the *quindim* while they are still warm and gently flip them out of the molds. Store in the refrigerator and serve at room temperature.

Lime Meringue Pie (*Torta de Limão*)

This tart and creamy lime pie is very similar to key lime pie.

INGREDIENTS | SERVES 8

1½ cups all-purpose flour
¼ teaspoon salt
2 teaspoons baking powder
9 tablespoons sugar, divided
6 tablespoons butter
6 tablespoons heavy cream
8 small limes
3 eggs, yolks and whites separated
2 (14-ounce) cans sweetened condensed milk

Juicing Limes

There are a couple of tricks for coaxing the maximum amount of juice from limes. First heat the limes in the microwave for 20–30 seconds, or until they just start to feel warm. Next roll the limes around on a flat surface, pressing down on them firmly with the palms of your hands. Then juice the limes as usual.

1. Preheat the oven to 350°F.

2. Place the flour, salt, baking powder, and 3 tablespoons sugar in the bowl of a food processor. Pulse once or twice to mix. Add the butter and process until mixture resembles coarse crumbs. Add the cream 1 tablespoon at a time, and process with short pulses until dough starts to come together. Press the dough into an ungreased tart pan with a removable base, covering the bottom and sides of the pan.

3. Prick the dough all over with a fork. Bake in the oven for 10–12 minutes, or until very light golden brown. Remove and let cool.

4. Zest the limes. Reserve 1 tablespoon of the lime zest for a garnish, and place the rest of the zest in a medium bowl. Add the egg yolks, the condensed milk, and the juice from the limes (about ⅓–½ cup) to the bowl and whisk together. Pour into the prebaked crust and bake for 15 minutes or until set (not jiggly).

5. Place the egg whites in a saucepan with remaining 6 tablespoons of sugar. Heat mixture over low heat, stirring constantly, for 3–4 minutes, until sugar is dissolved and mixture feels hot. Transfer to the bowl of a standing mixture and beat until stiff peaks form.

6. Spread the meringue over the tart (or use a pastry bag and tip to pipe the meringue). Use a knife to make decorative peaks and swirls in the meringue. Return the tart to the oven for 3–5 minutes (watch carefully), just until the meringue is lightly browned.

7. Sprinkle remaining lime zest over the meringue. Chill tart for 4–6 hours before serving.

Papaya Parfait (*Creme de Papaya*)

This popular Brazilian dessert is easy to make and perfect at the end of a summer meal.
Use frozen papaya if you can't find fresh fruit.

INGREDIENTS | SERVES 4

1½ cups papaya chunks

2 cups vanilla ice cream

1 tablespoon fresh lime juice

½ cup crème de cassis (black currant liqueur), divided

Mint leaves, for garnish

1. Place the papaya, vanilla ice cream, lime juice, and ⅓ cup of the crème de cassis in a blender.

2. Blend until smooth. Add a little bit of milk if the mixture is too thick to blend. Divide the mixture between 4 cups or glasses. Drizzle each with some of the remaining crème de cassis and garnish each with a mint leaf. Serve immediately.

Romeo and Juliet (*Queijo com Goiabada*)

Guava paste and salty minas cheese are a traditional combination in Brazil, dating back to the colonial era. This recipe substitues the easier-to-find cream cheese for minas cheese.

INGREDIENTS | SERVES 4

1 quart vanilla ice cream, softened

8 ounces cream cheese, softened

8 ounces guava paste

1 tablespoon fresh lime juice

1. Place the ice cream in a blender with the cream cheese. Blend until smooth. Return mixture to the freezer for at least 1 hour.

2. Just before serving, melt the guava paste with the lime juice in the microwave (or on the stove over very low heat) until soft enough to stir with a spoon.

3. Place 2 scoops of the ice cream in each of 4 bowls or serving dishes. Spoon softened guava paste over the ice cream and serve immediately.

Poached Meringues in Cream Sauce (*Farófias*)

*Farófias are the Brazilian version of the French dessert known as floating islands.
The fluffy meringue "islands" appear to float in sweet vanilla lime custard.*

INGREDIENTS | SERVES 6

3 cups milk

1 lime

4 large eggs

¾ cup sugar, divided

1 tablespoon cornstarch

¼ teaspoon salt

1 teaspoon vanilla

½ teaspoon cinnamon

About Meringue

Meringue is a mixture of raw egg whites and sugar, beaten until very stiff and glossy. In this recipe, the egg whites are cooked when they simmer in the hot milk. To make an Italian meringue, a very hot sugar syrup is poured into the egg whites as they are beaten, which cooks them and produces a very stable meringue that is great for pies. To prepare a Swiss meringue, the egg whites and sugar are gently heated to partially cook the egg whites before they are beaten (as in the recipe for Lime Meringue Pie in this chapter).

1. Place the milk in a large saucepan. Cut 3 or 4 strips of lime peel and add them to the milk. Bring the milk to a gentle boil, then remove from heat and set aside for 5 minutes.

2. Separate the eggs and reserve the eggs yolks. Place the egg whites in the bowl of a standing mixer and beat until soft peaks form. Gradually add ½ cup of the sugar while continuing to beat, until egg whites form stiff peaks.

3. Remove the lime peel from the milk, and heat milk over medium-low heat until just barely simmering. Use an ice cream scoop or 2 spoons to gather up scoops of meringue, and gently lower them into the milk, working in batches of 4 or 5 at a time. Cook for 2 minutes, then flip meringues and cook for 2 minutes more. Gently remove meringues from the milk with a slotted spoon and place them on a plate. Repeat with remaining meringue.

4. Place the cornstarch and the salt in a heatproof medium bowl and whisk in about ¼ cup of the hot milk until cornstarch is dissolved. Add the egg yolks and remaining sugar to the cornstarch mixture, and whisk until very smooth and pale yellow in color. Add a small amount of the hot milk to the egg yolk mixture and whisk until smooth, and then transfer all of the egg yolk mixture to the saucepan with the rest of the milk. Heat over low heat, stirring constantly, until mixture thickens (about 3–4 minutes). Do not boil. Remove from heat and stir in the vanilla.

5. Place the meringues in a serving dish and pour sauce over them. Sprinkle with cinnamon just before serving.

Coconut Flan (*Pudim de Leite de Coco*)

This popular variation on flan is very easy to make with a blender. Flan is typically served cold, but it is also delicious while still warm (though trickier to remove from the pan intact).

INGREDIENTS | SERVES 8

1 cup sugar

2 tablespoons water

8 large eggs

1 (14-ounce) can sweetened condensed milk

1 cup whole milk

1 (13.5-ounce) can coconut milk

1 teaspoon vanilla

1 tablespoon cornstarch

¼ teaspoon salt

1 cup grated fresh coconut (frozen is fine)

Baking Pan Options

Brazilian-style flan is almost always baked in a ring mold. If you don't have a ring mold, an angel food cake pan makes a good substitute, as does a 10" cake pan with tall sides. If you use a springform pan, make sure that it has a very tight seal, and wrap the outside of the pan tightly with aluminum foil to prevent the water bath from seeping into the flan.

1. Preheat the oven to 350°F. Place a baking pan inside of a larger pan with tall sides (such as a roasting pan). Fill a kettle with water and boil on the stove.

2. Place the sugar and 2 tablespoons water in a heavy saucepan and heat over medium heat. Swirl sugar occasionally as it starts to melt, and cook until sugar turns caramel in color. Remove from heat and quickly pour caramel into the baking pan, turning pan to allow caramel to coat the sides and bottom of the pan.

3. Place the eggs, condensed milk, whole milk, coconut milk, vanilla, cornstarch, salt, and coconut in a blender and blend until smooth. Pour the mixture into the prepared baking pan. Place both pans in the oven, then pour enough boiling water into the roasting pan to come halfway up the sides of the baking pan.

4. Bake flan in the water bath for 50–60 minutes, or until flan only jiggles slightly when you gently shake the pan.

5. Carefully remove from the oven, and let the flan cool in the water bath. Remove from water bath and refrigerate flan until ready to serve.

6. Use a knife to gently loosen edges of flan. Place a plate on top of the baking pan and invert the pan so that the flan slips out onto the plate, caramel side up. Drizzle any caramel sauce left in the pan over the flan and serve.

Bacon from Heaven (*Toucinho de Céu*)

Almond meal is the key ingredient in this intensely flavored, moist Portuguese cake.
The name may come from when lard was used in place of butter.

INGREDIENTS | SERVES 6

1¼ cups sugar

⅓ cup water

1 cup almond meal

¾ cup butter

6 large eggs

1 teaspoon almond extract

¾ cup all-purpose flour

¼ teaspoon salt

⅓ cup powdered sugar

1. Preheat the oven to 350°F. Grease and flour a 9" cake pan.

2. Place the sugar and water in a saucepan and bring to a boil over medium heat. Reduce heat to low and simmer gently for 3–4 minutes. Remove from heat and stir the almond meal and the butter into the mixture until well mixed. Set aside to cool.

3. Separate the eggs. Place the egg whites in the bowl of a standing mixer and beat until soft peaks form.

4. In a separate bowl, whisk the egg yolks until pale and creamy. Add the almond extract and mix well. Add the cooled sugar/almond mixture to the egg yolks and mix well. Fold in the flour and the salt. Gently fold the beaten egg whites into the mixture. Pour batter into prepared cake pan.

5. Bake for 25–30 minutes, or until cake springs back very lightly to the touch. Cool on a rack for 10–15 minutes. Loosen edges of cake with a knife, then place a large plate over the pan and invert cake to unmold. Dust cake generously with powdered sugar before serving.

Coconut Pudding Ring (*Manjar Branco*)

This beautiful dessert is typically prepared in a ring pan or decorative mold. The unmolded pudding is garnished with dried fruit in syrup, usually prunes.

INGREDIENTS | SERVES 8

1 tablespoon vegetable oil

6 tablespoons cornstarch

2 cups whole milk, divided

1 (14-ounce) can sweetened condensed milk

1 (13.5-ounce) can coconut milk

¼ teaspoon salt

1 teaspoon coconut flavoring

1 cup sugar

½ cup water

1 cup dried pitted prunes, peaches, or plums

Make It Chocolate

Manjar de chocolate is fun variation on this dessert—a molded chocolate pudding prepared in a ring mold. To make the chocolate version, melt 8 ounces of semisweet chocolate in a double boiler with 2 cups of cream. Whisk in 1 (14-ounce) can of condensed milk, 1 teaspoon of vanilla, and a package of unflavored gelatin dissolved in 3 tablespoons of water. Pour hot mixture into an oiled mold and chill for 4–6 hours before unmolding.

1. Carefully brush the inside of a ring mold or gelatin mold with the vegetable oil.

2. Place the cornstarch in a small bowl and whisk ⅓ cup of the milk into the cornstarch until smooth. Set aside.

3. Add the remaining milk, the condensed milk, the coconut milk, the salt, and the coconut flavoring to a saucepan. Whisk in the cornstarch mixture. Bring to a simmer over medium-low heat, stirring constantly, and cook until mixture thickens, about 15 minutes.

4. Remove from heat and pour mixture into mold. Chill in refrigerator for at least 4 hours.

5. Place the sugar and water in a saucepan. Bring to a simmer over medium heat and cook until sugar is dissolved. Add the dried fruit and simmer over low heat until fruit has softened. Remove from heat and let cool.

6. To unmold pudding, loosen the edges with a knife, then place a plate on top of the mold and invert mold and plate together, flipping the mold onto the plate. Drizzle fruit syrup and fruit over the pudding and serve.

Fried Bananas with Cheese (*Cartola*)

The word cartola means "top hat" in Portuguese, and this dessert must be so named because the bananas are topped with cheese. It's one of those unusual flavor combinations that just works.

INGREDIENTS | SERVES 4

½ cup sugar

1 tablespoon cinnamon

¼ cup mini chocolate chips

4 ripe bananas

2 tablespoons butter

8 ounces halloumi cheese or good-quality mozzarella

Melting Cheese

Brazilian recipes for *cartola* often call for a type of cheese called *queijo coalho,* which is very similar to Greek halloumi cheese. It's a "squeaky" cheese that holds its shape when heated and can even be placed on a skewer and grilled. Some people prefer a cheese that melts slightly over the sautéed bananas. A high-quality mozzarella cheese works well for that.

1. Preheat the broiler to 500°F. In a small bowl, mix together the sugar, cinnamon, and chocolate chips.

2. Peel the bananas and slice them lengthwise. Melt the butter in a skillet over medium-low heat. Sauté the bananas in the butter until browned on both sides.

3. Place the sliced bananas side by side in a baking sheet. Slice the cheese into ¼"-thick slices. Cover the bananas with the cheese. Broil for 3–5 minutes, or just until the cheese is lightly browned.

4. Remove bananas from the oven and immediately sprinkle the sugar/cinnamon/chocolate mixture over the bananas and cheese. Place bananas back in the oven for 1–2 minutes, then serve immediately.

Sweet Corn Ice Cream (*Sorvete de Milho Verde*)

Though Brazilians sometimes make this ice cream using canned corn, it's well worth waiting until fresh summer corn reaches its peak of sweetness to make this ice cream.

INGREDIENTS | SERVES 6

4 ears fresh sweet white or yellow corn

1 tablespoon cornstarch

1½ cups whole milk

1 (14-ounce) can sweetened condensed milk

¼ teaspoon salt

1½ cups heavy cream

1 teaspoon vanilla

Ice Cream Makers

Ice cream makers churn the ice cream as it freezes, reducing the size of the ice crystals and producing a creamier result. If you don't have an ice cream maker, substitute a can of evaporated milk for the whole milk, and place the prepared ice cream base in a bowl in the freezer. Stir the ice cream periodically as it freezes. Once the ice cream is frozen, place it in an airtight container and store it in the freezer.

1. Use a knife to cut the kernels of corn from the cob. Place the corn kernels in a blender with the cornstarch and the milk. Blend until smooth, then strain the mixture into a large saucepan.

2. Add the condensed milk and the salt to the corn mixture. Cook over medium-low heat, stirring constantly, until mixture thickens, about 6–8 minutes. Remove from heat and let cool for 5 minutes. Stir in the cream and the vanilla. Chill mixture in refrigerator until cold.

3. Freeze mixer in an ice cream maker, according to manufacturer's directions. Place the ice cream in an airtight container and store in the freezer for 4 hours before serving.

Red Wine Tapioca (*Sagu de Vinho*)

In this dessert, the tapioca pearls are soaked in spiced red wine, giving them a striking color. Use the largest pearls that you can find for this recipe.

INGREDIENTS | SERVES 4

6 cups water

1 cup tapioca pearls

3 cups red wine

1 cup plus 1 tablespoon sugar, divided

6 whole cloves

1 cinnamon stick

Pinch of salt

1 cup heavy cream

½ teaspoon vanilla

Tapioca Pearls

Tapioca pearls are made from the starch of the manioc (*mandioca*) root, a plant that is native to northeastern Brazil. Manioc is processed and consumed in many different forms in Brazil. Tapioca pearls (*bolinhas de mandioca*) are made by processing the manioc starch into small opaque balls that swell and become translucent when cooked. Confusingly, tapioca is also the name for a kind of crepe/pancake from northeastern Brazil that is made with manioc starch.

1. Place the water in a large saucepan and bring to a boil. Stir in the tapioca pearls and return to a boil. Cook, stirring for 2–3 minutes. Remove from heat and let the tapioca pearls soak in the water for 1 hour. Drain tapioca in a colander and rinse with fresh water.

2. Return the rinsed tapioca pearls to the saucepan. Add the red wine, 1 cup of sugar, cloves, cinnamon stick, and pinch of salt to the pot. Bring mixture to a boil and simmer for 3 minutes, stirring constantly. Remove from heat. Pour tapioca into a heatproof bowl and chill in the refrigerator until cold, about 1½ hours.

3. Remove the cloves and the cinnamon stick from the tapioca. Whip the cream with 1 tablespoon of sugar until soft peaks form. Fold the vanilla into the whipped cream. Divide the tapioca among 4 glasses or serving dishes, and top with some of the whipped cream. Serve cold.

Coconut Tapioca Pudding (*Cuscuz de Tapioca*)

Here, the tapicoca pearls are cooked in milk and combined with coconut to make a "pudding" that can be sliced into squares.

INGREDIENTS | SERVES 10

3 cups shredded unsweetened coconut (fresh or frozen), divided

3 cups large tapioca pearls

6 cups milk

1 cup sugar

¼ teaspoon salt

1 (14-ounce) can sweetened condensed milk

1. If you are using frozen coconut, thaw the coconut in a strainer over a saucepan. Reserve the liquid.

2. Place the tapioca pearls and 2 cups of the shredded coconut in a large bowl. Add the milk, sugar, and salt to a medium saucepan (with the drained liquid from the frozen coconut, if using) and bring to a boil.

3. Pour the boiling milk over the tapioca mixture and stir well. Set aside for 20 minutes, stirring occasionally. Transfer mixture to a 9" × 13" baking pan. Top with remaining 1 cup of shredded coconut.

4. Chill mixture until firm enough to slice. Serve cold, drizzled with condensed milk.

Chocolate Pudding Cups (*Brigadeiro de Colher*)

The brigadeiro is a popular Brazilian candy—a chocolate truffle named after a famous brigadier general. This version is more of a pudding, and is often served in small cups topped with small candies.

INGREDIENTS | SERVES 10

1 (14-ounce) can sweetened condensed milk

2 tablespoons butter

4 tablespoons cocoa powder

¼ teaspoon salt

1 cup heavy cream

1 cup assorted chocolate sprinkles, candies, and/or chocolate chips, for garnish

1. Place the condensed milk in a heavy saucepan with the butter, the cocoa powder, and the salt.

2. Cook mixture over low heat, stirring constantly, for 15 minutes, or until mixture is thick and shiny. It is ready when you drag a wooden spoon across the bottom of the pot and you see the bottom of the pot for 5–10 seconds before the mixture closes back over.

3. Remove the chocolate mixture from the heat and whisk in the cream. Pour the chocolate into 10 small clear cups or glasses (or 4 wine glasses). Let cool.

4. Cover the tops of each pudding with a layer of sprinkles, candies, chocolate chips, etc. Serve at room temperature.

Guava Cheesecake (*Cuca de Queijo com Goiabada*)

This delicious yet simple cheesecake is inspired by the famous combination of guava paste and cheese known as "Romeo and Juliet."

INGREDIENTS | SERVES 8

1¾ cups graham cracker crumbs or vanilla cookie crumbs

½ teaspoon salt, divided

1 cup sugar, divided

4 tablespoons butter, melted

2 (8-ounce) packages cream cheese, softened

1 teaspoon vanilla

1 teaspoon lime zest

4 large eggs

8 ounces guava paste

½ cup orange juice

1 tablespoon lime juice

Guava Paste (*Goiabada*)

The Portuguese brought their love of quince paste to Brazil, and guava became the tropical substitute for quince. The guava fruit is cooked with sugar over low heat until the mixture becomes very thick. Once cooled, *goiabada* can be cut into pieces and is enjoyed with cheese.

1. Place the crumbs, ¼ teaspoon salt, and ¼ cup sugar in a medium bowl. Stir in the melted butter until well mixed.

2. Preheat the oven to 350°F. Press the crumb mixture over the bottom and partly up the sides of a 9" springform or tart pan.

3. Place the cream cheese, remaining ¼ teaspoon salt, remaining ¾ cups sugar, vanilla, lime zest, and eggs in a food processor or blender and process until smooth. Pour mixture into the prebaked crust. Bake cheesecake for 35–40 minutes, or until edges are set but center still jiggles slightly. Remove from heat and let cool.

4. Place the guava paste in a small saucepan with the orange and lime juices. Heat over low heat, stirring constantly, until guava paste has melted and is smooth. Spread over the top of the cheesecake while still warm. Chill cheesecake until ready to serve.

Tropical Rice Pudding (*Arroz Doce de Coco com Abacaxi*)

In Brazil, rice pudding is often prepared with condensed milk or coconut milk, and flavored with cinnamon.

INGREDIENTS | SERVES 6

1 cup medium-grain rice

1¼ cups water

1 (13.5-ounce) can coconut milk, divided

1 teaspoon salt, divided

3 tablespoons butter, divided

2½ cups diced fresh pineapple

⅓ cup brown sugar

1 tablespoon fresh lime juice

2 tablespoons *cachaça* or rum (optional)

¾ cup sugar

2 tablespoons cornstarch

3 egg yolks

1 (14-ounce) can condensed milk

2 cups whole milk

1 cup flaked, sweetened coconut, divided

1 teaspoon vanilla

1. Place the rice in a medium saucepan with the water, 1 cup of the coconut milk, and ¼ teaspoon salt. Bring to a simmer over medium heat, reduce heat to low, cover, and cook for 10 minutes. Turn off heat and leave covered for 10 minutes.

2. Place 2 tablespoons butter, pineapple, brown sugar, lime juice, and ¼ teaspoon salt in a large skillet. Simmer for 10 minutes, until pineapple is softened and slightly browned. Remove from heat and stir in the *cachaça* or rum.

3. In a medium heatproof bowl, whisk together the sugar, cornstarch, egg yolks, and condensed milk.

4. Place the remaining coconut milk, whole milk, and remaining ½ teaspoon salt in a large saucepan and bring to a simmer. Pour half of the hot milk mixture into the sugar/egg mixture, whisking constantly.

5. Pour everything back into the saucepan and cook over low heat, stirring constantly, until mixture thickens (about 5 minutes). Remove from heat and stir the cooked rice, ½ cup coconut, 1 tablespoon butter, and vanilla into the hot pudding.

6. Make layers of rice pudding and pineapple in a serving bowl. Chill pudding until ready to serve.

7. Toast the remaining coconut in a 300°F oven until lightly browned, and use to garnish the pudding just before serving:

CHAPTER 13

Cookies and Cakes (*Biscoitos e Bolos*)

Chocolate-Dipped Honey Cakes (*Pão de Mel*)

These individual spiced honey cakes are filled with dulce de leche (doce de leite) and coated with chocolate. The cakes are baked in muffin tins, and are typically decorated with nuts or white icing.

INGREDIENTS | SERVES 18

1½ cups water

2 cinnamon sticks

1 teaspoon whole cloves

1 teaspoon anise seeds

1 cup honey

½ cup dark brown sugar

4 cups all-purpose flour

½ teaspoon salt

5 tablespoons cocoa powder, divided

1 teaspoon ground cinnamon

½ teaspoon ground nutmeg

½ teaspoon ground ginger

1 teaspoon baking soda

1 teaspoon baking powder

½ cup buttermilk

2 cups *Doce de Leite* (see sidebar) or filling of choice

1 pound semisweet chocolate chips

2 tablespoons vegetable shortening

White royal icing (optional)

18 walnut or pecan halves (optional)

Homemade Dulce de Leche (*Doce de Leite*)

Doce de leite is a mixture of sugar and milk that has been cooked over low heat until thick, creamy, and caramelized. The butter-scotch/caramel result is used in many different desserts. *Doce de leite* is easy to make, but it requires a long period of constant stirring to prevent the mixture from burning. Shortcut method: mix 1 (14-ounce) can of condensed milk, 1 (12-ounce) can of evaporated milk, and ¼ teaspoon salt and cook over low heat, stirring constantly, until mixture is thick and dark caramel in color, about 25–30 minutes.

1. Place the water in a medium saucepan. Add cinnamon sticks, cloves, and anise seeds and bring to a boil. Set aside, covered, for 30 minutes.

2. Preheat oven to 350°F. Strain the spice-infused water into the bowl of a standing mixer. Add honey and brown sugar and mix well with the whisk attachment.

3. In a separate medium bowl, whisk together the flour, salt, 4 tablespoons cocoa powder, ground cinnamon, ground nutmeg, ground ginger, baking soda, and baking powder. Add to the mixing bowl along with the buttermilk and mix until well blended. The mixture should have the texture of cake batter.

4. Grease 18 small round molds or muffin tins and sprinkle with remaining cocoa powder. Fill molds ½ full with the batter. Bake for 12–15 minutes. Remove from oven and let cool.

5. Split each cake in half horizontally. Spread 1–2 tablespoons of softened *doce de leite* or filling of choice (nutella, coconut cream, jam) on the bottom half of the cake and replace the top to enclose the filling. Chill cakes for 20 minutes.

6. Place the chocolate chips and vegetable shortening in a microwave-safe bowl. Heat for 30 seconds in the microwave, then remove and stir. Repeat until chocolate is completely melted.

7. Place a cake on the prongs of the fork and dip the cake in the melted chocolate, turning to coat all sides. Remove, letting excess chocolate drip off. Let cool on a wire rack or wax paper. Pipe royal icing decorations onto tops of cakes and garnish with nuts (optional).

Peanut Butter Cookies (*Biscoito Amanteigado de Amendoim*)

These tasty peanut rollout cookies can be cut into shapes with cookie cutters.
Toasted peanuts give these cookies lots of flavor.

INGREDIENTS | MAKES 25

½ cup raw shelled, skinned peanuts

1 cup butter, softened

½ cup sugar

1 large egg

1 teaspoon vanilla

2 cups all-purpose flour

½ teaspoon baking powder

½ teaspoon salt

⅓ cup powdered sugar

1. Preheat oven to 300°F. Place the peanuts in a shallow layer on a baking sheet and toast them until light brown and fragrant. Remove from the oven and let cool. Place peanuts in a food processor and process until very finely ground.

2. Place the butter in the bowl of a standing mixer. Add the sugar and beat until mixture is light and fluffy. Add the egg and the vanilla and mix well.

3. In a small bowl, whisk together the ground peanuts, flour, baking powder, and salt. Add the dry ingredients to the mixer and mix until just incorporated and mixture starts to come together as dough. (If mixture is too dry and crumbly, add 1–2 tablespoons of milk.) Wrap the dough in plastic wrap and chill for 30 minutes.

4. Preheat the oven to 350°F. On a floured surface, roll out the dough to ¼" thickness. Cut out cookies in desired shapes and place them on a baking sheet lined with parchment paper. Reroll scraps and cut out more cookies.

5. Bake cookies until firm and light brown, about 10–12 minutes. Remove from oven and cool for 5 minutes on the baking sheet, then transfer cookies to a wire rack.

6. Dust cookies with powdered sugar before serving.

Happily Married Cookies (*Bem-Casados*)

These beautiful cookies are given out at weddings wrapped in tissue paper with a little bow. Two sponge-cake cookies are "married" together with a special caramel cream and then dipped in a sugary glaze.

INGREDIENTS | MAKES 20

1 (14-ounce) can condensed milk
4 large eggs, separated
Pinch of salt
1 tablespoon butter
1½ teaspoons vanilla

¾ cup all-purpose flour
1 teaspoon baking powder
¼ teaspoon salt
⅓ cup granulated sugar
2 cups powdered sugar
¾ cup water

1. Place the condensed milk in a heavy saucepan along with 2 egg yolks, a pinch of salt, and the butter. Cook over medium-low heat, stirring constantly to prevent burning, until mixture thickens and turns light caramel in color, about 15 minutes. Stir in ½ teaspoon vanilla and set aside to cool.

2. In a small bowl, whisk together the flour, baking powder, and salt. Preheat the oven to 350°F. Grease a baking sheet with butter.

3. In a medium bowl, beat the egg whites until soft peaks form. Gradually add the granulated sugar to the egg whites while beating, until stiff peaks form. Beat in the remaining 2 egg yolks. Fold in remaining vanilla. Gently fold the flour mixture into the beaten egg mixture until just mixed, trying not to deflate the egg whites.

4. Place the batter in a pastry bag fitted with a wider round tip and pipe 2" circles of dough onto the baking sheet, spacing them about 1" apart. (Or use a small spoon to form circles of batter.)

5. Bake cookies until puffed and very light golden brown, about 8 minutes. Use a 2" cookie cutter to trim the cookies while they are still warm. Transfer cookies to a cooling rack.

6. Place 1–2 teaspoons of the caramel mixture on the bottom of 1 cookie and top with another cookie, facing the baking sheet sides of the cookies together. Repeat with remaining cookies.

7. Place the powdered sugar in a small saucepan with ¾ cup water. Bring to a boil, and simmer for 1–2 minutes or until mixture is slightly thickened and sugar is dissolved. Let cool slightly. Use a fork to dip each cookie sandwich into the syrup, then place cookies on a wire rack to dry. Store cookies in an airtight container for up to 5 days.

Lemon Cream Filling (*Creme de Limão*)

Other possible fillings for these sandwich cookies include chocolate ganache, passion fruit curd, guava, jams, and this lemon cream: Beat 6 tablespoons of softened butter with 2 teaspoons lemon zest until fluffy. Add a pinch of salt and 1 teaspoon of lemon juice. Gradually add 1½ cups powdered sugar while beating, or more to achieve desired texture.

Guava Shortbread Thumbprints (*Biscoito de Goiabada*)

The center of these elegant cookies is filled with goiabada, a fruit paste made with guava fruit. Goiabada is available in the Latin food section of most grocery stores, often packaged in metal tins.

INGREDIENTS | MAKES 30

1½ cups all-purpose flour

½ cup cornstarch

½ teaspoon salt

1 cup plus 2 tablespoons butter, softened

1 cup sugar, divided

1 teaspoon finely grated lime zest

8 ounces guava paste

Homemade Guava Paste (*Goiabada Caseira*)

If you are fortunate enough to have access to fresh guavas, you can make your own guava paste, which is delicious with cheese as well as in desserts. Peel the guava fruit and cut into chunks. Place fruit in the blender with a ½ cup of water and process. Strain the fruit through a fine-mesh sieve into a saucepan. Add about ¾ as much sugar as there is guava (for 1 cup guava, use ¾ cup sugar). Simmer over very low heat, stirring constantly, until mixture thickens to desired consistency. (Mixture will firm up even more as it cools.)

1. Place the flour, cornstarch, and salt in a medium bowl and mix well. Cream the butter in the bowl of a standing mixer until fluffy. Add ½ cup sugar and lime zest and beat well. Add the dry ingredients and mix well.

2. Preheat the oven to 350°F. Line a baking sheet with parchment paper. Divide the dough into 25 pieces. Take one of the pieces and roll it between your hands to form a smooth ball. Place the ball of dough on the baking sheet, and use your thumb to make a small well in the center, flatting the ball slightly. Repeat with remaining pieces of dough.

3. Cut the guava paste into 25 small squares, and place 1 in each cookie indentation.

4. Bake the cookies until just firm but not browned, about 10 minutes. Remove from heat and sprinkle with the remaining ½ cup of sugar while the cookies are still hot. Cookies will keep for several days in an airtight container.

Guava Roll (*Bolo de Rolo*)

This cake is a specialty of the city of Recife in northeastern Brazil. Very thin layers of delicate sponge cake are rolled around a filling of guava paste, and the cake is cut into slices crosswise so the layers are visible.

INGREDIENTS | SERVES 20

2 sticks butter, softened

1½ cups sugar, divided

4 large eggs, separated

½ teaspoon almond extract

1⅔ cups all-purpose flour

½ teaspoon salt

3 tablespoons powdered sugar

12 ounces guava paste

½ cup water

1. Preheat the oven to 350°F. Line a 12" × 18" baking sheet with parchment paper, and butter and lightly flour the parchment paper.

2. Beat the butter with 1 cup of the sugar until light and fluffy. Add the egg yolks and almond extract and beat until well mixed.

3. In a small bowl whisk together the flour and the salt. In a separate bowl, beat the egg whites until stiff peaks form. Carefully fold the egg whites into the egg/sugar mixture. Gently fold in the flour mixture.

4. Use a spatula (offset spatula works well for this) to spread about half of the batter into a ½"-thick layer over the buttered parchment paper. Bake for 5–8 minutes, until cake is just done but not browned.

5. While the cake is baking, sprinkle a clean dishtowel with 3 tablespoons powdered sugar. Remove cake from oven, let cool briefly, then gently flip cake out of the pan and onto the sugared dishtowel. Carefully peel off the parchment paper.

6. Dice the guava paste into pieces and place it in a blender with the water. Blend for several seconds, then empty mixture into a saucepan. Heat to a boil, stirring, then remove from heat and let cool.

7. Spread a thin layer of the cooled guava paste onto the cake. Roll cake up, starting with a short side and using the dishcloth to help. Set aside.

8. Make another thin cake layer with the remaining batter in the same manner. Spread the cake with guava paste and continue to roll the new cake onto the previous roll, enlarging it.

9. Slice the cake crosswise into thin slices and sprinkle slices with remaining sugar before serving.

Anthill Cake (*Bolo Formigueiro*)

Tiny chocolate sprinkles distributed throughout the batter represent ants, and the yellow pound cake is the anthill. The special trick is to use chocolate sprinkles instead of miniature chocolate chips—the sprinkles have an oblong shape that makes for a more convincing ant.

INGREDIENTS | SERVES 12

2 sticks softened butter, divided

1¾ cups sugar, divided

4 large eggs

2 teaspoons vanilla

3 cups all-purpose flour

1 teaspoon baking powder

¾ teaspoon salt

1 cup buttermilk

1½ cups chocolate sprinkles, divided

4 tablespoons cocoa powder

2 tablespoons milk

1. Preheat the oven to 350°F. Grease and flour an angel food cake pan with a removable bottom, or bundt pan.

2. Place all but 1 tablespoon of the butter in the bowl of a standing mixer. Add 1½ cups of sugar and beat until mixture is light and fluffy. Add the eggs one at a time and the vanilla and mix well.

3. In a small bowl, whisk together the flour, baking powder, and salt. Add to the butter/sugar mixture in parts, alternating with the buttermilk. Fold in 1 cup of the chocolate sprinkles.

4. Pour the batter into the cake pan. Bake for 45–55 minutes, or until a toothpick inserted in the center of the cake comes out clean. Remove from oven and let cool on a rack. Once the cake has cooled, remove it from the pan.

5. Prepare the glaze: Place remaining 1 tablespoon butter, remaining ¼ cup sugar, cocoa powder, and milk in a small saucepan and bring to a simmer over medium-low heat, stirring constantly. Cook for 1–2 minutes, then remove from heat and let cool for 5 minutes.

6. Drizzle the glaze over the top of the cake, and sprinkle the remaining ½ cup of chocolate sprinkles over the glaze.

Orange Snack Cake (*Bolo de Laranja*)

This cake is quick and easy to make. The batter is mixed entirely in the blender and the oranges are simply cut into chunks before they go straight in. No need to get out the juicer.

INGREDIENTS | SERVES 12

2 thin-skinned oranges, ends and seeds removed, cut into coarse chunks

2 limes

8 tablespoons butter, melted, plus 1 tablespoon

½ cup vegetable oil

3 large eggs

1 teaspoon vanilla

1 teaspoon orange flavoring (optional)

½ teaspoon salt

2 cups sugar, divided

2½ cups all-purpose flour

5 tablespoons orange juice

Candied Orange Slices

This cake is sometimes decorated with slices of candied orange, which are placed in the bottom of the pan before adding the batter. When the cake is flipped out of the pan, the orange slices make a built-in decoration. Slice an orange very thinly. Place the slices in a saucepan with ½ cup sugar and 1 cup water. Simmer for about 10 minutes, or until orange slices are tender. Place orange slices in the bottom of cake pan (greased, floured, and lined with parchment) before adding batter to the pan.

1. Preheat the oven to 350°F. Grease and flour an angel food cake pan with a removable bottom, or bundt pan.

2. Add the orange chunks to a blender along with the juice of 1 lime. Blend until finely chopped.

3. Add 8 tablespoons of butter (melted), vegetable oil, eggs, vanilla, and orange flavoring (if using) to the blender and mix well.

4. Combine the salt, 1½ cups sugar, and flour in a bowl, then add mixture to the blender in three parts, mixing briefly after each addition, until batter is well mixed.

5. Pour the batter into the cake pan. Bake for 45–55 minutes, or until a toothpick inserted in the center of the cake comes out clean. Remove from oven and let cool on a rack.

6. Prepare the glaze: Place the orange juice, juice of 1 lime, 1 tablespoon butter, and ½ cup sugar in a small saucepan and bring to a simmer over medium-low heat, stirring constantly. Cook for 1–2 minutes, then remove from heat and let cool for 5 minutes.

7. Prick holes in the cake (still in the pan) with a wooden skewer. Drizzle half of the glaze over the cake and set aside until cake is completely cool. Remove cake from pan and drizzle remaining glaze over the top of the cake.

Cassava Coconut Cake (*Bolo Souza Leão*)

This is a very traditional dessert from Pernambuco that dates back to the colonial period. This rich cake has a creamy, custard-like texture and is served at weddings and other special occasions.

INGREDIENTS | SERVES 12

2 pounds frozen manioc root, thawed
12 egg yolks
1 teaspoon salt
1 cup water
2½ cups sugar
2 sticks butter
1 (13.5-ounce) can coconut milk

1. Cook the manioc until tender in boiling water. Drain and when cool enough to handle, press manioc through a food mill. Wrap the pressed manioc in cheesecloth and twist the cloth very firmly, pressing on the manioc, to remove as much liquid as possible. Discard liquid.

2. Preheat oven to 350°F. Place the manioc in a large bowl, add the egg yolks and the salt, and mix well.

3. Place the water and the sugar in a saucepan and bring to a boil. Reduce heat to low and simmer for 6–8 minutes, or until the thread stage is reached (syrup thickens and forms fine threads when a fork is dipped in the mixture and removed). Remove from heat and stir the butter into the sugar syrup.

4. Add the syrup to the manioc, along with the coconut milk, and mix well. Pour batter into a 9" or 10" springform pan.

5. Bake for 40–50 minutes, or until a toothpick inserted into the middle comes out clean.

6. Let cake cool on a rack in a pan for 10–15 minutes before removing from pan. Serve warm or at room temperature.

Apple Crumb Cake (*Cuca de Maçã*)

This German-style coffee cake with its cinnamon crumb topping is very popular in Brazil, especially in southern Brazil where apples are cultivated. Banana (cuca de banana) and pineapple (cuca de abacaxi) are other popular versions of this cake.

INGREDIENTS | SERVES 12

3 apples, peeled, cored, and thinly sliced
1 tablespoon fresh lemon juice
2 cups sugar, divided
3½ cups all-purpose flour, divided
2 teaspoons cinnamon
¾ teaspoon salt, divided
6 tablespoons cold butter
8 tablespoons room-temperature butter
4 large eggs, separated
1 teaspoon vanilla
2 teaspoons baking powder
¾ cup buttermilk

1. Toss the apple slices with the lemon juice and 2 tablespoons of sugar in a bowl and set aside.

2. In a small bowl, whisk together ½ cup flour, ½ cup sugar, cinnamon, and ¼ teaspoon salt. Cut cold butter into small pieces, and use a pastry cutter (or your fingers) to mix butter into the flour/sugar mixture until it has the texture of coarse crumbs. Set aside.

3. Preheat oven to 350°F. Grease the bottom and sides of a 10" springform pan. Place room-temperature butter in the bowl of a standing mixer. Add remaining sugar and beat until light and fluffy. Add the egg yolks one at a time (reserve whites) and vanilla and mix well.

4. In a small bowl, whisk together remaining flour, baking powder, and remaining salt. Add the dry ingredients to the mixer in 2 parts, alternating with the buttermilk.

5. In a large, clean bowl, beat the egg whites until stiff peaks form. Carefully fold the egg whites into the batter. Spread mixture into the prepared cake pan. Layer the sliced apples on top of the batter. Sprinkle the reserved crumb mixture over the apples.

6. Bake for 40–45 minutes, or until a toothpick inserted into the middle comes out clean.

7. Let cake cool on a rack in a pan for 10–15 minutes before removing from pan.

Peanut Cream Cookie Cake (*Torta Paulista*)

Layers of cream, cookies, dulce de leche, and toasted peanuts make up this delicious and unusual cake, a favorite in São Paulo.

INGREDIENTS | SERVES 10

3½ cups roasted peanuts (salted or unsalted)

8 ounces whipped cream cheese

¾ cup creamy peanut butter

¼ teaspoon salt

1 cup powdered sugar, sifted

2 tablespoons milk

1 teaspoon vanilla

1½ cups heavy cream

2 tablespoons sugar

1½ cups dulce de leche

20 ounces vanilla wafers or graham crackers (about 1½ boxes)

1. Place 2 cups of the peanuts in the food processor and process until finely ground. Coarsely chop the remaining 1½ cups.

2. Place the cream cheese, peanut butter, and salt in the bowl of a standing mixer. Beat until fluffy. Add the powdered sugar, milk, and vanilla and beat until very well mixed.

3. In a medium bowl, beat the cream and the sugar until stiff peaks form. Gently fold cream/sugar mixture into the peanut-butter mixture.

4. Soften the dulce de leche by heating it in the microwave for 20 seconds or until it is spreadable.

5. Spread ¼ of the peanut-butter cream in the bottom of a 9" square baking dish. Top with a layer of wafers. Spread ½ cup of dulce de leche over the wafers, and sprinkle with ⅓ of the ground peanuts. Top with another layer of wafers.

6. Spread a layer of peanut-butter cream over the wafers. Top with another layer of wafers. Spread ½ cup dulce de leche over the wafers, and sprinkle another ⅓ of the peanuts over top. Add another layer of wafers. Repeat layers once more. Top with remaining peanut-butter cream.

7. Garnish top of cake with coarsely chopped peanuts and chill for at least 2 hours, or overnight. Cut into squares to serve.

Coconut Chocolate Layer Cake (*Bolo de Prestígio*)

This cake is named after a Brazilian candy bar called Prestígio, *which has a center of chewy coconut surrounded by chocolate.*

INGREDIENTS | SERVES 10

6 ounces semisweet chocolate, chopped
½ cup heavy cream
2 teaspoons vanilla, divided
5 large eggs, separated
½ cup butter, softened
2 cups sugar, divided
1½ cups all-purpose flour
1 teaspoon baking powder
1 teaspoon salt, divided

1 cup cocoa powder
½ cup buttermilk
¼ cup water
½ cup coconut milk
1 cup milk
1 tablespoon cornstarch
1 (14-ounce) can condensed milk
2 tablespoons butter
1½ cups sweetened flaked coconut
⅓ cup chocolate sprinkles (optional)

1. Preheat the oven to 350°F. Butter and flour 2 (9") cake pans and line the bottom of each pan with a circle of wax paper.

2. Place chopped chocolate in a heatproof bowl. In a small saucepan, bring the cream to a simmer over medium-low heat. Pour hot cream over chocolate, and stir gently with a spatula until chocolate melts. Stir in 1 teaspoon vanilla. Set aside.

3. In a large bowl, beat the egg whites until stiff peaks form and set aside.

4. Beat butter with 1½ cups sugar until light and creamy. Add egg yolks and remaining vanilla. In a separate bowl, whisk together flour, baking powder, ½ teaspoon salt, and cocoa powder. Add dry ingredients to the egg/sugar mixture, alternating with the buttermilk. Carefully fold in egg whites.

5. Divide the batter between the pans. Bake for 20 minutes, or until cake just springs back to the touch. Remove from oven and let cool.

6. In a small saucepan, bring ½ cup sugar, ¼ cup water, and coconut milk to a simmer over medium-low heat, stirring until sugar is dissolved. Remove from heat. Brush syrup over cake layers while they are still in the pans.

7. In a large saucepan, whisk together the milk, cornstarch, condensed milk, butter, coconut, and remaining ½ teaspoon salt. Cook over medium-low heat until mixture thickens and begins to pull away from the sides of the pan, about 5–7 minutes. Remove from heat.

8. Remove cake layers from pans and peel off wax paper. Place one cake layer on serving platter. Spread the coconut filling filling over the cake. Top with second cake layer.

9. Frost top and sides of cake with ganache. Cover top of cake with chocolate sprinkles, if desired.

Sweet Cornmeal Cake (*Bolo de Fubá*)

Very finely ground cornmeal (fubá) is the secret to this sweet, light cake. Bolo de fubá has the taste and texture of a cake, and is very different from corn bread. Look for finely ground yellow cornmeal, often labeled "corn flour" (but not cornstarch).

INGREDIENTS | SERVES 12

3 large eggs

1 cup corn oil

1½ cups buttermilk

1½ cups sugar

2 cups very fine cornmeal

1 cup all-purpose flour

1 teaspoon salt

1 tablespoon baking powder

¼ cup powdered sugar

Blenders and Tube Pans

Brazilian cuisine includes a huge variety of cakes, and many of the recipes call for mixing the batter in a blender. Brazilians use blenders in place of standing mixers or food processors for many kitchen tasks, which can be a convenient alternative (especially if you need to free up counter space in your kitchen). Tube pans are the most popular kind of cake pan in Brazil. These cakes are served plain or with a simple glaze and enjoyed on a daily basis, even for breakfast.

1. Preheat the oven to 350°F. Grease and flour a tube pan, angel food cake pan, or bundt pan.

2. Place the eggs, corn oil, and buttermilk in a blender and mix well.

3. In a small bowl, whisk together the sugar, cornmeal, flour, salt, and baking powder. Add dry ingredients to the blender in 3 parts, blending well after each addition. (If your blender is small, place the dry ingredients in a large bowl and whisk in the wet ingredients (from the blender) until well mixed.)

4. Pour batter into prepared pan. Bake cake for 40–45 minutes, or until a toothpick inserted in the middle comes out clean.

5. Remove cake from oven and let cool in pan for 10 minutes. Remove cake from pan and sprinkle top of cake with powdered sugar while it is still warm.

Chocolate Fudge Layer Cake (*Bolo de Brigadeiro*)

The brigadeiro is a Brazilian candy, a creamy chocolate fudge truffle rolled in chocolate sprinkles. This rich chocolate layer cake has a filling made of the same chocolate fudge, and is decorated with chocolate sprinkles.

INGREDIENTS | SERVES 10

5 large eggs, separated
2 cups sugar, divided
¾ cup vegetable oil
1 teaspoon vanilla
2 cups all-purpose flour
1 teaspoon baking powder
1 teaspoon salt, divided

1 cup plus 2 tablespoons cocoa powder, divided
¾ cup buttermilk
½ cup water
2 (14-ounce) cans sweetened condensed milk
2 tablespoons heavy cream
2 tablespoons butter
¾ cup chocolate sprinkles

1. Preheat the oven to 350°F. Butter and flour 2 (9") cake pans and line the bottom of each pan with a circle of wax paper.

2. In a large bowl, beat the egg whites until stiff peaks form and set aside.

3. Mix the egg yolks with 1½ cups of sugar until light and creamy. Add the oil and vanilla. In a separate bowl, whisk together the flour, baking powder, ½ teaspoon salt, and ¾ cup cocoa powder. Add dry ingredients to the egg/sugar mixture, alternating with the buttermilk. Carefully fold the egg whites into the batter until just mixed.

4. Divide the batter between the pans. Bake for 20 minutes, or until cake just springs back to the touch. Remove from oven and let cool.

5. In a small saucepan, combine remaining ½ cup sugar, ½ cup water, and 2 tablespoons cocoa powder and bring to a simmer over medium-low, stirring until sugar is dissolved.

Remove from heat. Brush syrup over cake layers while they are still in the pans.

6. In a large saucepan, place the condensed milk, cream, butter, remaining ¼ cup cocoa powder, and remaining ½ teaspoon salt. Cook over medium-low heat until mixture thickens and begins to pull away from the sides of the pan, about 5–7 minutes. Remove from heat.

7. Remove cake from pans, and peel off the wax paper. Place one cake layer on serving platter. Spread about a fourth of the chocolate filling over the cake. Top with second cake layer. Spread remaining chocolate filling over the top and sides of the cake while it is still warm. (Microwave chocolate filling briefly if it becomes too stiff to spread easily.)

8. Cover top and sides of frosted cake with chocolate sprinkles. Let cool before serving.

Carrot Cake with Chocolate Frosting
(*Bolo de Cenoura com Cobertura de Chocolate*)

Brazilian carrot cake is very different from American carrot cake. This cake is golden and light, rather than dense and moist. A shiny chocolate glaze tops it off.

INGREDIENTS | SERVES 10

5 medium carrots, peeled

1⅓ cup vegetable oil

4 large eggs

3 cups sugar, divided

1 teaspoon salt, divided

2 teaspoons baking powder

2 teaspoons vanilla, divided

3 cups all-purpose flour

1 cup milk

¼ cup cocoa powder

1 tablespoon cornstarch

Make It in a Mug (*Bolo de Cenoura de Caneca*)

This carrot cake is a popular afterschool snack in Brazil. To make 2 quick mugs of cake, mix 1 egg, 4 tablespoons grated carrot, 2 tablespoons vegetable oil, 4 tablespoons each sugar and flour, and ½ teaspoon each salt and baking powder in a medium bowl. Divide batter between 2 large mugs. Microwave for 2–3 minutes. In a separate bowl, melt 1 chocolate bar in the microwave with half of a 14-ounce can of condensed milk. Mix until smooth. Make a hole in center of carrot cakes, and pour chocolate over cakes.

1. Grease and flour a 9" × 13" cake pan. Preheat the oven to 350°F.

2. Finely shred the carrots in a food processor. Add the vegetable oil, eggs, 2 cups sugar, ¾ teaspoon salt, baking powder, and 1 teaspoon vanilla to the food processor and mix well. Add flour in 2 parts and pulse briefly to mix.

3. Transfer batter to prepared pan. Bake for 25–30 minutes or until cake springs back lightly to the touch.

4. While the cake is baking, prepare the chocolate glaze: Place milk, 1 cup sugar, cocoa powder, cornstarch, and remaining ¼ teaspoon salt in a medium saucepan. Bring to a simmer over medium-low heat and cook, stirring, until mixture is shiny and slightly thickened, about 4–5 minutes.

5. Remove cake from oven and let cool for 5 minutes, then pour warm glaze over the cake (still in the pan). Let cool and cut into squares to serve.

Portuguese Custard Pastries (*Pastel de Nata*)

*These tarts are baked at a high temperature so that the tops almost blacken,
and they are then sprinkled with cinnamon and powdered sugar.*

INGREDIENTS | MAKES 24

1⅔ cups all-purpose flour

1 teaspoon salt, divided

⅓–½ cup water

12 tablespoons butter, softened

6 egg yolks

¾ cup sugar

3 tablespoons cornstarch

2 cups whole milk

1 cinnamon stick

1 teaspoon vanilla

⅓ cup powdered sugar

1 tablespoon ground cinnamon

1. Whisk together the flour and ½ teaspoon salt in a medium bowl. Add the water gradually, stirring until mixture just comes together into a smooth dough. (You may need slightly more or less water.) Knead briefly then wrap with plastic wrap and chill for 15 minutes.

2. Roll out dough on a floured surface to an 18" square. Spread 4 tablespoons of the softened butter over the dough. Fold the dough neatly into thirds, like a letter.

3. Turn the dough 90° and roll out into another 18" square. Spread 4 tablespoons of the softened butter over the dough. Fold the dough neatly into thirds. Rewrap dough and chill for 15 minutes.

4. Roll dough into an 18" × 20" rectangle. Spread remaining butter over dough, leaving 1" free of butter along one short side. Starting with the other short side, roll the dough up into a log. Wrap with plastic wrap and chill for 1 hour.

5. To make the custard, place the egg yolks in a heatproof bowl. Add the sugar, remaining ½ teaspoon salt, and cornstarch and whisk until creamy and light.

6. Place the milk and cinnamon stick in a large saucepan and bring to a simmer over medium-low heat. Remove cinnamon stick from milk, then gradually pour hot milk into the egg mixture, stirring. Return everything to the saucepan and cook over low heat, stirring, until mixture thickens. Remove from heat, stir in vanilla, and cover with plastic wrap. Keep warm.

7. Preheat oven to 500°F. Remove pastry from refrigerator and roll dough log on counter until it is about 1½" in diameter. Cut crosswise into 24 pieces.

8. Place each piece of dough in the bottom of the wells of a mini muffin pan. Press dough down and up sides of well, so that it rises a bit over the top. Fill each pastry ¾ full with the custard.

9. Bake pastries until browned on top in spots, about 7–10 minutes. Remove from oven, and place on rack to cool.

10. Sprinkle pastries with powdered sugar and cinnamon. Serve warm.

Sweet Potato Cake with Orange Glaze (*Bolo de Batata-Doce*)

*This delicious cake has a moist texture and distinctive sweetness,
thanks to mashed sweet potatoes in the batter.*

INGREDIENTS | SERVES 10

1½ cups mashed sweet potato (1 large sweet potato)

1½ cups vegetable oil

2 cups sugar

1 tablespoon orange zest

1 teaspoon vanilla

4 large eggs

1 cup all-purpose flour

1 cup cornstarch

1 teaspoon salt

1½ teaspoons baking powder

1 teaspoon baking soda

½ cup chopped walnuts or pecans (optional)

¼ cup orange juice

2 cups powdered sugar, divided

2 tablespoons *cachaça* or rum (optional)

1. Grease and flour a tube pan, angel food cake pan, or bundt pan. Preheat the oven to 350°F.

2. Place the mashed potato, vegetable oil, sugar, orange zest, and vanilla in the bowl of a standing mixer and beat until well mixed. Add eggs one at a time.

3. In a medium bowl, whisk together flour, cornstarch, salt, baking powder, and baking soda. Gradually add dry ingredients to egg mixture until just mixed. Stir in nuts if using.

4. Spread batter into the prepared pan. Bake for 40–45 minutes, or until cake springs back lightly to the touch.

5. Whisk orange juice with 1 cup powdered sugar and rum (if using). While cake is still hot, pierce cake with a wooden skewer and drizzle half of the glaze over the cake. Let cake cool in pan for 30–35 minutes.

6. Remove cake from pan. Whisk remaining powdered sugar into remaining glaze and drizzle over cake before serving.

Portuguese Almond Cookies (*Pastel de Santa Clara*)

These pretty cookies are a Portuguese sweet that has remained popular in Brazil.

INGREDIENTS | MAKES 24

2 cups all-purpose flour

¼ teaspoon salt

¾ cup sugar, divided

10 tablespoons cold butter, cut into ½" pieces

3–4 tablespoons ice water

2 tablespoons water

¾ cup ground almonds

4 egg yolks

½ teaspoon almond extract (optional)

1 large egg

1 tablespoon milk

½ cup powdered sugar

1. Place the flour, salt, and 1 teaspoon of sugar in a medium bowl. Add the butter and use a pastry cutter or 2 knives to blend it into the flour until mixture is crumbly. Stir in the ice water 1 tablespoon at a time until mixture comes together as a shaggy dough. Knead 2 or 3 times until just barely smooth. Shape dough into a disk, wrap with plastic wrap, and chill.

2. Add the remaining sugar to a small saucepan with 2 tablespoons water. Heat over medium-low heat until sugar melts, then thickens to the thread stage. Add the almonds and stir well. Add the egg yolks, stirring constantly, and cook until it thickens and starts to pull away from the sides of the pan. Remove from heat and set aside. Stir in almond extract, if using.

3. Preheat the oven to 350°F. On a floured surface, roll out the pastry dough very thin (about ¼–⅛"). Use a round biscuit cutter to make circles of dough 3–4" in diameter.

4. Place a generous teaspoon of the almond mixture in the middle of each circle of dough. Lightly wet the edges of each dough circle, then lift the edges up slightly around the filling (but not closing over it), crimping the edges of the circle of dough, to make a fluted cup, with the filling inside.

5. Whisk the egg with 1 tablespoon of milk or water. Place the pastries on a baking sheet and brush them with the egg/milk mixture.

6. Bake the pastries for about 15–20 minutes, until very lightly browned.

7. Sprinkle the pastries with powdered sugar as soon as they come out of the oven.

Guava Sandwich Cookies (*Casadinho de Goiabada*)

These shortbread cookie sandwiches filled with guava paste are a popular sweet at weddings and other celebrations.

INGREDIENTS | MAKES 20

2 cups all-purpose flour

1 cup cornstarch

⅓ cup sugar

¾ teaspoon salt

14 tablespoons butter, slightly softened

1 egg yolk

1 teaspoon vanilla

1 teaspoon lime zest

2–3 tablespoons rum

1 cup guava paste

2 tablespoons lime juice

½ cup powdered sugar

1. Place the flour, cornstarch, sugar, and salt in a large bowl. Cut the butter into small pieces and mix it into the dry ingredients with your fingers.

2. Add the egg yolk, vanilla, lime zest, and 2 tablespoons rum and continue to mix and knead until mixture forms a smooth dough. It will seem crumbly at first but should gradually come together. Add another tablespoon of rum if mixture is still too crumbly. Set dough aside for 15 minutes.

3. Preheat oven to 350°F. Roll out the dough on a floured surface to ¼" thickness. Cut out small rounds of dough (2–3" in diameter) and place them on baking sheets lined with parchment paper.

4. Bake cookies until they just barely start to turn golden brown around the edges, about 8 minutes. Remove from oven and transfer cookies to a rack to cool.

5. Place the guava paste and lime juice in a small saucepan over low heat. Stir until guava paste is softened and spreadable (add 1 or 2 tablespoons water to thin mixture if needed).

6. Spread 1–2 teaspoons of guava paste on the bottom of a cookie, and top with another cookie.

7. Dust cookies lightly with powdered sugar before serving. Store in an airtight container.

CHAPTER 14

Candy (*Doces*)

Chocolate Fudge Truffles (*Brigadeiros*)

Brigadeiros *are very simple to make and delicious. These truffles are named after a famous 1940s brigadier general named Eduardo Gomes, who must have liked chocolate.*

INGREDIENTS | MAKES 16

1 (14-ounce) can sweetened condensed milk

¼ cup cocoa powder

¼ teaspoon salt

2 tablespoons butter

½ cup chocolate sprinkles

1. Place the condensed milk, cocoa powder, and salt in a heavy saucepan. Cook over low heat, stirring constantly. Mixture should not boil. Cook until mixture thickens, turns shiny, and starts to come together and pull away from the sides of the pan (about 10–15 minutes).

2. Remove from heat and stir in the butter. Set mixture aside until cool enough to handle.

3. With buttered hands, take some of the chocolate mixture and roll it between the palms of your hands to form a 1" ball. Repeat with remaining chocolate mixture.

4. Roll each candy in the chocolate sprinkles to coat. Place in individual fluted paper cups to serve. Store candies in an airtight container for up to 1 week.

Dulce de Leche (*Doce de Leite*)

This creamy caramelized milk is delicious on its own, but it is often used in cakes, cookies, puddings, ice cream, and many other desserts.

INGREDIENTS | MAKES 1½ CUPS

4 cups milk

2 cups sugar

½ teaspoon salt

1 tablespoon corn syrup

1. Place all of the ingredients in a saucepan. Heat over medium heat, stirring constantly. Reduce heat to low and cook, stirring constantly, for 45 minutes to 1 hour, until mixture is caramel brown and thick. Do not let mixture boil after the first 15 minutes or it will burn.

2. The caramel is done when you can scrape a spatula across the bottom of the pot and it takes several seconds for the mixture to close back over the track.

3. Remove from heat and let cool. Store caramel in an airtight container or glass jar in the refrigerator for up to 10 days.

Chocolate Peanut "Cashews"
(*Cajuzinho de Amendoim com Chocolate*)

These candies are shaped to resemble whole cashew nuts, though they are typically made with toasted peanuts instead of cashews. Other nuts work well in this recipe, such as pecans or walnuts.

INGREDIENTS | MAKES 25

8 ounces peanuts (peeled), or other nuts

Pinch of salt

1 (14-ounce) can sweetened condensed milk

1 tablespoon butter

4 ounces chocolate, chopped

½ teaspoon vanilla

25 whole cocktail peanuts

½ cup sugar

1. Preheat the oven to 300°F. Scatter the peanuts on a baking sheet and toast in the oven until lightly browned and fragrant, about 5–8 minutes. Remove from oven and let cool. Place the toasted peanuts and the salt in a food processor and process until finely ground.

2. Place the condensed milk and the butter in a heavy saucepan. Cook over medium-low heat, stirring constantly, until mixture thickens and darkens in color. When you can scrape the bottom of the pan with a wooden spoon and it takes 7–10 seconds for the mixture to close back over the bottom of the pan, the mixture has thickened enough. Remove from heat and let cool for 5 minutes before stirring in the chocolate and the vanilla. Stir gently until chocolate has melted. Stir in ground peanuts. Set aside until mixture is cool enough to handle.

3. Take 1½ tablespoons of the candy mixture and mold it into an oblong shape, similar to that of a butternut squash—slightly narrower at one end, fatter at the other, and slightly curved. Push a whole cocktail peanut about halfway into the top of the narrow end to resemble a stem.

4. Roll each piece of candy in the sugar to coat. Place each candy in a small fluted paper cup to serve. Store candies in an airtight container for up to 1 week.

Chocolate-Covered Peanut Truffles (*Bom Bom de Paçoca*)

Paçoca is a traditional peanut candy from northeastern Brazil. Paçoca tastes like a soft, crumbly version of peanut brittle, and can be molded or cut into shapes.

INGREDIENTS | MAKES 25

1½ cups raw peanuts

1 cup manioc meal (or substitute 4 tablespoons cornstarch)

1 cup sugar

1 teaspoon salt

1 (14-ounce) can sweetened condensed milk, divided

½ teaspoon vanilla

12 ounces semisweet chocolate chips

1 tablespoon vegetable shortening

1. Preheat the oven to 300°F. Scatter the peanuts on a baking sheet and toast in the oven until lightly browned and fragrant, about 5–8 minutes. Remove from oven and let cool. Rub the peanuts with a dishtowel to remove any skins.

2. Place the peanuts in a food processor. Process with short pulses until they are finely ground. Add the manioc meal (or cornstarch), sugar, and salt to the food processor and mix until smooth and very finely ground. Add 2 tablespoons of condensed milk and process until mixture starts comes together like a dough.

3. Grease a 9" square baking pan and press peanut mixture into the pan. Chill for 2 hours in the refrigerator.

4. Place the remaining condensed milk in a medium heavy saucepan and cook over low heat, stirring constantly, until mixture thickens (about 10–15 minutes) and starts to pull away from the sides of the pan. Remove from heat and stir in the vanilla. Crumble the *paçoca* candy and add to the condensed milk. Set mixture aside until cool enough to handle.

5. With buttered hands, take some of the candy mixture and roll it to form a 1" ball. Repeat with remaining mixture. Chill candies for 30 minutes.

6. Place chocolate chips and vegetable shortening in a microwave-safe bowl. Heat for 30 seconds in the microwave, then remove and stir. Repeat until chocolate is completely melted. Use a fork to dip the candies into the chocolate, letting excess chocolate drip back into the bowl. Set candies on a piece of wax paper or wire rack to cool until chocolate hardens.

Pistachio Truffles (*Brigadeiros de Pistache*)

These pistachio truffles are made just like the chocolate brigadeiros, but they are rolled in chopped pistachios instead of chocolate sprinkles.

INGREDIENTS | MAKES 20

1 (14-ounce) can sweetened condensed milk

6 ounces shelled pistachios, finely chopped, divided

½ teaspoon salt

2 tablespoons pistachio paste, or 2 tablespoons butter

1. Place the condensed milk, half of the chopped pistachios, and salt in a heavy saucepan. Cook over low heat, stirring constantly. Mixture should not boil. Cook until mixture thickens, turns shiny, and starts to come together and pull away from the sides of the pan (about 10–15 minutes).

2. Remove from heat and stir in the pistachio paste or butter. Set mixture aside until completely cooled.

3. With buttered hands, take some of the candy mixture and roll it between the palms of your hands to form a 1" ball. Repeat with remaining mixture.

4. Roll each candy in the remaining chopped pistachios. Place in individual fluted paper cups to serve. Store candies in an airtight container for up to 1 week.

Mother-in-Law's Eyes (*Olho de Sogra*)

These coconut sweets wrapped in dried prunes definitely resemble watchful eyes.

1 (14-ounce) can condensed milk

1 cup sugar

2 egg yolks

½ cup shredded, sweetened coconut

½ cup coconut milk

½ teaspoon salt

1 teaspoon vanilla

24 dried prunes

½ cup course sprinkling sugar

Caramelized Candies (*Olho-de-Sogra Caramelizado*)

These candies are very attractive when given a clear candy shell, which is easier to do than you might think. Bring 2 cups sugar and 2 cups water to a boil, and cook to the thread stage (230°F—sugar syrup forms threads in cold water). Remove from heat. Place each candy on a toothpick and dip it in the hot sugar syrup, letting excess drip off. Use toothpick to stick candies into a piece of Styrofoam until the sugar coating cools and hardens (or place candies on a piece of wax paper). Candies keep in an airtight, humidity-free container for 1–2 days.

1. Place the condensed milk, sugar, egg yolks, coconut, coconut milk, and salt in a heavy saucepan. Heat over medium heat, stirring constantly, until mixture thickens and slightly darkens, about 10–15 minutes. When you can scrape a spatula across the bottom of the pot and it takes several seconds for the mixture to close back over the track of the spatula, the mixture is ready. Remove from heat and stir in vanilla. Set aside until cool enough to handle.

2. Slice each prune almost in half. Roll pieces of the coconut mixture into 1" ovals (or size needed to fill the prune). Roll each piece of candy in the coarse sprinkling sugar, and place it inside of a prune in such a way that most of candy is visible, bulging out of the prune.

3. Place each candy in a mini paper cup to serve.

Guava Paste (*Goiabada*)

If you happen to come by a bushel of guava fruit, now you will know what to do with it:
Make a batch of this delicious candy.

INGREDIENTS | MAKES 20

2 pounds ripe guava fruit
½ cup water
3 cups sugar
¼ teaspoon salt

Spreadable Guava Paste (*Goiabada de Colher*)

You can cook the guava paste to a softer, more spreadable consistency. Remove it from the heat a bit earlier, after about 25 minutes of cooking, and place it in a glass casserole dish to cool. Serve with cheese and crackers, with a knife or spoon for spreading.

1. Peel the guava fruit and cut it into cubes.

2. Place the cubes in a blender with ½ cup water (working in batches if necessary) and process until smooth, adding a bit more water if needed.

3. Strain the mixture through a fine-mesh sieve (to remove the seeds) into a heavy saucepan. Add the sugar and salt and simmer over low heat, stirring constantly, until mixture thickens, darkens in color, and pulls away from the pan, about 35–45 minutes.

4. Pour guava paste into lightly oiled (heatproof) container and let cool until set. Slice into pieces to serve.

Italian Fudge (*Palha Italiana*)

Even though the name of this candy implies that it is Italian in origin, it's actually a Brazilian version of the Portuguese candy called salame de chocolate *(so named because it is shaped into a log and sliced like salami).*

INGREDIENTS | MAKES 20

2 (14-ounce) cans condensed milk

4 tablespoons cocoa powder

½ teaspoon salt

2 tablespoons butter

½ teaspoon vanilla (optional)

8 ounces Maria cookies or vanilla wafer cookies, broken into ½" pieces

1½ cups powdered sugar

1. Place the condensed milk, cocoa powder, and salt in a heavy saucepan. Cook over low heat, stirring constantly. Mixture should not boil. Cook until mixture thickens, turns shiny, and starts to come together and pull away from the sides of the pan (about 10–15 minutes).

2. Remove from heat and stir in the butter, vanilla (if using), and cookie pieces.

3. Transfer mixture to a buttered 8" × 8" cake pan. Place candy in the refrigerator until completely cool, about 1 hour.

4. Cut candy into small squares, and roll each square in the powdered sugar.

5. Store candies in an airtight container for up to 1 week.

Brazilian Coconut Kisses (*Beijinhos*)

The name of these very sweet coconut candies means "little kisses."
The candies are rolled in dried coconut and decorated with a clove or small piece of candy.

INGREDIENTS | MAKES 20

1 (14-ounce) can sweetened condensed milk

2 cups shredded unsweetened dried coconut, divided

¼ teaspoon salt

2 tablespoons butter

½ teaspoon coconut flavoring

Strawberry *Beijinhos* (*Bicho-de-pé*)

Strawberry gelatin can be added to this recipe to produce bright pink strawberry-coconut candies (which are humorously named after a type of flea that leaves itchy red bite marks!). Prepare the recipe in the same manner, but add 4 tablespoons of strawberry gelatin to the condensed-milk mixture. Roll the finished candies in sparkly sugar instead of shredded coconut to show off their pretty pink color.

1. Place the condensed milk, 1½ cups of the coconut, and salt in a heavy saucepan. Cook over low heat, stirring constantly. Mixture should not boil. Cook until mixture thickens, turns shiny, and starts to come together and pull away from the sides of the pan (about 10–15 minutes).

2. Remove from heat and stir in the butter and coconut flavoring. Set mixture aside until cool enough to handle.

3. With buttered hands, take some of the coconut mixture and roll it between the palms of your hands to form a 1" ball. Repeat with remaining coconut mixture.

4. Roll each candy in the remaining coconut to coat. Place *beijinhos* in individual fluted paper cups to serve. Store candies in an airtight container for up to 1 week.

Walnut Cameos (*Camafeu de Nozes*)

These very pretty candies are popular for weddings and fancy occasions.
They look beautiful, and they are easy and fun to make.

INGREDIENTS | MAKES 20

1 (14-ounce) can sweetened condensed milk

¼ teaspoon salt

7 ounces walnuts, finely chopped

½ teaspoon vanilla, divided

⅓ cup milk

4 cups powdered sugar

10 walnut halves, cut in half lengthwise

1. Place the condensed milk, salt, and walnuts in a heavy saucepan. Cook over medium-low heat, stirring, until mixture thickens and darkens slightly, about 10 minutes.

2. Remove from heat and stir in ½ teaspoon vanilla. Refrigerate mixture until completely cooled, about 45 minutes. Divide mixture into 20 portions and shape each into a 2" cylinder with rounded edges.

3. In a medium bowl, whisk 3–4 tablespoons of the milk into the powdered sugar, until mixture is thick but smooth, like a thick glaze. Add more milk, 1 tablespoon at a time, if needed.

4. Use a fork to dip the candies one at a time into the glaze to coat. Let excess glaze drip off, then place the candy on a piece of wax paper. Top each with a walnut quarter and set aside until glaze dries.

5. Serve candies in individual paper cups.

Brazilian Marshmallows (*Maria-mole*)

Maria-mole translates literally to "soft Mary," and this pillow-like candy is soft enough to melt in your mouth. Roll these candies in toasted coconut or chocolate sprinkles. A favorite with kids!

INGREDIENTS | MAKES 20

1 cup flaked sweetened coconut
¼ cup warm water
1 packet unflavored gelatin (¼-ounce)
3 egg whites
1 cup sugar
2 tablespoons corn syrup
¼ teaspoon salt
½ cup water
1 teaspoon vanilla

1. Preheat oven to 300°F. Toast the coconut until light brown, stirring occasionally.

2. Lightly butter a 9" square baking pan. Sprinkle ⅓ of the toasted coconut over the bottom of the pan.

3. Place ¼ cup of warm water in a small bowl and sprinkle the gelatin over the water. Set aside.

4. Place the egg whites in the bowl of a standing mixer fitted with the whisk attachment.

5. Place the sugar, corn syrup, salt, and ½ cup water in a medium saucepan. Bring to a simmer over medium heat and cook until it reaches a temperature of 240°F. At this point, turn on the mixer and beat the egg whites just until they start to form stiff peaks.

6. When the sugar syrup reaches 248°F, remove it from the heat and carefully pour it in a thin stream into the egg whites, with the mixer running. Immediately add the melted gelatin, and beat meringue for 3 minutes or until it forms shiny peaks. Stir in the vanilla.

7. Spread meringue into the prepared pan. Sprinkle ⅓ of the toasted coconut over the mixture. Cover with plastic wrap and chill for 1 hour.

8. Cut into squares and roll edges in remaining toasted coconut before serving.

Hazelnut Truffles (*Trufas de Avelã*)

These elegant, decadent truffles are surprisingly easy to make.

INGREDIENTS | MAKES 25

16 ounces good-quality semisweet chocolate

½ cup heavy cream

2 tablespoons hazelnut spread

¼ teaspoon salt

1 tablespoon hazelnut liqueur (optional)

½ teaspoon vanilla

½ cup toasted hazelnuts, finely chopped, divided

16 ounces couverture chocolate or chocolate chips

1. Place the semisweet chocolate, cream, and hazelnut spread in the top of a double boiler, or in a heatproof bowl placed over a pot of simmering water (bowl should not touch the water). Stir occasionally until chocolate is melted.

2. Remove from heat and stir in the salt, liqueur, vanilla, and all but 1 tablespoon of the hazelnuts.

3. Let mixture cool to room temperature, stirring briefly once or twice. Once chocolate has cooled, place in the refrigerator for 30–45 minutes.

4. Form the chocolate ganache into 1" balls by quickly rolling them in your hand (dust hands with cocoa powder if needed). Chill truffles for 30 minutes.

5. Melt the couverture chocolate or chocolate chips in the top of a double boiler, or in a heatproof bowl placed over a pot of simmering water (bowl should not touch the water). Use a fork to dip each truffle into the melted chocolate, letting excess chocolate drip off. Carefully slide truffle off of the fork onto a piece of wax paper. Sprinkle the top of each truffle with a small amount of the remaining chopped hazelnuts. Let truffles cool until chocolate hardens.

6. Store truffles in the refrigerator until ready to serve. Serve at room temperature.

Angel Chin (*Papo de Anjo*)

Portuguese nuns invented this dessert to use up extra egg yolks. The round, dumpling-like shape of this pastry must have reminded the nuns of the double chins and plump cheeks of cherubic angels.

INGREDIENTS | MAKES 12

2 cups sugar

2 cups water

1 cinnamon stick

½ cup rum

1 teaspoon vanilla

12 egg yolks

½ teaspoon salt

1 teaspoon baking powder

12 whole cloves

1. Place the sugar, water, and cinnamon stick in a heavy saucepan and bring to a boil. Reduce heat to low and simmer until syrup thickens slightly, about 20 minutes. Remove from heat, let cool, remove cinnamon stick, and stir in the rum and vanilla.

2. Preheat the oven to 350°F. Place the egg yolks, salt, and baking powder in the bowl of a standing mixer. Beat mixture on a high speed until doubled in volume and very light and fluffy, about 5–10 minutes.

3. Lightly grease a 12-cup muffin tin. Divide the batter between the tins. Bake for about 15 minutes, or until puffed.

4. Remove pastries from the tin, place 1 clove in the center of each pastry, and submerge them in the syrup until ready to serve.

5. Serve pastries in a bowl with the syrup.

Dulce de Leche Candy Cones
(*Canudinho de Doce de Leite e Amendoim*)

These sweet, crunchy cones are similar to Italian cannoli. Brazilians use special metal cone-shaped forms to make these pastries. If you don't have the special forms, large metal tips for pastry bags (about 3" long) will work in their place.

INGREDIENTS | MAKES 25

¼ cup sugar

3 tablespoons butter

1 teaspoon salt

2 tablespoons rum

1½ cups all-purpose flour

½ cup warm water

Vegetable oil, for frying

1 cup Dulce de Leche (see recipe in this chapter)

1 cup coarsely chopped roasted salted peanuts (optional)

Coconut Filling
(*Canudinhos de Coco*)

You can also fill your cones with this delicious coconut filling. Place 1 cup sugar and ½ cup water in a saucepan and simmer until it thickens, about 15 minutes. Add 1 cup grated fresh (or frozen) coconut, ½ teaspoon salt, and 1 (14-ounce) can sweetened condensed milk and cook over low heat, stirring constantly, for 15 minutes more, or until mixture starts to pull away from the side of the pan. Remove from heat and stir in 1 teaspoon vanilla. Fill cones with coconut mixture and dip tops of cones in mini chocolate chips (optional).

1. Place the sugar, butter, salt, rum, and flour in a medium bowl and mix well, working the butter into the flour with your fingers. Add the water slowly while stirring, until mixture comes together as a dough. Knead until smooth and set aside for 15 minutes.

2. Roll out dough on a floured surface into a large, very thin (¼") rectangle. Use a pizza cutter or sharp knife to cut the dough into ¾" strips.

3. Lightly grease the metal cones or pastry tips. Wrap a strip of dough around each cone, overlapping the edges, starting at the bottom and finishing at the tip, trimming off excess and pressing down to seal. Repeat with remaining dough (working in batches if needed).

4. Heat several inches of vegetable oil in a heavy pot to 350°F (or until dough sizzles when placed in the oil). Cook the pastry cones (still on the molds) until lightly browned and crisp.

5. Remove cones with a slotted spoon and place them on paper towels to drain. When cool, gently remove the metal molds.

6. Soften the Dulce de Leche by heating it in the microwave for a few seconds. Stir the peanuts into the dulce de leche.

7. Spoon the Dulce de Leche into the cones just before serving. Store unfilled cones in an airtight container for up to 3 days.

Candied Pumpkin with Coconut (*Doce de Abóbora com Coco*)

This spiced candied pumpkin is a very popular dessert in Brazil, especially in Rio Grande do Sul. Either sugar pumpkin (small sweet pumpkin for baking) or butternut squash will work in this recipe.

INGREDIENTS | MAKES 3 CUPS

2 pounds cubed sugar pumpkin or butternut squash

½ cup water

2 cups sugar

½ teaspoon salt

2 cinnamon sticks

5 whole cloves

1 cup sweetened dried grated coconut

1. Place the pumpkin in a large stockpot with the water, sugar, salt, cinnamon sticks, and cloves. Bring to a simmer over medium heat and cook until pumpkin is soft. Mash pumpkin with a potato masher until all the larger pieces are broken up and mixture is only slightly lumpy.

2. Add the coconut and cook over low heat, stirring constantly, until mixture thickens and almost all of the liquid has evaporated. Candied pumpkin is ready when you can scrape a spatula across the bottom of the pot and it takes a second or two for the mixture to close back over the track of the spatula.

3. Let candied pumpkin cool. Remove cinnamon sticks and cloves before serving.

CHAPTER 15

Brazilian BBQ (*Churrasco*)

Brazilian BBQ (*Churrasco*)

Brazil has a long tradition of barbecue, dating back to the gaúchos (cowboys) who drove cattle across southern Brazil. The gaucho BBQ method involved skewering the meat and then staking the skewer in the ground leaning over the embers.

INGREDIENTS | SERVES 12

3 pounds *linguiça* or other smoked sausages

5 pounds top sirloin steak

Coarse salt

4 pounds boneless leg of lamb

8 beef short ribs

4 pounds thick-cut skirt steak

8 boneless, skinless chicken breasts, marinated overnight in marinade of choice

1. Prepare charcoal grill: Light charcoal and remove grill rack. Have on hand 12 large Brazilian-style skewers (large, flat blades with a handle, like swords). Make sure skewers can rest across the grill (where the rack would be) so that skewered meat is positioned over the coals.

2. Cut the sausages into 4" lengths and place them crosswise on 2 parallel skewers.

3. Cut the sirloin steak into 3–4" pieces, and evenly place on two parallel skewers so that steak can lay flat over the heat on both sides. Sprinkle meat with coarse salt on both sides.

4. Cut the lamb into 3–4" pieces, and evently distribute on 2 parallel skewers in the same way as the steak. Sprinkle with coarse salt on both sides.

5. Place the short ribs on 2 skewers using the same procedure and sprinkle with salt.

6. Slice the skirt steak crosswise into 1" strips. Skewer top and bottom of each strip, forming a "C" shape with the meat as you place the strips on a skewer. Sprinkle with salt.

7. Place the chicken breasts on 2 skewers in the same fashion as the sirloin steak.

8. Place the chicken, sausages, and ribs on the grill, turning to cook both sides, until they are cooked as desired. Serve chicken and sausages first, as they become ready. Bring the skewers to the table and slice off pieces of meat for the guests.

9. Replace the space on the grill with the beef and the lamb, and cook to desired doneness. Bring skewers of meat to the table and serve as they become ready. Enjoy! (*Bom churrasco!*)

A Complete *Churrasco*

A complete *churrasco* might include sausage, several different cuts of beef or lamb, chicken, and pork ribs. Garlic bread is toasted on the grill after the meat is removed. Sauces for the meat, like Creamy Garlic Sauce (see recipe in Chapter 9) and Tomato and Onion Vinaigrette Salsa (see recipe in this chapter), Brazilian-Style Potato Salad (see recipe in Chapter 3), and *farofa* (see recipes in this chapter) are all part of the feast, along with rice, green salad, fruit, and dessert. Guests enjoy beer, *guaraná* soda, and *caipirinha* cocktails to drink.

Grilled Pork Tenderloin with Parmesan
(*Lombo com Parmesão*)

This is an unusual but delicious way to grill pork tenderloin. Most Brazilian churrasco meats are not marinated or seasoned with anything other than salt, but pork and chicken are the exception to the rule.

INGREDIENTS | SERVES 6

1 (14-ounce) pork tenderloin
Juice of 1 lime
2 teaspoons minced fresh garlic
Coarse salt
1 cup finely grated Parmesan cheese
Lime wedges, for garnish

1. Clean grill and light the charcoal. Remove grill rack.

2. Place the pork lengthwise on 2 large skewers so that the meat lays flat and can be cooked on both sides by flipping the skewers.

3. Sprinkle the meat on both sides with the lime juice and garlic, and sprinkle generously with coarse salt.

4. Cook the pork over the charcoal by resting the skewers across the grill opening. When meat is browned and almost finished cooking (5–6 minutes per side, pork should be slightly pink in the center), remove from heat and place on a heatproof pan. Generously sprinkle Parmesan cheese on both sides of the meat, pressing on it a bit so that it sticks. Return meat to the grill and cook until cheese is golden brown and crispy.

5. Slice pork into thin slices across the grain, and serve with lime wedges, as well as the usual *churrasco* accompaniments (rice, *farofa*, salad, and tomato-onion vinaigrette (see recipes later in this chapter).

Chicken Skewers with Pineapple and Bacon
(*Espetinho de Frango com Bacon*)

This chicken is marinated and then wrapped in bacon and grilled. The bacon fat helps to tenderize the chicken, while adding lots of smoky flavor. Serve with white rice and orange slices.

INGREDIENTS | SERVES 8

¼ cup teriyaki sauce

⅓ cup orange juice

3 tablespoons honey

1 teaspoon sesame oil

1 teaspoon minced fresh garlic

1 teaspoon minced fresh ginger

2 pounds chicken breasts, cut into 1½" pieces

¼ cup vegetable oil

1 pound bacon

1 pineapple, peeled, cored, and cut into 1½" pieces

1. In a blender, mix the teriyaki sauce, orange juice, honey, sesame oil, garlic, and ginger until well blended.

2. Place the chicken in a shallow dish or zip-top bag. Pour half of the teriyaki mixture over the chicken, plus vegetable oil. (Reserve other half for basting.) Toss the chicken to mix well. Marinate in the refrigerator for several hours or overnight. Soak wooden grilling skewers in water for 30 minutes before using.

3. Heat the grill. Cut the strips of bacon in half. Remove the chicken from the marinade. Wrap a piece of bacon around each piece of chicken. Place the bacon-wrapped chicken pieces on the wooden skewers, alternating the chicken with pieces of pineapple.

4. Place the skewers on the grill. Baste with reserved marinade. Cook, turning skewers and basting them occasionally, until bacon is browned and crispy and chicken is cooked through (test a piece or two by cutting into it with a knife), about 6–10 minutes, depending on grill temperature.

Beef and Vegetable Skewers (*Espetinho de Carne*)

Everyone will love these beef and vegetable skewers. Serve them with vinaigrette salsa (molho vinagrete).

INGREDIENTS | SERVES 4

1 pound top sirloin steak

12 mushrooms, rinsed, stems trimmed

12 cherry tomatoes

2 medium green bell peppers, seeded and sliced into 1" squares

8 slices bacon, cut into 3" pieces

12 small onions, peeled, or 2 large onions, peeled and cut into chunks

2 tablespoons olive oil

Coarse salt

Vinaigrette Salsa for Grilled Meat (*Molho Vinagrete*)

Finely dice 2 onions, 2 tomatoes, and 1 red bell pepper. Place them in a bowl with 1 tablespoon minced parsley, ¼ cup red wine vinegar, and ¼ cup olive oil. Season with salt and freshly ground pepper to taste.

1. Clean grill and light the charcoal. Lightly oil the grill rack if using. Remove rack if using skewers.

2. Cut the steak into 1–2" pieces. Place 3 or 4 pieces of steak on each a skewer, alternating with mushrooms, tomatoes, bell pepper, pieces of bacon folded in half, and onions.

3. Brush meat and vegetables with the olive oil, and sprinkle generously with coarse salt.

4. Grill skewers over high heat until well browned on all sides and steak is cooked to your liking.

5. Serve skewers with Vinaigrette Salsa (see sidebar), white rice, *farofa*, and a green salad.

Farofa with Plantains (*Farofa de Banana*)

Choose ripe plantains, which are yellowish (not green) with black spots, because they are sweeter and less starchy than unripe ones.

INGREDIENTS | SERVES 4

Vegetable oil, for frying

2 ripe plantains, peeled and cut into ½" slices

4 ounces bacon, chopped

1 medium onion, peeled and finely chopped

2 cloves garlic, minced

1 teaspoon salt

3 tablespoons butter

2 cups coarse manioc flour (*farinha de mandioca*)

¼ cup chopped fresh parsley

¼ cup chopped scallions

How to Peel Plantains

Plantains do not peel as easily as regular bananas, even when they are ripe. To peel them, cut off each end. Use a knife to make lengthwise cuts though the peel in several places, then pull the peel from the plantain in sections.

1. Heat several inches of oil in a heavy stockpot or deep skillet until plantains sizzle upon touching the oil (about 350°F).

2. Fry plantain slices until golden brown. Remove them with a slotted spoon to a plate lined with paper towels and set aside.

3. Place the bacon in a medium skillet and cook over medium heat until crispy. Remove bacon and reserve. Add the onion to the skillet and cook over medium heat until soft and translucent, about 5–8 minutes. Add the garlic and salt and cook for 2–3 minutes.

4. Add the butter. Once the butter is melted, add the manioc meal and stir until it is heated through and evenly moistened with the butter.

5. Chop the bacon and add it to the skillet with the fried plantains, parsley, and scallions. Stir until just heated through.

6. Serve warm.

Grilled Spiced Pineapple (*Abacaxi Grelhado*)

Grilled pineapple goes very well with churrasco because it's not too filling after a heavy meal.

INGREDIENTS | SERVES 8

4 tablespoons brown sugar
1 teaspoon ground cinnamon
½ teaspoon ground nutmeg
½ teaspoon ground ginger
¼ teaspoon salt
4 tablespoons rum or *cachaça*
1 large pineapple
1 pint vanilla ice cream

Chocolate Sauce (*Calda de Chocolate*)

Drizzle warm chocolate sauce over grilled pineapple for an extra-special treat. To make the sauce, heat ½ cup water, ¼ cup sugar, 3 tablespoons corn syrup, and ¼ cup cocoa powder in a small saucepan until mixture just comes to a boil. Pour the hot mixture over 2 tablespoons of semisweet chocolate chips. Stir gently until chocolate is melted. Sauce will thicken slightly as it cools.

1. In a medium bowl, whisk together the brown sugar, cinnamon, nutmeg, ginger, salt, and rum.

2. Slice the top off of the pineapple, and remove the rind. Slice pineapple crosswise into ¾"-thick rings.

3. Place the rings on a cutting board. Use a small cookie cutter to cut out the inner core from each slice of pineapple. Place the pineapple slices in a shallow casserole dish and pour the brown sugar mixture over them. Turn pineapples to coat them on both sides.

4. Place pineapple slices on a (very clean) preheated grill. (Or place them on a skewer and prop skewer over the charcoal.) Cook 3–5 minutes on each side, brushing them with the marinade from time to time, or until pineapple is caramelized and lightly browned on both sides.

5. Serve warm with a scoop of vanilla ice cream on each slice.

Ground Beef Kebabs (*Kafta no Espeto*)

*Kofka (ground beef with spices) are typically shaped as meatballs,
but the grilled kebab form is a natural fit for Brazil.*

INGREDIENTS | SERVES 4

Wooden sticks for kebabs

2 pounds ground beef

4 slices bacon, finely chopped

1 small onion, peeled and grated

2 tablespoons minced fresh parsley

1 tablespoon minced fresh mint

2 cloves garlic, finely minced

1 teaspoon cumin

1 teaspoon smoked paprika

1 teaspoon salt

1 teaspoon freshly ground black pepper

½ teaspoon cinnamon (optional)

Yogurt Tahini Sauce (*Molho de Tahine e Iogurte*)

Whisk 1 cup Greek yogurt with ½ cup tahini (sesame seed paste). Mash 3 cloves garlic with 1 teaspoon salt and add to yogurt mixture. Stir in 3 tablespoons fresh lemon juice, 1 tablespoon minced fresh parsley, and 1 teaspoon freshly ground black pepper.

1. Soak the wooden sticks in water for 30 minutes. Heat the grill.

2. Place the ground beef, bacon, onion, parsley, mint, garlic, and seasonings in a large bowl and mix well. If you have a meat grinder, pass the mixture through once or twice.

3. Shape the ground-beef mixture onto the wooden skewers, forming it into the shape of thin sausages.

4. When grill is ready, place the kebabs on the grill and cook until well browned on all sides and cooked through, about 6–10 minutes total, depending on grill temperature.

5. Serve kebabs with Yogurt Tahini Sauce (see sidebar).

Grilled Salmon with Passion Fruit Glaze (*Salmão Grelhado*)

Salmon steaks are very quick and easy to grill. Serve these steaks with white rice and a green salad with Grilled Hearts of Palm (see sidebar).

INGREDIENTS | SERVES 4

½ cup passion fruit pulp

¼ cup sugar

3 tablespoons fresh lime juice

1 tablespoon soy sauce

1½ teaspoons freshly ground black pepper, divided

1 tablespoon minced fresh cilantro

4 (6-ounce) salmon steaks, about 1" thick

3 tablespoons butter, melted

½ teaspoon salt

Grilled Hearts of Palm

Drain a jar of hearts of palm. Pat the hearts of palm dry, then brush them with 2 table-spoons olive oil. Season palm hearts with 1 teaspoon salt and 1 teaspoon pepper and place them on the grill. Cook, turning often, until slightly charred on all sides. Place them on a plate, drizzle with the juice of 1 lime, and serve.

1. In a small saucepan, heat the passion fruit pulp and sugar over low heat until sugar is dissolved, about 2 minutes. Remove from heat and whisk in the lime juice, soy sauce, 1 teaspoon pepper, and cilantro. Divide the sauce between 2 bowls.

2. Heat the grill. Clean the grilling surface and brush with oil. Brush the salmon steaks with the melted butter and sprinkle with the salt and remaining ½ teaspoon pepper.

3. When grill is hot, place the salmon steaks on the grill. Cook for about 5 minutes on each side, using 1 bowl of the passion fruit sauce to baste frequently.

4. Place salmon on a serving platter and drizzle with remaining passion fruit sauce.

Toasted Manioc Meal (*Farofa para Churrasco*)

Farofa is manioc meal, toasted in butter or oil with vegetables and other seasonings. It is often served as a condiment, to be sprinkled over food. Gauchos used to carry manioc meal with them and sprinkle it onto pieces of grilled meat, so serving farofa with churrasco continues that tradition.

INGREDIENTS | SERVES 4

2 tablespoons butter

2 tablespoons olive oil

1 medium onion, peeled and finely diced

4 large carrots, peeled and shredded

1 cup manioc meal

½ teaspoon salt

½ teaspoon freshly ground black pepper

10 green olives, sliced

¼ cup golden raisins

2 tablespoons minced fresh parsley

1. Place the butter and the olive oil in a medium skillet. Add the onion and carrots and cook over medium-low heat until soft and fragrant, about 5–8 minutes.

2. Add the manioc meal and cook, stirring, until manioc is slightly browned and toasted, about 3–4 minutes. Add the salt, pepper, olives, and raisins and cook until everything is heated through.

3. Garnish with the parsley and serve.

Rice "Farofa" (*Farofa de Arroz*)

Manioc meal (*farinha de mandioca*) can be hard to find in the United States (look for it at Latin food markets or order it online), but you can make a similar dish using rice or couscous. Just add 1 cup cooked rice or couscous in place of the manioc meal and cook until rice/couscous is slightly toasted.

Grilled Red Pepper and Eggplant Antipasto
(*Antipasto de Berinjela*)

*This Italian-style grilled eggplant salad can be prepared a day ahead of time
and marinated overnight in the refrigerator.*

INGREDIENTS | SERVES 6

¾ cup olive oil, divided

3 cloves garlic, minced

3 tablespoons red wine vinegar

1 teaspoon dried oregano

¼ cup chopped dried parsley

2 large eggplants

1 teaspoon kosher salt

2 medium red bell peppers

Salt and pepper, to taste

1. In a small bowl, whisk ½ cup olive oil together with the garlic, vinegar, oregano, and parsley.

2. Slice the eggplants from top to bottom into very thin slices. Brush them on both sides with the remaining olive oil and sprinkle them with kosher salt

3. Place the bell peppers on a preheated grill. Cook, turning frequently, until charred on all sides. Remove and set aside to cool.

4. Place the eggplant slices on the grill (in batches if necessary) and cook until softened with grill marks on each side.

5. Peel the charred skin from the peppers. Remove the stems and seeds, and cut peppers into 1" strips.

6. Place the eggplant slices and pepper strips together in a large bowl and toss with the olive-oil mixture. Season with salt and pepper to taste.

7. Serve warm or at room temperature.

Marinated New Potatoes (*Batatinha em Conserva*)

Serve these potatoes as an appetizer, with toothpicks for spearing the potatoes and olives.

INGREDIENTS | SERVES 4

2 pounds bite-size yellow potatoes

1 cup olive oil

½ cup red wine vinegar

1 teaspoon dried oregano

1 teaspoon kosher salt

1 teaspoon freshly ground black pepper

1 medium onion, peeled and finely diced

2 cloves garlic, minced

1 medium red bell pepper, seeded and minced

1 small red chili pepper, seeded and minced

1 cup assorted large pitted olives

2 tablespoons minced fresh parsley

1. Place the potatoes in a large pot of boiling salted water and cook until very tender. Drain well and place in a large bowl.

2. In a small bowl, whisk together the olive oil, vinegar, oregano, salt, and black pepper. Pour dressing over potatoes and toss to mix.

3. Add onion, garlic, red pepper, chili pepper, olives, and parsley to the potatoes and mix well. Let potato mixture marinate in refrigerator for several hours or overnight before serving.

4. Serve warm or at room temperature.

Tomato and Onion Vinaigrette Salsa
(*Molho Vinagrete para Churrasco*)

Make a large bowl of this salsa and enjoy it with the grilled meats or on toasted garlic bread.

INGREDIENTS | SERVES 8

3 tomatoes, seeded and diced

2 medium onions, peeled and diced

1 medium green bell pepper, seeded and diced

¼ cup minced scallions

¼ cup chopped fresh parsley

2 tablespoons chopped fresh cilantro

½ cup chopped green olives (optional)

1 cup olive oil

½ cup white wine vinegar

1 teaspoon kosher salt

1 teaspoon freshly ground black pepper

1. In a medium bowl, mix together the tomatoes, onions, green pepper, scallions, parsley, cilantro, and green olives (if using).

2. In a small bowl, whisk together the olive oil, vinegar, salt, and pepper.

3. Toss the vegetables with the dressing. Refrigerate until ready to serve, or for up to 4 days.

Colorful Molded Gelatin (*Gelatina Colorida*)

Make this dessert a day ahead of time so that it has plenty of time to chill and set before the dramatic unmolding.

INGREDIENTS | SERVES 8

1½ cups sweetened condensed milk

¾ cups coconut milk

1 teaspoon vanilla

¼ teaspoon salt

6 (3-ounce) packages assorted fruit-flavored gelatin

2 packets plain gelatin (½ ounce)

4½ cups hot water

3 cups assorted fruit juices (½ cup each), such as pineapple, guava, mango, or orange

Grownup Version (*Gelatina Alcoólica*)

For special occasions when the children are not included, you can add rum to some or all of the gelatin flavors. This is especially good with tropical fruit flavors like pineapple. Just substitute rum for the fruit juice in one or all of the gelatin layers, and proceed according to directions.

1. Lightly spray a bundt pan or other mold (10-cup capacity) with nonstick cooking spray, or wipe inside of the mold lightly with vegetable oil.

2. In a small bowl, whisk together the condensed milk, coconut milk, vanilla, and salt.

3. Place 1 package of flavored gelatin plus 1 teaspoon plain gelatin in a 2-cup glass measuring cup or heatproof bowl. Pour in ¾ cup hot (almost boiling) water and stir until the gelatin is dissolved. Stir in ½ cup fruit juice of choice.

4. Pour half of the gelatin mixture into the mold. Place the mold in the refrigerator to set. Once the first layer is just set (about 15–20 minutes), whisk 3 tablespoons of the condensed-milk mixture into the other half of the gelatin mixture and pour it over the first layer. Chill until set (about 15–20 minutes). Add the second layer once the first layer is just barely firm but not completely set. Otherwise the layers will not adhere to one another.

5. Repeat with remaining flavors, chilling each layer in the refrigerator for 15–20 minutes before adding the next. You will have a layer of plain gelatin and a layer of gelatin with cream for each flavor/color, making 12 layers total. Chill gelatin overnight.

6. To unmold, loosen the edges with a sharp knife all the way around the mold. Place the mold in a warm water bath for 15 seconds. Dry the bottom of the mold quickly, and invert the mold onto the serving platter.

Tropical Chicken Salad (*Maionese Tropical*)

This delicious chicken salad is served in a pineapple bowl, a very tropical presentation that is perfect for summer gatherings.

INGREDIENTS | SERVES 6

1 large pineapple

1 cup mayonnaise

½ cup heavy cream

1 teaspoon salt

1 tablespoon fresh lime juice

½ teaspoon curry powder

2 poached chicken breasts, shredded or cut into small cubes

1 cup grapes, halved

1 green apple, peeled and cut into small cubes

1 (14-ounce) jar hearts of palm, drained and cut into rounds

½ cup chopped cashews

1. Carefully cut the pineapple in half lengthwise, from top to bottom (leaving the fronds attached). Scoop out the inside, leaving about ½" of rind and fruit in one of the halves, which will become the bowl. Remove core and chop pineapple fruit into small cubes. Place chopped pineapple in a large bowl.

2. In a small bowl, whisk together the mayonnaise, cream, salt, lime juice, and curry powder.

3. Add the shredded chicken, grapes, green apple, hearts of palm, and cashews to the bowl with the pineapple. Add the mayonnaise dressing and toss everything together well.

4. Arrange salad in the pineapple bowl. Chill until ready to serve. Can be made 1 day ahead.

Grilled Garlic Bread with Cheese (*Torradas de Alho*)

Garlic bread is an essential accompaniment to churrasco,
and it is usually toasted right on the grill, alongside the meats.

INGREDIENTS | SERVES 6

1 loaf crusty Italian or French bread, or 6 French bread rolls

2 cloves garlic

1½ teaspoons garlic salt

2 teaspoons dried oregano

¾ cup butter, melted

6 tablespoons olive oil

1 cup grated mozzarella cheese

1 cup grated provolone cheese

¼ cup grated Parmesan cheese

1. Slice the bread diagonally into 1"-thick slices. If using rolls, slice each roll in half horizontally.

2. In a small bowl, mash the garlic cloves with the garlic salt and oregano. Add the melted butter and olive oil and mix well.

3. In a separate small bowl, mix together the three cheeses.

4. Brush both sides of the bread slices with the garlic/butter mixture.

5. Place the bread slices on a preheated grill. Sprinkle some of the cheese over each slice. Close the grill cover and cook until the bread is toasted and cheese is melted, about 3–5 minutes.

6. Serve warm.

CHAPTER 16

Vegetarian Recipes (*Comida Vegetariana*)

Rice and Tofu Croquettes (*Bolinho de Arroz com Tofu*)

These brown rice fritters are seasoned with garlic and ginger, and stuffed with a piece of creamy marinated tofu. Serve them with sweet and sour chili sauce for dipping.

INGREDIENTS | SERVES 6

8 ounces soft or medium-soft tofu, cut into ½" cubes

½ cup soy sauce, divided

2 tablespoons rice vinegar

1 teaspoon sugar

1 tablespoon chili oil

2 tablespoons vegetable oil

¼ cup finely diced onion

1 clove garlic, minced

1 tablespoon minced fresh ginger

1 tablespoon teriyaki sauce

2 cups cooked brown rice

2 tablespoons minced scallions

2 tablespoons fresh parsley

1 large egg

½ cup cornstarch

⅓ cup cornmeal

1 teaspoon salt

Vegetable oil, for frying

Best Brown Rice (*Arroz Integral*)

Heat 2 tablespoons vegetable oil, ¼ cup finely chopped onion, 1 teaspoon minced fresh ginger (optional), and 1 teaspoon sesame oil in a heavy saucepan until onion is soft and starting to brown. Add 1 teaspoon minced fresh garlic and cook for 1 minute. Add 1 cup rinsed brown rice and stir over medium heat for 1 minute. Add 2 cups water and 1 teaspoon salt. Cover and simmer for 35–40 minutes, or until rice is tender and water is absorbed. Fluff and serve. Makes 2 cups.

1. Place the tofu in a dish with ¼ cup soy sauce and toss to coat. Set aside.

2. Make the dipping sauce: In a small bowl, whisk together remaining ¼ cup soy sauce, rice vinegar, sugar, and chili oil. Set aside.

3. Heat 2 tablespoons vegetable oil in a medium skillet and add the onion. Cook until soft and fragrant, about 5–8 minutes. Add the garlic, ginger, and teriyaki sauce and cook for 2 minutes more.

4. Place the brown rice in a medium bowl. Add the cooked onion mixture, scallions, parsley, and egg and mix well. Add 1–2 tablespoons of the cornstarch if mixture is too wet to form into balls. Shape balls of rice with your hands (dampen your hands with water to prevent sticking), and press a piece of tofu into the middle of each ball.

5. In a shallow dish, combine the remaining cornstarch, cornmeal, and salt. Roll rice balls in the cornmeal mixture to coat.

6. Heat several inches of vegetable oil in a heavy saucepan to 350°F. Fry rice balls until browned and crispy.

7. Serve croquettes warm, with chili sauce for dipping.

Vegetarian Bobo (*Bobó Vegetariano*)

Bobo is a shrimp and manioc stew from Bahia. This vegetarian version of bobo uses vegetables and cashew nuts as a substitute for the shrimp. Serve with white rice.

INGREDIENTS | SERVES 6

1 pound fresh or frozen manioc (also called yuca or cassava), peeled

2 teaspoons salt, divided

1 (13.5-ounce) can coconut milk, divided

4 tablespoons *dendê* oil, or 4 tablespoons olive oil mixed with 1 teaspoon annatto powder, divided

1 medium onion, peeled and finely chopped

1 medium red bell pepper, seeded and finely chopped

1 medium green bell pepper, seeded and finely chopped

1 medium tomato, seeded and chopped

½ cup diced hearts of palm

½ cup chopped cashews

½ cup peas

¼ cup chopped scallions

¼ cup chopped fresh parsley

1. Cut the manioc into large chunks, removing inner fibrous core, and place in a large pot. Cover with water. Add 1 teaspoon salt and simmer until manioc is very tender. Drain.

2. Place the manioc in a food processor while still hot with ½ cup of the coconut milk, and process until smooth. Set aside.

3. Place 2 tablespoons of the *dendê* oil in a stockpot. Add the onion and sauté until the onion is soft and fragrant, about 5–8 minutes.

4. Add the bell peppers. Cook over medium heat until soft, about 5 minutes. Add the tomatoes and cook until liquid has evaporated. Add the hearts of palm, cashews, peas, and remaining salt and cook for 2 minutes more.

5. Add the manioc cream and the remaining coconut milk to the pan. Cook, stirring, until mixture thickens slightly, about 5 minutes.

6. Add the scallions and parsley to the pot. Drizzle with remaining *dendê* oil and serve.

Polenta and Ricotta Roll (*Rocambole de Polenta*)

Rocambole are typically rolled cakes with cream fillings, but they can be savory as well. Polenta takes the place of sponge cake in this recipe, and the filling is a mixture of ricotta, mozzarella, and Parmesan.

INGREDIENTS | SERVES 8

2 cups ricotta cheese

¾ cups grated Parmesan cheese, divided

1 cup grated mozzarella cheese

2 tablespoons heavy cream

1 tablespoon minced basil

1 teaspoon dried oregano

1 tablespoon minced fresh parsley

1½ teaspoons salt, divided

1 teaspoon freshly ground black pepper

4 cups water or vegetable stock

2 cups coarse cornmeal

2 tablespoons butter

2 cups tomato sauce

1. In a medium bowl, whisk together the ricotta, ½ cup Parmesan, mozzarella, cream, basil, oregano, parsley, ½ teaspoon salt, and pepper. Set aside.

2. Place the water or vegetable stock in a saucepan and bring to a simmer over medium heat. Whisk in the cornmeal and 1 teaspoon of salt. Reduce heat to low and cook, stirring, until mixture thickens and starts to stick to the pan, about 10 minutes. Remove from heat and stir in the butter and 2 tablespoons of Parmesan.

3. Line a baking sheet with plastic wrap. Spread the polenta on the plastic wrap, forming a 8" square. Spread cheese mixture onto the polenta, leaving a 1" border at the top.

4. Working quickly, while polenta is still warm, carefully roll up the polenta, starting with the bottom edge, using the plastic wrap to guide the polenta. Wrap the "roll" in plastic wrap and chill until firm.

5. Preheat the oven to 350°F. Place the tomato sauce in a medium casserole dish and place polenta roll on top. Spoon some of the sauce on top of the roll, and sprinkle with remaining Parmesan.

6. Bake until heated through, about 20 minutes. Slice crosswise into spirals and serve warm with sauce.

Hearts of Palm Fondue in a Pumpkin Shell
(*Palmito na Moranga*)

Serve this dish with white rice, as well as bread sticks and vegetables for dipping, if desired.

INGREDIENTS | SERVES 8

1 small pumpkin (8" in diameter, about 5 pounds)

2 tablespoons olive oil

2 tablespoons butter

½ cup minced onion

2 cloves garlic, minced

1 medium red bell pepper, seeded and chopped

1 medium tomato, seeded and chopped

1 (14-ounce) can hearts of palm, drained and chopped into ½" rounds

½ teaspoon salt

1 teaspoon freshly ground black pepper

2 tablespoons all-purpose flour

1 cup vegetable stock

½ cup heavy cream

1 cup coconut milk

¼ cup chopped scallions

¼ cup chopped fresh parsley

8 ounces cream cheese

¼ cup Parmesan cheese, divided

1. Cut a circle around the stem and remove the top of the pumpkin. Scoop out the inside of the pumpkin, scraping the sides to remove all the fibrous material and seeds. Brush the inside of the pumpkin with olive oil. Wrap the outside of the pumpkin in foil, leaving the top opening uncovered. Place on a baking sheet and set aside. Preheat oven to 375°F.

2. Add butter, onion, garlic, and bell pepper to a large skillet and cook over medium heat until soft, about 5–8 minutes. Add the tomato, hearts of palm, and salt and pepper (to taste) and cook until liquid has evaporated. Add the flour and cook for 1 minute. Add the vegetable stock and simmer until thickened.

3. Add the cream, coconut milk, scallions, and parsley and cook, stirring, until everything is well mixed and heated through, about 3 minutes. Remove from heat and stir in the cream cheese and 2 tablespoons of Parmesan.

4. Use a ladle to spoon mixture into the pumpkin. Replace the top of the pumpkin, and loosely cover top with foil. Bake pumpkin for 30 minutes. Carefully remove top of pumpkin, and sprinkle the top of the filling with the Parmesan. Return to the oven until cheese is browned.

5. Carefully unwrap foil from pumpkin, and gently transfer pumpkin to a platter (support the bottom of the pumpkin as it may be soft).

Lentil and Potato Casserole (*Torta de Batata com Lentilha*)

This is hearty vegetarian comfort food at its best. Cheesy, creamy potatoes top a layer of savory lentils cooked with tomatoes and onions.

INGREDIENTS | SERVES 6

1½ cups uncooked lentils

1 bay leaf

2 medium onions, peeled

3 cups water

2 tablespoons olive oil

2 cloves garlic, minced

½ cup sun-dried tomatoes, chopped

1 tomato, seeded and chopped

2 teaspoons salt, divided

1 teaspoon freshly ground black pepper, divided

1 cup vegetable stock

3 cups mashed potatoes

2 tablespoons butter

¼ cup heavy cream

½ cup grated cheese (Cheddar, mozzarella, or Monterey jack)

1 teaspoon dried oregano

1 tablespoon minced fresh parsley

1. Place the lentils in a medium bowl, cover with water, and soak for 1 hour. Drain.

2. Place the lentils in a medium saucepan with the bay leaf. Quarter 1 onion and place it in the pot. Add the water and bring to a simmer over medium heat. Reduce heat to low, cover, and cook until lentils are just tender, about 30 minutes. Remove onion and bay leaf.

3. Add the olive oil to a large skillet. Chop the remaining onion and place in the skillet. Cook over medium heat until onion is very soft and slightly browned, about 5–8 minutes. Add the garlic, sun-dried tomatoes, chopped tomato, 1 teaspoon salt (or to taste), and ½ teaspoon pepper. Cook until tomato is soft, about 4 minutes.

4. Add the lentils and the vegetable stock to the skillet and cook until most of liquid has evaporated, about 10 minutes.

5. Preheat the oven to 350°F. Place the lentils in a greased casserole dish. Heat the mashed potatoes in the microwave until hot. Stir in butter, cream, and remaining salt and pepper (or to taste). Smooth the mashed potatoes over the lentils, covering them completely. Top with the grated cheese. Sprinkle with oregano and parsley.

6. Bake casserole for 25–30 minutes, or until cheese is melted and casserole is heated through. Serve warm.

Cheese and Artichoke Tart (*Torta de Alcachofra*)

This is a special-occasion dish, for when company is coming over or a celebration is in order.

INGREDIENTS | SERVES 6

1¼ cups all-purpose flour
½ teaspoon salt
½ teaspoon sugar
8 tablespoons cold butter
2 tablespoons cream cheese
¼ cup ice water
2 tablespoons olive oil
2 cloves garlic, minced
2 tablespoons chopped scallions
½ cup diced sun-dried tomatoes
¾ teaspoon salt
½ teaspoon freshly ground black pepper
2 (14-ounce) cans artichoke hearts, drained and coarsely chopped
½ cup ricotta cheese
1 egg yolk
¼ cup crumbled goat cheese
¼ cup sour cream
¼ cup grated Parmesan cheese

1. Place the flour, salt, and sugar in a medium bowl. Cut the butter and cream cheese into small pieces and add it to the flour mixture. Mix with your fingers or a pastry cutter until mixture is crumbly. Stir in the ice water with a fork, 1 tablespoon at a time, until mixture just comes together as a dough. Shape dough into a flat disk, wrap in plastic wrap, and chill for 1 hour.

2. Heat the olive oil in a medium skillet over medium heat. Add the garlic and sauté until fragrant, about 2–3 minutes. Add the scallions, sun-dried tomatoes, salt and pepper (to taste), and cook for 2–3 minutes. Add the artichoke hearts and sauté for 3–4 minutes.

3. In a small bowl, combine the ricotta, egg yolk, goat cheese, sour cream, and Parmesan.

4. Preheat the oven to 350°F. Roll out the dough on a floured surface into an 11" circle. Line a lightly buttered 9" tart pan with the dough, and trim the edges.

5. Spread the cheese mixture into the tart pan and top with the vegetables.

6. Bake tart for 30–40 minutes, or until filling is puffed, lightly browned, and heated through.

Hearts of Palm Bahian Stew (*Moqueca de Palmito*)

Hearts of palm are a natural choice to replace the traditional fish in this recipe, since red palm oil already provides some of the signature flavor and color to Bahian-style moquecas.

INGREDIENTS | SERVES 6

4 tablespoons *dendê* oil, or 4 tablespoons olive oil plus 1 teaspoon achiote powder

1 large onion, peeled and sliced into thin rings

4 cloves garlic, minced

1–2 teaspoons minced red chili pepper

1 teaspoon paprika

2 medium tomatoes, diced (reserve 2 small slices for garnish)

1 medium green bell pepper, seeded and sliced crosswise into thin rings

1 medium red bell pepper, seeded and sliced crosswise into thin rings

1 (14-ounce) jar hearts of palm, drained and sliced crosswise into ½" pieces

1 tablespoon cornstarch

1 (13.5-ounce) can coconut milk

1 cup vegetable stock

Salt and pepper, to taste

1 small bunch fresh cilantro, finely chopped, divided

3 scallions, chopped

1. Add the *dendê* oil (or olive oil) to a deep skillet or medium stew pot. Add the onion and cook over medium-low heat until soft and fragrant, about 5–8 minutes. Add the garlic, chili pepper, and paprika and cook over medium heat until garlic is soft, about 2 minutes. Add tomatoes and cook until soft, about 4 more minutes.

2. Add the bell peppers and the hearts of palm and cook for 2–3 minutes. Stir 1 tablespoon of cornstarch into the vegetables.

3. Add the coconut milk and vegetable stock and simmer for 5 minutes. Taste for seasoning and add salt and pepper. Add the cilantro (reserve 1 tablespoon for garnish) and half of the scallions. Cover and simmer over low heat for 10 minutes.

4. Garnish with remaining cilantro, reserved tomato slices, and remaining scallions.

Black Bean Stew (*Feijoada Vegetariana*)

Add a fried egg to the plate, or serve the feijoada *with egg-enriched* farofa *(farofa de ovos) and you will have a complete meal on your plate that is loaded with protein—a* feijoada vegetariana completa.

INGREDIENTS | SERVES 8

1 pound dried black beans

3 tablespoons olive oil

12 ounces sausage made with soy protein, such as soy *chouriço* or soy Italian-style sausage

2 large onions, peeled and chopped

4 cloves garlic, minced

2 medium carrots, peeled and diced

1 large sweet potato, peeled and cut into ½" cubes

1 tablespoon smoked paprika

1 teaspoon cumin

6 cups vegetable stock

¼ cup chopped fresh cilantro

1 teaspoon salt

½ teaspoon ground cayenne pepper (optional) or 1 teaspoon ground black pepper

¼ cup chopped scallions

1. Place the beans in a bowl, cover with 2" of water, and soak overnight.

2. Drain the beans and set aside. Place the olive oil in a stockpot. Slice the sausages crosswise into bite-size pieces and brown them in the oil over medium heat. Remove from heat and reserve.

3. Add the onions and cook over low heat until onion is browned and caramelized, about 15–20 minutes. Add the garlic, carrots, sweet potato, paprika, and cumin and cook, turning often, until lightly browned.

4. Add the beans and the vegetable stock. Turn heat to low. Cover and simmer for 1 hour, or until beans are just tender. Add the cilantro and salt and pepper (to taste) and cook for 45–60 minutes more, until beans reach desired texture.

5. Garnish stew with the scallions before serving.

Farofa with Eggs (*Farofa de Ovos*)

Whisk 4 eggs with ½ teaspoons each salt and pepper, 2 tablespoons minced parsley, and 2 tablespoons grated Parmesan cheese. Place 2 tablespoons butter and ¼ cup minced onion in a medium skillet, and cook over medium-low heat until soft. Add eggs and cook until scrambled, then remove to a plate. Add 1 cup manioc meal to skillet and sauté until well toasted and lightly browned. Add eggs back to skillet and mix well.

Hot Zucchini and Cheese Sandwich
(*Sanduíche Quente de Abobrinha e Queijo*)

This vegetarian sandwich is a hot mix of garlicky sautéed zucchini, artichokes, goat cheese, olives, and sun-dried tomatoes, toasted in the oven until the cheese melts and the bread is crispy.

INGREDIENTS | SERVES 2

2 crusty French bread rolls

2 tablespoons mayonnaise

4 ounces goat cheese

1 tablespoon minced fresh parsley

4 tablespoons grated Parmesan, divided

¼ cup sun-dried tomatoes, chopped

¼ cup green or black olives, sliced

2 medium zucchini

1 teaspoon salt

1 teaspoon freshly ground black pepper

2 tablespoons olive oil

4 cloves garlic, minced

4 artichoke hearts, quartered

¼ cup grated mozzarella

Chimichurri-Style Sandwich Spread (*Molho de Ervas*)

Place 2 peeled garlic cloves in a food processor and pulse until finely chopped. Add 1 large bunch parsley and 1 teaspoon minced hot pepper and pulse until chopped. Transfer mixture to a bowl. Add the juice of 1 lime, 1 teaspoon dried oregano, ¼ cup olive oil, ½ cup cream cheese (or *requeijão*, Brazilian-style cream cheese), ½ teaspoon salt, and ½ teaspoon black pepper (or to taste) and stir until well mixed. Store in an airtight container in the refrigerator until ready to use.

1. Slice the rolls halfway through lengthwise, and split open almost all the way.

2. In a small bowl, mix together the mayonnaise, goat cheese, parsley, and 2 tablespoons Parmesan. Spread the inside of the rolls with the mayonnaise mixture (top and bottom).

3. Place the sun-dried tomatoes and olives on the bottom half of each roll, dividing them between the 2 rolls. Turn on the oven broiler.

4. Slice the ends off of the zucchini. Slice each zucchini lengthwise into ¼"-thick slices. Place the zucchini slices on a plate and season both sides with the salt and pepper.

5. Heat the oil in a large skillet over medium heat. Add the garlic and cook for 1 minute. Add the zucchini slices (working in batches, if needed) and cook until lightly browned on both sides. Remove zucchini slices from skillet and place on the rolls, dividing them between the two.

6. Add the artichoke hearts to the skillet and cook until lightly browned. Divide them between the rolls, placing them on top of the zucchini slices.

7. Sprinkle the mozzarella over the artichoke and zucchini slices. Sprinkle the remaining Parmesan over the mozzarella. Toast sandwiches, still open, under the broiler for 1–2 minutes, watching carefully, until Parmesan is lightly browned and cheese is melted. Remove from oven, close sandwiches, and serve.

Eggplant Parmesan (*Berinjela a Parmigiana*)

This Italian dish is very popular in Brazil. It's often served with grilled meats, but it also works well as a vegetarian main course.

1. Sprinkle the eggplant slices on both sides with 1 teaspoon of salt, and place in a colander for 30 minutes.

2. Place the flour in a shallow dish. Whisk the eggs in a shallow bowl. Mix the bread crumbs with 1 teaspoon oregano, 2 tablespoons Parmesan, remaining salt, and pepper in a shallow dish.

3. Dip the eggplant slices in the flour, then in the egg, and then in the bread crumbs to coat.

4. Preheat the oven to 350°F. Heat half of the oil in a large skillet over medium heat. Fry the eggplant until golden on both sides, working in batches, then drain on paper towels. Add more oil as needed.

5. Spread 1 cup of the tomato sauce in the bottom of a casserole dish. Place half of the fried eggplant on top of the tomato sauce, overlapping slightly if needed. Spread 1 cup of tomato sauce on top of the eggplant, then sprinkle ½ cup mozzarella and ⅓ cup Parmesan over the sauce. Top with another layer of eggplant, another cup of tomato sauce, remaining mozzarella and remaining Parmesan, and 1 teaspoon oregano.

6. Bake casserole for 25–30 minutes, until cheese is melted and sauce is bubbly.

Black Bean Veggie Burger (*Hambúrguer de Feijão Preto*)

*You can enjoy these black bean burgers with a wide variety of toppings,
though they are especially good with guacamole and/or a slice of fried plantain.*

INGREDIENTS | SERVES 4

4 tablespoons olive oil, divided

¼ cup finely chopped onion

2 cloves garlic, minced

½ medium red bell pepper, seeded and finely chopped

1 tablespoon minced cilantro

1 teaspoon chili powder

1 teaspoon cumin

1 teaspoon salt

1 teaspoon freshly ground black pepper

1 (16-ounce) can black beans, drained and rinsed, or 2 cups cooked black beans, divided

1 large egg

1 cup cooked rice

1 cup bread crumbs

4 hamburger buns

Avocado Spread (*Molho de Abacate*)

Place a handful of fresh basil leaves, some fresh parsley leaves, and 2 or 3 scallions in a food processor and pulse until chopped. Add the flesh of 1 ripe avocado, ⅓ cup cream cheese, 2 tablespoons mayonnaise, 1 tablespoon fresh lime juice, 1 tablespoon olive oil, 1 teaspoon honey, and ½ teaspoon each of salt and black pepper. Process until smooth. Store covered with a thin layer of olive oil in an airtight container in the refrigerator for up to 1 day.

1. Heat 2 tablespoons olive oil in a medium skillet over medium-low heat. Add the onion and cook until soft and slightly browned, about 5–8 minutes. Add the garlic, bell pepper, and cilantro and cook until soft and fragrant, about 4 minutes. Add the chili powder, cumin, salt, and black pepper and mix well.

2. Add 1½ cups of the black beans and mash beans in the skillet with a potato masher, until beans are well mashed and heated through.

3. Transfer mixture to a medium bowl. Wipe out the skillet and set aside. Add the egg, rice, and remaining beans to the bowl and mix well. Let mixture cool, then shape into 4 patties. Roll each patty in bread crumbs.

4. Heat the remaining 2 tablespoons of oil in the same skillet and cook the patties over medium-low heat until browned on both sides, about 3–4 minutes per side.

5. Serve in hamburger buns with Avocado Spread (see sidebar) and toppings of choice.

Cornmeal and Vegetable Couscous Ring
(*Cuscuz Paulista Vegetariano*)

This elaborate molded cornmeal and manioc ring (cusuz paulista) is a specialty of São Paulo. Cuscuz paulista normally has shrimp and/or chicken inside, but this version has lots of vegetables instead.

INGREDIENTS | SERVES 8

3 tablespoons butter

1 small onion, peeled and chopped

2 cloves garlic, minced

¼ cup diced scallions

1 medium zucchini, diced

1 medium carrot, peeled and diced

1 medium tomato, seeded and diced

1 cup fresh or frozen corn kernels

1 cup fresh or frozen peas

3 cups vegetable stock

1 cup manioc meal (*farinha de mandioca*)

2½ cups cornmeal

1 teaspoon salt

1 teaspoon freshly ground black pepper

1 plum tomato, sliced crosswise

1 large hard-cooked egg, peeled and sliced

3 or 4 green olives with pimento, sliced crosswise

3 or 4 parsley sprigs

1. Heat the butter in a large saucepan over medium heat. Add the onion and cook until soft and fragrant, about 5–8 minutes. Add the garlic, scallions, zucchini, and carrots and cook for 2–3 minutes. Add the tomato, corn, and peas and cook until most of the liquid has evaporated.

2. Add the vegetable stock and bring to a simmer. Slowly stir in the manioc meal. Gradually add the cornmeal, stirring constantly. Add salt and black pepper. Cook over medium-low heat, stirring constantly, until mixture is very thick and is starting to stick to the bottom of the pan, about 10 minutes. Remove from heat.

3. Generously oil the inside of a ring mold. Decorate the bottom and sides of the mold with the sliced plum tomato, egg, olives, and parsley sprigs. Carefully add the cornmeal mixture to the mold, filling the mold evenly and pressing down firmly on the cornmeal to pack it well.

4. Invert mold onto a serving plate and slice to serve. Serve warm or at room temperature.

Corn and Cheese Empanada Pie (*Empadão de Milho e Queijo*)

This savory pie is filled with creamy fresh corn, onions, and Cheddar cheese. The dough and filling can also be used to make 8–10 individual empandinhas, the Brazilian version of empanadas.

INGREDIENTS | SERVES 8

2⅓ cups all-purpose flour

1½ teaspoons salt, divided

1 large egg

6 tablespoons vegetable shortening

14 tablespoons butter, divided

1 medium onion, peeled and finely chopped

3 cups fresh or frozen corn kernels

⅓ cup heavy cream

½ cup vegetable stock

2 tablespoons minced fresh cilantro

1 teaspoon freshly ground black pepper

1 cup grated Cheddar cheese

2 tablespoons grated Parmesan cheese

1 egg yolk

1. Make the pastry dough: Place 2¼ cups of the flour and ½ teaspoon salt in a large bowl. Make a well in the center and add the egg. Work the shortening and 10 tablespoons of butter into the flour with your hands, or use a pastry cutter. Knead the dough until smooth. Wrap dough in plastic wrap and refrigerate for at least 30 minutes.

2. Place the remaining 4 tablespoons butter in a large saucepan. Add the onion and cook over medium heat until onion is very soft, about 5–8 minutes. Stir 1 tablespoon of flour into the onions. Purée the corn in a blender with the cream, vegetable stock, and ½ teaspoon salt. Add corn mixture, cilantro, and black pepper to the onions and simmer, stirring constantly, until mixture thickens (about 5 minutes).

3. Remove from heat and stir in the cheeses. Set aside to cool.

4. Preheat oven to 350°F. On a floured surface, roll out ⅔ of the dough into an 11" circle. Use dough circle to line a 9" tart pan. Press dough into the sides and bottom of the pan, and trim excess.

5. Pour the cooled filling into the tart shell. Roll out the remaining dough into a 9" circle and use it to cover the filling, sealing the edges. Decorate the crust with scraps of dough, if desired, and make a few vents in the top crust. Brush the tart lightly with the egg yolk.

6. Bake for 35–40 minutes, or until crust is golden brown.

Good Luck Lentil Loaf (*Bolo Salgado de Lentilha*)

This dish is very tasty, as the lentils have a lot of flavor. And just like meatloaf, slices of this lentil loaf are great in sandwiches.

INGREDIENTS | SERVES 8

1 cup lentils

3 cups vegetable stock

2 tablespoons olive oil

1 medium onion, peeled and finely chopped

2 cloves garlic, minced

1 teaspoon garlic salt

1 teaspoon smoked paprika

1 teaspoon cumin

1 teaspoon freshly ground black pepper

3 slices whole-wheat sandwich bread, lightly toasted

1 cup cooked brown rice

1 large egg

¼ cup chopped scallions

¼ cup chopped fresh parsley

1 tablespoon soy sauce

2 tablespoons ketchup

1 tablespoon vinegar

1 tablespoon brown sugar

1. Place the lentils in a pot and cover with the vegetable stock. Bring to a simmer over medium heat, then reduce heat to low, cover, and cook for 40 minutes, or until lentils are tender.

2. Place the olive oil in a medium saucepan. Add the onion and cook over medium heat until onion is very soft, about 5–8 minutes. Add the garlic and cook for 1 minute. Add the garlic salt, smoked paprika, cumin, and black pepper and cook for 1 minute. Remove from heat.

3. Place toasted bread in a food processor and process until you have coarse crumbs. Place ⅔ of the cooked lentils in a large bowl, and mash them with a potato masher. Add the remaining lentils, bread crumbs, rice, egg, scallions, parsley, and soy sauce. Mix everything together well.

4. Preheat oven to 350°F. Lightly oil a 4" × 8" loaf pan. Place the lentil mixture into the pan, packing it down gently. Whisk together the ketchup, vinegar, and brown sugar and brush mixture over the top of the loaf.

5. Bake for 40 minutes, or until glaze is dark caramel brown and loaf is heated through.

Cheesy Sandwich Spiral (*Rocambole Salgado*)

This savory rocambole (cake roll) is sliced crosswise into spirals for serving.
Rocambole salgado makes a pretty and unique lunch or brunch entrée.

INGREDIENTS | SERVES 8

7 large eggs

1 tablespoon sugar

6 tablespoons all-purpose flour

4 tablespoons grated Parmesan cheese, divided

1 teaspoon salt

1 teaspoon baking powder

1 cup ricotta cheese

1 cup cream cheese, softened

½ cup crumbled blue cheese

¾ cup mayonnaise, divided

¼ cup finely chopped green olives

1 teaspoon dried oregano

¼ cup chopped scallions

Ketchup and/or mustard, for garnish (optional)

1 tablespoon minced fresh parsley, for garnish (optional)

Rocambole with Pastry Crust (*Rocambole com Massa de Pastel*)

You can use the same pastry that is used to make *pastéis* (fried pastries) to make a calzone-like *rocambole*—warm flaky pastry baked in the oven with melted cheese inside. Use the recipe for Pastel Dough (see sidebar for Fried Beef Pastries recipe in Chapter 11), or use puff pastry. Roll out the pastry into a 10" × 14" rectangle. Spread tomato sauce, slices of mozzarella and provolone cheese, grated Parmesan, oregano, and other fillings of your choice on the pastry. Roll it into a log, starting with a long end. Place seam side down on a baking sheet, brush with egg yolk, and sprinkle with Parmesan and oregano. Bake at 350°F until golden brown (about 30 minutes).

1. Preheat oven to 350°F. Place the eggs and sugar in the bowl of a standing mixer and beat on a high speed until doubled in volume, about 5–8 minutes.

2. Whisk together the flour, 2 tablespoons Parmesan, salt, and baking powder and carefully fold dry ingredients into the egg/sugar mixture. Line a 12" × 18" baking pan with parchment paper. Generously butter and flour the paper. Spread the batter into the pan as evenly as possible.

3. Bake for 10 minutes, or until cake springs back to the touch. Remove from oven and immediately flip cake out of the pan onto a clean, floured dishtowel. Peel the parchment paper off of the cake and sprinkle cake with flour. Loosely roll up the cake with the towel, starting with a short end.

4. In a medium bowl, beat the ricotta with the cream cheese. Add the blue cheese, ½ cup mayonnaise, olives, oregano, and scallions.

5. Unroll cake and spread filling over the inside of the cake roll, leaving a 1" border at the top of a short side. Roll up cake around filling. Place on clean baking sheet, seam side down. Brush cake lightly with remaining mayonnaise and sprinkle with remaining Parmesan. Place cake in the oven briefly, just to brown the Parmesan slightly.

6. Decorate cake roll with drizzles of ketchup and/or mustard if desired, or garnish with parsley. Slice crosswise to serve.

CHAPTER 17

Breakfast (*Café da Manhã*)

Tapioca Crepes with Cheese and Guava
(*Tapioca Romeu e Julieta*)

Manioc starch is available in two forms: sweet (doce) or sour (azedo). Either kind will work in this recipe, but the sweet starch works best with sweeter fillings, such as guava paste or fruit.

INGREDIENTS | SERVES 4

8 ounces guava paste

2 tablespoons orange juice

2 cups tapioca starch (*polvilho de mandioca doce*)

⅓ teaspoon salt

½ cup water, plus more if needed

1½ cups grated cheese (mozzarella, Cheddar, Monterey jack, or a combination)

1. Place the guava paste in a small saucepan with 2 tablespoons of orange juice over low heat. Cook guava paste, stirring, until softened and smooth.

2. Place the tapioca starch and salt in a medium bowl and stir to mix.

3. Add the water a few tablespoons at a time, mixing well with your hands and crumbling the tapioca. Continue to add water until all of the starch resembles coarse crumbs. If you add too much water, the starch will start to flow together—if this happens, just add some more starch.

4. Sift the dampened starch through a fine-mesh sieve into a clean bowl, using a wooden spoon to help push it through the sieve.

5. Heat a nonstick skillet over medium heat. Sprinkle about 5 tablespoons of the sifted starch onto the skillet in an even layer (you can use a sieve to do this step). Cook for 1 minute, and as soon as crepe will move and slide in the skillet, flip the crepe to the other side. Sprinkle with ¼ cup cheese and cook for 1 minute more. Remove from skillet, add 2–3 tablespoons of the guava paste on top of the grated cheese, then fold crepe in half to enclose fillings.

6. Repeat with remaining starch, cheese, and guava. Serve warm.

Açaí Breakfast Bowl (*Açaí na Tigela*)

Açaí (pronounced "ah-sigh-EE") is a dark purple berry with a sweet, blackberry-like flavor that grows on a South American species of palm tree.

INGREDIENTS | SERVES 1

7 ounces frozen açaí purée (look for açaí smoothie "packets" (3.5 ounces each) in the frozen food section)

1 banana, peeled and sliced

¼ cup *guaraná* syrup (*xarope de guaraná*), or substitute blackberry syrup

1 tablespoon fresh lime juice

2 or 3 ice cubes

Granola, for garnish

1. Place the frozen açaí pulp in a blender with half of the banana slices, syrup, lime juice, and ice.

2. Blend until mixture has a very thick, smooth texture, similar to that of sorbet.

3. Place mixture in a bowl. Top with remaining banana slices and granola and serve immediately.

Baked Cinnamon Toast (*Rabanada de Forno*)

Rabanadas are the Portuguese version of what Americans call French toast, and are very similar to Spanish torrijas. This is also a great way to use up stale bread.

INGREDIENTS | SERVES 4

2 cups milk

½ cup sweetened condensed milk

2 large eggs

½ teaspoon salt

1 teaspoon vanilla

1 cup sugar

2 tablespoons cinnamon

1 tablespoon melted butter

8 (1½"-thick) diagonal slices French baguette or other crusty bread loaf

1. In a medium bowl, whisk together the milk, condensed milk, eggs, salt, and vanilla.

2. In another bowl, stir together the sugar and the cinnamon.

3. Grease a 9" square baking pan with melted butter.

4. Soak each slice of bread in the milk/egg mixture, then lift it out and let it drain slightly. Dip it in the sugar mixture. Place in the baking pan. Repeat with remaining bread slices.

5. Bake bread at 350°F for 20 minutes or until golden brown. Serve warm.

Cinnamon "Raindrop" Doughnuts (*Bolinho de Chuva*)

The name of these bite-size doughnuts in Portuguese means "raindrop" because they have a droplet-like shape that forms when the batter is spooned into the hot oil.

INGREDIENTS | MAKES 25

2½ cups all-purpose flour
1 tablespoon baking powder
½ teaspoon salt
1 cup sugar, divided
2 tablespoons butter, melted
2 large eggs
½ teaspoon vanilla
1¼ cups milk
Vegetable oil, for frying
1 tablespoon cinnamon

Chocolate Raindrops (*Bolinho de Chuva Recheado com Chocolate*)

These doughnuts can be filled with a variety of delicious things before they are cooked. Popular choices include banana slices, *doce de leite* (dulce de leche), chocolate, and guava paste. To make a simple chocolate filling, cut a thick chocolate bar into small (½") squares. Place a square of chocolate in the middle of a spoonful of batter before you drop it into the oil, making sure that the batter completely surrounds the chocolate. The same procedure will work with banana slices and cubes of guava paste. To fill the doughnuts with dulce de leche, shape teaspoons of chilled dulce de leche into small balls. Freeze the balls of dulce de leche for a half hour, and then place them in the doughnut batter using the same method.

1. Place the flour, baking powder, salt, and ⅓ cup sugar in a medium bowl.

2. Add the butter, eggs, and vanilla and stir to mix.

3. Add the milk in two parts, stirring after each addition, until batter is smooth and has the texture of a thick cake batter. You may need to add a bit more or a bit less milk.

4. Heat 2" of vegetable oil in a large saucepan over medium heat to 350°F. Take a spoonful of batter and use a second spoon to help drop the batter into the oil. Repeat several times, being careful not to overcrowd the doughnuts. Use a slotted spoon to flip the doughnuts in the oil, and once they are evenly browned, remove them to a plate lined with paper towels. Continue to cook the doughnuts in batches.

5. Mix the cinnamon and remaining sugar together in a shallow dish and roll the doughnuts in the mixture to coat.

6. Serve warm.

Doughnut "Dreams" (*Sonhos*)

*Once cooked, these doughnuts are split in half and filled with pastry cream,
doce de leite (dulce de leche), or guava paste, and then sprinkled with sugar.*

INGREDIENTS | MAKES 20

2¼ cups all-purpose flour

1 tablespoon active dry yeast

½ cup warm water

¾ cup sugar, divided

6 tablespoons butter, softened

3 large eggs

½ teaspoon salt

1 teaspoon vanilla

Vegetable oil, for frying

1½ cups Vanilla Cream Filling (see sidebar) or dulce de leche

Vanilla Cream Filling (*Creme*)

Place 1½ cups milk, ¼ cup sugar, and a pinch of salt in a small saucepan and bring to a simmer over medium-low heat. In a heatproof bowl, whisk together 2 egg yolks with ¼ cup sugar and 2 tablespoons cornstarch. Add the hot milk/sugar mixture to the egg mixture, stirring constantly. Return everything to saucepan and cook over low heat, stirring, until thickened and smooth. Remove from heat. Stir in 1 teaspoon vanilla and 1 tablespoon butter. Transfer to a bowl, cover surface with plastic wrap, and chill until ready to use.

1. Place ½ cup flour, the yeast, and the warm water in the bowl of a standing mixer and stir to mix. Set aside for 15 minutes.

2. Add the remaining flour to the bowl. Add ½ cup sugar, butter, eggs, salt, and vanilla and mix with the dough hook attachment until a smooth dough forms. Let rise in a warm place, covered loosely, for 30 minutes.

3. Divide dough into 20 pieces and roll each piece with the palms of your hands to form a ball. Place balls of dough 2" apart on a baking sheet and let rise in a warm place for 20–30 minutes.

4. Heat 2" of oil in a heavy saucepan to 350°F. Fry doughnuts in batches until golden brown. Drain on paper towels.

5. Once doughnuts have cooled, slice them in half horizontally, and fill with a tablespoon of Vanilla Cream Filling (see sidebar) or dulce de leche.

6. Sprinkle doughnuts with remaining sugar before serving.

Cornmeal Muffins with Guava
(*Bolinho de Fubá com Goiabada*)

These sweet and tender corn muffins have a surprise center of guava paste.
This batter can also be prepared the day before and refrigerated overnight.

INGREDIENTS | SERVES 18

½ cup plus 1 tablespoon butter, melted (divided)

2 tablespoons sugar

1½ cups milk

½ cup vegetable oil

3 large eggs

1 teaspoon salt

2 cups finely ground yellow cornmeal

1 cup all-purpose flour

1 tablespoon baking powder

8 ounces guava paste, cut into 18 pieces

2 tablespoons powdered sugar

Guava Cake (*Bolo de Fubá com Goiabada*)

This same batter can be used to make a cake. Butter and flour a ring mold or angel food cake pan. Fold the pieces of guava paste into the batter (add small cubes of cheese also, if desired). Bake at 350°F until cake springs back to the touch. Remove from oven and let cool before removing from pan. Sprinkle with powdered sugar.

1. Brush the wells of an 18-cup muffin tin with 1 tablespoon of the melted butter, and sprinkle them with the granulated sugar. (Or line the muffin tin with paper liners.) Preheat the oven to 350°F.

2. Place the milk, oil, remaining butter, eggs, and salt in a blender and mix well. Add the cornmeal, flour, and baking powder and blend until smooth.

3. Fill muffin cups about ⅔ of the way full. Place a piece of guava paste in the middle of each one. Distribute the remaining batter to cover the guava paste and until the muffin tins are almost full.

4. Bake for 20–25 minutes until muffins spring back lightly to the touch.

5. Remove from oven, let cool for 5 minutes, then sift powdered sugar over the tops of the muffins.

Cheesy Tapioca Bread Ring (*Bolo Pão de Queijo*)

Brazilians love their delicious cheese puff–style rolls called pão de queijo (see recipe for Gluten-Free Cheese Rolls in Chapter 10). This is a sliceable bread version, which is very quick to make and ideal for breakfast.

INGREDIENTS | SERVES 8

½ cup vegetable oil

½ cup butter, melted

1 cup milk

4 large eggs

1 teaspoon salt

¾ cup grated Cheddar cheese

¾ cup grated mozzarella cheese

3 cups tapioca starch (*polvinho de mandioca*)

2 tablespoons baking powder

2 tablespoons grated Parmesan cheese

1. Butter and flour a 10" ring mold or angel food cake pan. Preheat the oven to 350°F.

2. Place the oil, butter, milk, eggs, and salt in a blender and process until mixed. Add the Cheddar and mozzarella cheeses and process briefly.

3. Place the tapioca starch and baking powder in a large bowl. Add the mixture from the blender and stir until smooth.

4. Pour batter into prepared mold or pan. Sprinkle with the Parmesan.

5. Bake for 25–30 minutes until bread is puffed and has small browned spots. Serve warm.

Cheesy Muffins (*Queijadinha*)

These gluten-free cheese muffins have a creamy texture and are delicious when they are warm from the oven. They go very well with coffee in the morning.

INGREDIENTS | MAKES 12

4 large eggs

1 (14-ounce) can sweetened condensed milk

2 tablespoons butter, melted

1 cup grated Cheddar cheese

1 cup grated mozzarella cheese

⅓ cup grated Parmesan cheese

½ cup grated coconut (optional)

3 tablespoons all-purpose flour

1 teaspoon baking powder

1. Preheat the oven to 350°F.

2. Beat the eggs with the condensed milk and the melted butter. Add remaining ingredients and mix well.

3. Distribute the batter between 12 muffin molds.

4. Bake for 25–30 minutes until muffins have risen and are lightly browned on top.

5. Let cool for 5 minutes before unmolding. Serve warm.

Cinnamon Crumb Cake (*Cuca de Canela*)

This traditional German-style cake from Rio Grande du Sul has a yeasted dough and a cinnamon streusel topping.

INGREDIENTS | SERVES 10

½ cup warm water

1 tablespoon active dry yeast

2 cups sugar, divided

4½ cups all-purpose flour, divided

1 teaspoon salt

3 large eggs

3 tablespoons softened butter

1 cup milk

2 teaspoons vanilla

Pinch of salt

3 tablespoons cold butter

1 tablespoon cinnamon

Optional Strawberry Filling (*Cuca Recheada de Morango*)

In a heatproof bowl, whisk 1 egg yolk with 1 tablespoon cornstarch and ¼ cup sugar until pale and smooth. Bring 1 cup milk to a simmer in a small saucepan. Slowly stir hot milk into egg mixture. Return everything to the saucepan and heat over low heat, stirring constantly, until mixture thickens. Remove from heat and stir in ½ tablespoon butter and ½ teaspoon vanilla. Once the yeasted cake batter has risen in the pan (about an hour), spread all of the cream lightly over the top of the cake, leaving a 1" border all the way around. Top with ¾ cup strawberry jam (softened in the microwave). Cover the top of the cake with the streusel and bake.

1. Butter and flour a 10" ring mold or springform pan.

2. Place the warm water, yeast, and 1 tablespoon sugar in the bowl of a standing mixer and set aside for 5 minutes.

3. Add 1½ cups sugar, 1 cup flour, salt, eggs, and 3 tablespoons softened butter and mix well with the dough hook attachment. Add the milk, vanilla, and 3 cups of flour and mix until you have a soft, smooth dough (about 3–5 minutes). It should be stretchy and soft in texture. If dough is too stiff, add a bit more milk. Cover bowl loosely with a dishtowel and let dough rise in a warm place for 1 hour.

4. Punch down dough and place it in the mold or pan, using your fingers to press it evenly in the pan. Let rise in warm place for 45 minutes.

5. Prepare the streusel: In a small bowl, place ½ cup flour, the remaining sugar, a pinch of salt, 3 tablespoons cold butter, and cinnamon. Mix with your fingers until mixture is crumbly.

6. Preheat oven to 350°F. Sprinkle streusel over risen dough. Place in the oven to bake for 30–40 minutes until cake has risen and streusel is lightly browned. Let cool for 10 minutes before removing cake from the pan.

Cornmeal and Cheese Empanadas
(*Pastel de Angu com Queijo*)

The cornmeal dough makes the empanadas extra crispy on the outside but nice and creamy on the inside.

INGREDIENTS | MAKES 16

4 cups water

1 teaspoon salt

2 tablespoons butter

4 cups yellow cornmeal

2 tablespoons tapioca starch

12 ounces Monterey jack and/or mozzarella cheese, grated

Vegetable oil, for frying

1. Place the water in a large saucepan. Add the salt and butter and bring to a simmer over medium-low heat. Gradually stir in the cornmeal.

2. Cook over low heat, stirring, until mixture comes together and forms a dough. Turn mixture out onto a counter and sprinkle the tapioca starch over the dough. Knead until dough is very smooth.

3. Take golf ball–size portions of dough and shape them into balls. Use your fingers to hollow out each ball of dough into the shape of a cup, making the walls of the cup fairly thin. Fill the cup with 1–2 tablespoons shredded cheese, then fold closed into a half-moon shape. Seal edges and crimp decoratively.

4. Heat 2" of oil in a heavy saucepan or deep skillet to 350°F. Fry *pastéis* in batches until golden brown on both sides. Drain on paper towels. Serve warm.

Yogurt Cake (*Bolo de Iogurte*)

The yogurt adds a nice tang and moist texture to this cake.

INGREDIENTS | SERVES 8

½ cup vegetable oil
½ cup butter, melted
5 large eggs
1 teaspoon vanilla
1½ cups plain Greek yogurt
3 cups all-purpose flour
2 cups sugar
1 tablespoon baking powder
½ cup fruit jam of choice (optional)
2 tablespoons powdered sugar

1. Butter and flour a 10" ring mold, bundt, or angel food cake pan. Preheat the oven to 350°F.

2. Place the oil, butter, eggs, vanilla, and yogurt in a blender or food processor and process until mixed. Add the flour and sugar and mix until batter is very smooth.

3. Add the baking powder and mix briefly.

4. Pour the batter into the prepared pan. Soften fruit jam in microwave for 10 seconds, then gently swirl into the batter with a knife (optional). Bake for 35–40 minutes, or until cake springs back lightly to the touch.

5. Sprinkle cake with powdered sugar while still warm.

Toasted French Bread Roll (*Pão na Chapa*)

To be authentic, you should enjoy these rolls with a glass of pingado (sweetened milk and coffee—see sidebar).

INGREDIENTS | SERVES 1

1 crusty French bread roll
2 tablespoons butter
1 teaspoon dried oregano (optional)
1 teaspoon grated Parmesan cheese (optional)

Milk with Coffee (*Pingado*)

Heat about ½ cup milk with 2 teaspoons sugar in a small saucepan until steaming. Do not boil. Pour the milk into a glass. Add hot brewed coffee to desired color (light or dark caramel), up to a fifty-fifty mix. Sweeten with more sugar if desired.

1. Slice the roll in half lengthwise. Spread each half with 1 tablespoon of butter. Sprinkle with oregano and Parmesan if desired.

2. Heat a skillet over medium heat. Place the rolls, buttered side down on the skillet. Toast rolls, pressing down on them with a spatula to flatten them slightly.

3. Once rolls are lightly browned on the buttered side, flip them and toast them on the other side to desired doneness. Serve warm.

Steamed Cornmeal "Couscous" (*Cuscuz com Queijo*)

In Brazil you can buy a form of precooked, coarsely flaked cornmeal called milharina, but regular coarse yellow cornmeal works for this recipe as well. You can order milharina online from Brazilian food vendors (see Appendix C).

INGREDIENTS | SERVES 4

2 cups yellow cornmeal or *milharina* (*farinha de milho flocada*)

1 teaspoon salt

1¼ cups water

8 ounces Monterey jack or mozzarella cheese, cubed

Melted butter, for topping (optional)

1. Place the cornmeal in a bowl with the salt and the water. Mix well and set aside, covered with a dish-towel, for 10 minutes.

2. Butter the inside of a 16-ounce soufflé ramekin or bowl. Fold the cheese cubes into the cornmeal, then place the cornmeal in the ramekin. Cover the top of the bowl with a double layer of cheesecloth, and secure it with a rubber band.

3. Place a colander over a large pot of simmering water, making sure the colander does not touch the water. Place the casserole upside down (cheesecloth facing down) in the colander. Steam cornmeal for 30 minutes.

4. Unmold cornmeal, cut into loose slices, and serve warm, drizzled with some melted butter or coconut milk if desired.

Creamy Cornmeal Cake (*Bolo de Fubá Cremoso*)

This unusual cornmeal cake does something surprising in the oven—it separates into layers with different textures. The top and the bottom layers are tender sweet corn bread with a hint of Parmesan cheese, while the middle layer is more like a cheesy soufflé.

INGREDIENTS | SERVES 10

4 cups milk

4 large eggs

2 tablespoons butter, melted

4 tablespoons cream cheese, softened

½ teaspoon salt

1½ cups sugar

1½ cups very fine cornmeal

3 tablespoons all-purpose flour

1 teaspoon baking powder

¾ cup grated mozzarella cheese

2 tablespoons grated Parmesan cheese

1. Butter and flour a 10" ring mold or angel food cake pan, or a 9" × 13" rectangular pan. Preheat the oven to 325°F.

2. Place the milk, eggs, butter, cream cheese, and salt in a blender or food processor and process until mixed.

3. Place the sugar, cornmeal, flour, and baking powder in a large bowl. Add the mixture from the blender and stir until very smooth.

4. Add the cheeses and mix briefly.

5. Pour the batter into the prepared mold or pan and bake for 45–50 minutes, or until cake springs back lightly to the touch.

6. Let cake cool for 5–10 minutes before slicing. Serve warm or at room temperature. Cake can be reheated in the microwave.

Cheesy Manioc Biscuits (*Biscoitinho de Queijo*)

These cheese "biscuits" are similar to the more well-known cheese rolls called pão de queijo, but these are crispier and more cookie-like.

INGREDIENTS | MAKES 16

2 cups sweet tapioca starch (*polvinho de mandioca doce*)

½ cup milk

⅓ cup vegetable oil, heated until very warm to the touch

1 large egg

½ cup grated Cheddar cheese

½ cup grated mozzarella cheese

½ cup grated Parmesan cheese

½ teaspoon salt

1. Preheat the oven to 375°F. Place the tapioca starch in a medium bowl and add the milk. Stir with a spoon or your fingers until milk is incorporated and mixture is crumbly.

2. Add the hot vegetable oil and stir well. Add the egg, cheeses, and salt and stir until mixture comes together as a dough. Knead mixture well until very smooth.

3. Divide the dough into 16 pieces. Roll each piece between your palms to form a 6" rope. Shape the rope into a circle and seal the ends.

4. Place the rings on a greased baking sheet, and bake until they are puffed and start to brown slightly around the edges, about 10–12 minutes. Once cooled, store biscuits in an airtight container.

CHAPTER 18

Drinks and Cocktails (*Bebidas e Cocktails*)

Caipirinha Cocktail (*Caipirinha*)

The caipirinha is Brazil's national cocktail. Serve this cocktail in an old-fashioned glass, preferably one that is narrow at the bottom and wide at the top, with a stirring stick.

INGREDIENTS | SERVES 1

1 lime
1½ tablespoons cane sugar or regular white sugar
Ice cubes
2 ounces *cachaça*

1. Trim the ends off the lime. Slice the lime in half lengthwise. Remove the white pith and the seeds from the lime, and cut each half into 4 equal pieces.

2. Place the limes in the bottom of an old-fashioned glass. Add the sugar, and "muddle" the limes with the sugar using a pestle.

3. Add the ice cubes, slightly overfilling the glass.

4. Slowly pour the *cachaça* over the ice. Stir well, until the ice settles into the glass.

5. Serve with a stirring stick or straw.

Brazilian Iced Tea (*Chá Mate Gelado*)

Brazilian iced tea is quite similar to American iced tea, except that Brazilians use toasted erva-mate leaves (chá mate).

INGREDIENTS | SERVES 4

2 tablespoons *chá mate* (toasted erva-mate tea leaves)
4 cups water
⅔ cup sugar
Juice of 2 limes

1. Place the tea in a heatproof pitcher, carafe, or jar. Bring the water to a boil. Pour the hot water over the tea and set aside to steep for 5 minutes.

2. Place the sugar and the lime juice in a blender. Strain the tea mixture and add it the strained liquid to the blender. Blend well.

3. Store tea in the refrigerator until ready to serve. Serve over ice.

Pineapple *Caipirinha* (*Caipirinha de Abacaxi*)

This frozen tropical version of a caipirinha is often served in a hollowed-out pineapple (don't forget the paper umbrella!).

INGREDIENTS | SERVES 1

1 small pineapple

Ice cubes

2–3 ounces *cachaça* or vodka

4 tablespoons cane sugar or regular white sugar

Juice of 1 lime

Several fresh mint leaves

Nonalcoholic *Caipifruta*

Make sugar syrup by boiling 1 cup sugar with 1 cup water until sugar is dissolved. Let cool. Muddle ½ cup fruit in the bottom of a tall glass with a few small pieces of lime. Add a few mint leaves. Add some of the sugar syrup (to taste). Fill the glass with ice cubes. Pour seltzer water over the ice to fill glass. Stir with a straw and enjoy.

1. Cut a circle around the top of the pineapple, removing the fronds. Remove the inside of the pineapple, leaving about ½–1" thickness all the way around.

2. Remove the core and chop the pineapple fruit into small cubes. Place half of the cubes in the blender with 1 cup of ice, the *cachaça*, 2 tablespoons of the sugar, and the lime juice. Process until smooth, adding a little water if needed.

3. Place the remaining pineapple cubes into the hollowed-out pineapple and use a pestle to mash them with the mint leaves and remaining sugar.

4. Pour the mixture from the blender into the pineapple and stir to mix.

5. Serve with a straw.

Strawberry Shaved Ice (*Raspadinha de Morango*)

This simple recipe is bursting with strawberry flavor. Kids and adults alike will enjoy cooling off with this icy yet creamy drink.

INGREDIENTS | SERVES 4

3 cups strawberries, stems removed

1 (14-ounce) can sweetened condensed milk

Juice of 1 lime

½ teaspoon vanilla

4–6 cups crushed ice

4 strawberries, for garnish

1. Place 3 cups strawberries, condensed milk, lime juice, and vanilla in a blender and process until creamy and smooth.

2. Fill 4 glasses with crushed ice.

3. Pour strawberry mixture over the crushed ice. Garnish each glass with a strawberry, and serve immediately.

Gaucho-Style Erva-Mate Tea (*Chimarrão*)

A cula is a dried, hollow gourd, which serves as the cup for chimarrão, and the bomba is a metal straw with a filter at one end to keep out the finely ground tea. People drink chimarrão socially, and the cula is passed from one person to the next, after being refilled with hot water from a thermos.

INGREDIENTS | SERVES 1

1 *cula* (special gourd cup)

Enough erva-mate tea leaves to fill ⅔ of *cula*

1 cup warm water

1 *bomba* (metal straw)

1 thermos hot (not boiling) water, for refilling cula

1. Fill the *cula* ⅔ of the way full with the erva-mate. Place one hand over the mouth of the *cula*, and turn it on its side. Tap the cup so that the tea falls to the bottom. Carefully turn the cup so that it is at a 45-degree angle. There should now be a space between the tea and one side of the inside of the cup.

2. Pour enough warm water into that space to moisten the tea (about ½ cup) and wait 1 minute for the tea to absorb the water.

3. Pressing your thumb firmly over the nonfilter end of the *bomba*, place the filter end of the *bomba* into the space, then carefully give the *bomba* a quarter turn/twist toward the tea.

4. Pour enough hot water from the thermos to fill the *cula*. Drink the tea. Refill with hot water as needed.

Frozen Iced Tea (*Mate Gelado Batido*)

When it's really hot outside, this frozen iced tea will hit the spot.

INGREDIENTS | SERVES 3

2 tablespoons *chá mate* (toasted erva-mate tea leaves)

4 cups water

Ice

Juice of 1 lime

½ cup sweetened condensed milk (optional) or ⅓ cup sugar or to taste

1. Place the tea in a heatproof pitcher, carafe, or jar. Bring the water to a boil. Pour the hot water over the tea and set aside to steep until tea has a dark color. Strain and chill.

2. Place about 1 cup of ice in a blender. Add the lime juice and condensed milk (if using) or sugar. Pour in the tea. Blend until smooth and very frothy.

3. Immediately pour into glasses to serve, so that a layer of froth forms at the top of the glass.

Pineapple Tea (*Chá de Abacaxi*)

This sweet tea is the perfect accompaniment to a slice of cake. This is a great way to use the pineapple rind that is normally discarded when you cut up a pineapple.

INGREDIENTS | SERVES 6

1 pineapple
4–6 cups water
2 cinnamon sticks
6 whole cloves
1 cup sugar

Iced Pineapple Tea

To enjoy this tea on a hot summer day, prepare as usual, but after simmering the tea, strain it into a jar or glass pitcher and chill. Place the cold tea in a blender with some ice and a few mint leaves. Blend until slushy and serve.

1. Cut off the top and the bottom of the pineapple and discard.

2. Stand the pineapple upright. Use a knife to slice off the pineapple rind in strips, cutting from top to bottom. Place the strips of pineapple rind in a pot and cover with water. Cut the pineapple into cubes, removing the core. Add several cubes of pineapple to the water and reserve the rest.

3. Add cinnamon sticks and cloves to the water. Add sugar and bring to a low simmer over medium-low heat for 10–15 minutes.

4. Remove from heat and serve hot. (Remove rind, cinnamon sticks, and cloves before serving.)

Milk with Coffee (*Pingado*)

Pingado is a particular Brazilian form of café au lait. Pingado tends to be more milk than coffee (it should be caramel in color). For some reason, the pingado is served in a wide glass, rather than a mug.

INGREDIENTS | SERVES 3

4 tablespoons freshly ground coffee beans
3 teaspoons sugar, divided
1½ cups milk

1. Brew the coffee normally, and sweeten with 2 teaspoons sugar. Keep coffee hot.

2. Heat the milk and remaining sugar in a small saucepan over low heat until steaming. Do not boil.

3. Divide the hot milk between 2 glasses. Add coffee to desired color (light or dark caramel), up to a fifty-fifty mix. Serve warm.

Creamy Hot Chocolate (*Chocolate Quente Cremoso*)

Brazilian-style hot chocolate tends to be extra creamy and thick with a touch of cinnamon, the perfect vehicle for dipping churros (doughnut sticks).

INGREDIENTS | SERVES 2

2 cups milk

4 tablespoons sugar

3 tablespoons cocoa powder

1 tablespoon cornstarch

¼ teaspoon salt

1 cinnamon stick

½ cup heavy cream

½ teaspoon vanilla

Whipped cream

1. Place the milk, sugar, cocoa powder, cornstarch, and salt in a blender, and process until smooth.

2. Pour the mixture into a small saucepan. Add the cinnamon stick and heat mixture over medium-low heat, stirring constantly, until it comes to a simmer and thickens.

3. Remove from heat and discard cinnamon stick. Stir in the cream and the vanilla until smooth.

4. Serve warm, with a dollop of whipped cream.

Mulled Hot Caramel (*Quentão*)

This spiced alcoholic drink is a popular winter treat. Quentão is something like mulled cider, but the first and most important ingredient is caramelized sugar.

INGREDIENTS | SERVES 6

1½ cups sugar

2 cups water

2" piece fresh ginger, peeled and diced

1 lime, sliced into rounds

1 orange, sliced

2 cinnamon sticks

6 whole cloves

4 cups *cachaça* or red wine

1 apple, diced

1. Place the sugar in a medium saucepan and heat over medium heat until sugar melts and caramelizes (swirling pan to stir) to a golden brown.

2. Add the water, ginger, lime, orange, cinnamon, and cloves, and bring to a simmer. Simmer for 5 minutes.

3. Add the *cachaça* or wine and diced apple. Simmer for 5 minutes, then turn heat down to low. Keep warm until ready to serve.

Frozen Coconut Cocktail (*Batida de Coco*)

Batidas are cocktails made with cachaça *(a Brazilian white rum–like spirit),
which is blended with tropical fruit and sugar and served chilled or over ice.*

INGREDIENTS | SERVES 4

1 (13.5-ounce) can coconut milk

1 (14-ounce) can sweetened condensed milk

¾ cup grated fresh or frozen coconut

1½ cups *cachaça* or vodka

1 cup crushed ice (optional)

1. Place all of the ingredients except for the ice in a blender and process until smooth.

2. Chill mixture and serve very cold, or add the ice to the blender and process until smooth.

Guava Smoothie (*Vitamina de Goiaba*)

If you are lucky enough to find fresh guavas, process the whole fruit (skin included) in the blender with the other ingredients to save time, then strain the mixture to remove the seeds.

INGREDIENTS | SERVES 4

5 ripe (soft) guava fruits, or 1½ cups (frozen) guava pulp

1 (14-ounce) can sweetened condensed milk

1 cup orange juice

½ cup cold water

Juice of 1 lime

1 cup crushed ice (optional)

1. Place all of the ingredients except ice in a blender and process until smooth.

2. Chill mixture until ready to serve. If using ice, blend ice into mixture just before serving.

Strawberry Caipirinha with a Tangerine Popsicle
(*Caipilé de Morongo e Tangerina*)

This cocktail is a fun but grown-up combination of the famous caipirinha cocktail with the addition of a picolé, or fruit popsicle. (Caipirinha plus picolé = caipilé.)

INGREDIENTS | SERVES 1

½ lime, cut into 8 pieces

6 strawberries, stems removed

1½ tablespoons sugar

Ice cubes

¼ cup vodka or *cachaça*

1 tangerine popsicle

Tangerine Popsicle (*Picolé de Tangerina*)

Peel 8–10 tangerines and place them in the blender. Add 4–6 tablespoons of simple syrup (1 cup sugar plus 1 cup water, simmered until sugar dissolves and cooled), and the juice of 1 or 2 limes (to taste). Process until smooth. Strain mixture and pour into 6 popsicle molds. Freeze.

1. Place the lime pieces and strawberries in the bottom of an old-fashioned glass. Add the sugar, and "muddle" the fruit with the sugar using a pestle.

2. Add the ice cubes, slightly overfilling the glass.

3. Slowly pour the vodka or *cachaça* over the ice. Stir well, until the ice settles into the glass and melts a bit.

4. Place the popsicle upside down in the glass and serve immediately.

Brazilian Limeade (*Limonada Suíça*)

Brazilian limeade differs slightly from other versions because the lime is left unpeeled, adding extra flavor. This tasty limeade does not keep well, since the rind becomes a bit bitter over time, so enjoy immediately.

INGREDIENTS | SERVES 4

5 Mexican limes, washed and quartered, seeds and pith removed

¼ cup sweetened condensed milk

⅓ cup sugar

4 cups water, divided

1 cup crushed ice

Lime slices, for garnish

1. Place the lime quarters in a blender with the condensed milk, sugar, and 1 cup water.

2. Blend until smooth. Add remaining water and ice and blend until smooth.

3. Strain mixture into glasses or a serving pitcher. Serve immediately, garnished with lime slices.

CHAPTER 19

Fusion Cuisine
(*Cozinha de Fusão*)

Pizza with Chicken and Hearts of Palm
(*Pizza de Frango com Palmito*)

Brazilians love pizza, and tend to pile all kinds of exotic toppings onto their pies. This combination of creamy chicken and hearts of palm is very typically Brazilian and quite tasty on pizza.

INGREDIENTS | SERVES 6

2 teaspoons active dry yeast

1 teaspoon sugar

½ cup warm milk

3½ cups all-purpose flour

1 teaspoon salt

3 tablespoons olive oil, divided

1 large egg

½ cup diced onion

1 tomato, seeded and diced

1 (14-ounce) jar hearts of palm, drained and chopped

½ teaspoon salt

½ teaspoon freshly ground black pepper

1 tablespoon cornstarch

½ cup chicken broth

1 cup shredded poached or roasted chicken breast

2 tablespoons cream cheese

1 cup grated mozzarella cheese

1 teaspoon dried oregano

1 tablespoon minced fresh parsley

Sliced green olives (optional)

1. Mix the yeast and sugar with the warm milk and set aside for 5 minutes. Place 3 cups of flour and the salt in a large bowl. Add 2 tablespoons olive oil, egg, and yeast mixture and mix until smooth. Knead dough, adding more flour if needed, until smooth and elastic. Cover and set aside to rise in a warm place for about an hour.

2. Place remaining 1 tablespoon olive oil in a large skillet. Add the onion and cook over medium-low heat until soft, about 5–8 minutes. Add the tomato, hearts of palm, salt, and pepper, and cook until the liquid has evaporated and tomato is soft, about 5 minutes.

3. Add cornstarch and stir well. Add the chicken broth and cook until mixture has thickened, about 3–5 minutes. Remove from heat. Stir in the shredded chicken and the cream cheese. Set aside to cool.

4. Preheat oven to 450°F. Roll out the dough into a 14" circle on a floured surface and place on a large round oiled pizza pan. Bake crust until it just starts to crisp and is pulling away from the sides of the pan, about 10 minutes.

5. Remove crust from the oven. Spread the chicken mixture over the pizza and top with the mozzarella cheese. Sprinkle with oregano and parsley, and olives, if using.

6. Return pizza to oven until cheese is melted and lightly browned. Remove and serve warm.

Gluten-Free Cheese Bread Pizza
(*Pizza com Massa de Pão de Queijo*)

Pão de queijo are gooey cheese rolls made with tapioca flour, eggs, cheese, and oil.
This same dough makes a very tasty pizza crust, which happens to be gluten-free.

INGREDIENTS | SERVES 6

½ cups milk or buttermilk

4 tablespoons butter

¼ cup vegetable oil

½ teaspoon salt

2 cups sweet tapioca starch (*polvilho de mandioca doce*)

2 large eggs

1 cup grated farmer cheese (or a combination of Monterey jack and Cheddar)

¼ cup grated Parmesan cheese

1 cup grated mozzarella cheese

¼ cup chopped ham

¼ cup chopped sun-dried tomatoes

4–6 thin slices of tomato

4–6 thin slices of onion

¼ cup sliced olives

1 teaspoon dried oregano

1 tablespoon chopped fresh basil leaves

1. Preheat oven to 400°F. Lightly oil a 14" pizza pan.

2. Place the milk or buttermilk, butter, vegetable oil, and salt in a medium saucepan. Bring to a simmer over medium heat, stirring constantly.

3. In a large bowl, place the tapioca starch. Pour the hot milk mixture into the bowl and mix well with a wooden spoon.

4. Stir in the eggs and the farmer and Parmesan cheeses and mix well. Knead mixture to form a smooth dough, adding more tapioca starch if mixture is too sticky.

5. Roll out the dough into a 14" circle on a countertop dusted with tapioca starch, or simply press it into the oiled pizza pan.

6. Bake the dough for 20 minutes, or until lightly browned, then remove from the oven.

7. Add toppings: mozzarella, ham, chopped sun-dried tomatoes, tomato slices, onion slices, olives, oregano, basil, or toppings of choice.

8. Return pizza to oven until cheese is melted.

Fried Pizza (*Pizza Frita*)

Brazilian cooks use a variety of different cooking techniques that sometimes cross over from one tradition to another. This delicious fried pizza is an example: The dough is similar to the dough for pastéis, but the pastries are filled with traditional pizza ingredients.

INGREDIENTS | SERVES 3

2 teaspoons active dry yeast

1 cup warm water, divided

1 teaspoon sugar

3½ cups all-purpose flour

1 teaspoon salt

2 tablespoons vegetable oil

1 tablespoon *cachaça* or rum

¾ cup tomato sauce

1 teaspoon oregano

3 cups grated mozzarella cheese

Vegetable oil, for frying

Skillet Pizza (*Pizza na Frigideira*)

For speed and convenience, cook the pizza in a large skillet. Prepare and roll out the dough as directed in this recipe. Heat a 12" nonstick skillet with 2 tablespoons of oil over medium heat. Place the dough in the skillet and cook until the bottom of the crust is lightly browned. Remove from skillet, flip the crust over, and add the toppings of your choice to the side of the dough that was cooked. Cook pizza until bottom of crust is browned and cheese is melted.

1. Sprinkle the yeast over ½ cup warm water mixed with the sugar and set aside for 5 minutes.

2. Place the flour in the bowl of a standing mixer fitted with the dough hook attachment. Add the salt and mix briefly. Add yeast/water mixture, oil, and *cachaça* or rum. Add the remaining ½ cup of warm water slowly, while kneading, until mixture forms a smooth ball (you may not need all of the water). Knead for 3–5 minutes. Cover dough and set aside to rise in a warm place for 1½ hours.

3. Divide the dough into 3 pieces. On a floured surface, roll out each piece into a very thin 10" circle. Place ¼ cup of tomato sauce in the middle of each circle, sprinkle with ⅓ of the oregano, and make a mound of 1 cup of mozzarella cheese on top of the sauce. Fold the dough over the filling to form a semicircle, trim edges, and seal firmly. Repeat with remaining pieces of dough.

4. Heat several inches of vegetable oil in a large pot to 350°F. Fry each pizza until golden brown, turning once or twice.

5. Let cool for several minutes before serving.

Romeo and Juliet Dessert Pizza (*Pizza de Goiabada e Queijo*)

Dessert pizzas are very popular in Brazil. The pairing of guava paste with queijo coalho, a salty white cheese, is called Romeo and Juliet (Romeo is the cheese and Juliet is the guava paste).

INGREDIENTS | SERVES 6

2 teaspoons active dry yeast

⅓ cup warm water

1 tablespoon sugar

2 cups all-purpose flour

1 teaspoon salt

1 tablespoon oil

2 tablespoons rum or *cachaça*

1 cup grated halloumi cheese or another firm, white, salty cheese

6 ounces guava paste, cut into small cubes

Banana Pizza (*Pizza de Banana*)

Pizza topped with bananas, cinnamon, and mozzarella cheese is another favorite dessert pizza, inspired by a traditional dessert of fried bananas and cheese called *Cartola* (see recipe in Chapter 12). Prepare the pizza dough in the same way as in this recipe. Spread dough lightly with ¼ cup condensed milk, and sprinkle with grated mozzarella cheese. Top cheese with thin slices of banana and sprinkle the bananas with 3 tablespoons brown sugar, 1 teaspoon cinnamon, and ¼ cup mini chocolate chips. Bake until bananas are caramelized and cheese is melted.

1. In a small bowl, sprinkle the yeast over ½ cup warm water mixed with the sugar and set aside for 5 minutes.

2. Place the flour in the bowl of a standing mixer fitted with the dough hook attachment. Add the salt and mix briefly. Add yeast/water mixture, oil, and rum or *cachaça*. Knead for 3–5 minutes, adding more flour if dough it too sticky. Cover dough and set aside to rise for 1½ hours.

3. Preheat the oven to 450°F. Roll out the dough on a floured surface into a 13" circle. Brush a little water around the edge of the dough and roll the edge toward the inside to form a small border. Press to seal. Place dough on a baking sheet (or directly on a pizza stone in the oven). Bake pizza for 8–10 minutes or until crust is puffed and lightly browned.

4. Remove crust from oven and spread the cheese over the dough. Scatter the guava paste over the cheese, or arrange it into decorative forms, such as a spiral or stripes.

5. Return pizza to oven until cheese is melted and lightly browned. Slice and serve warm.

Ham and Cheese Swiss Crepes (*Crepe Suíço*)

These stuffed crepes are very popular at Brazilian fairs and carnivals. At home, you can use a waffle maker to make these. Fill crepes/waffles with any filling of your choice.

INGREDIENTS | SERVES 4

2 large eggs
4 tablespoons butter, melted
1 cup milk
1½ cups all-purpose flour
¾ teaspoon salt
1 teaspoon baking powder
8 slices mozzarella cheese
4 teaspoons mayonnaise
8 slices smoked deli ham
4 very thin slices tomato

1. Place the eggs, butter, milk, flour, salt, and baking powder in a blender and blend until smooth.

2. Preheat the waffle maker. Once it is hot, pour about ¼ cup of batter into the bottom of the waffle maker. Top with 2 slices of cheese, 1 teaspoon mayonnaise (spread over the cheese), 2 slices of ham, and 1 slice of tomato. Pour another ¼ cup of batter on top of the fillings (don't worry if they are not completely covered). Repeat with the rest of the batter and fillings.

3. Close the waffle maker and cook until waffle is browned on both sides.

4. Serve warm.

Kiwi Sakeirinha (*Caipirinha de Saquê com Kiwi*)

Kiwi is a popular choice of fruit for this cocktail and gives it a pretty green color, but pineapple, lime, and strawberry are also very good.

INGREDIENTS | SERVES 1

1 kiwi, peeled and cut into cubes (reserve 1 slice for garnish)
1½ tablespoons cane sugar or regular white sugar
Ice cubes
1½ ounces sake

1. Place the kiwi in the bottom of an old-fashioned glass. Add the sugar and muddle the fruit and sugar together with a pestle.

2. Fill the glass with ice cubes. Pour the sake over the ice and stir well.

3. Serve with a stirrer and a slice of kiwi as garnish.

Hearts of Palm Fried Pies (*Pastel de Palmito*)

Brazilian pastels (pastéis) are fried pastries, usually rectangular in shape, with a thin crispy crust that is similar to a Chinese wonton.

INGREDIENTS | SERVES 9

3½ cups plus 2 tablespoons all-purpose flour, divided

4 tablespoons vegetable shortening, softened

1½ teaspoons salt, divided

1 tablespoon rum or *cachaça*

1 teaspoon vinegar

1 large egg

8–10 tablespoons water

2 tablespoon butter

1 small onion, peeled and minced

1 (14-ounce) jar hearts of palm, drained and chopped

½ teaspoon freshly ground black pepper

2 tablespoons tomato paste

¾ cup milk or heavy cream

2 tablespoons cream cheese

3 tablespoons grated Parmesan cheese

Vegetable oil, for frying

1. Place 3½ cups of flour in a large bowl. Add vegetable shortening, 1 teaspoon of salt, rum or *cachaça*, and vinegar.

2. In a small bowl, lightly beat the egg with 8 tablespoons warm water and add to flour mixture. Mix everything together, kneading mixture with your hands until you have a smooth dough. Add more water if needed, or more flour if dough is too sticky. Wrap in plastic wrap and refrigerate until ready to use.

3. Place the butter in a medium skillet over medium-low heat and cook the onion until soft, about 5–8 minutes. Add the hearts of palm, ½ teaspoon salt, pepper, and tomato paste and cook for 3–4 minutes.

4. Add 2 tablespoons flour and mix well. Add the milk or cream and simmer until mixture is thick and creamy. Remove from heat and stir in the cream cheese and Parmesan. Let cool.

5. Roll out the dough on a floured surface into a large (21") square about ¼" thick. Let dough rest for 5 minutes.

6. Cut dough into 7" squares (a pizza cutter works well for this). Place 2 tablespoons of filling on each. Brush a little water on the edges of each dough square and fold in half, pressing the seal closed with a fork.

7. Heat vegetable oil to 350°F in a deep skillet. Fry pastels (*pastéis*) in batches, letting one side turn brown before flipping. Remove pastels with a slotted spoon and drain on paper towels. Serve warm.

Deep-Fried Philadelphia Sushi Roll (*Hot Filadelfia*)

Tropical fruits, quinoa, mayonnaise, and potato sticks are some of the more unusual ingredients that might appear in your sushi roll at a Japanese–Latin American fusion restaurant. This classic Brazilian-Japanese sushi roll is very popular and fun to make at home.

INGREDIENTS | MAKES 24

5 tablespoons rice vinegar
1 teaspoon salt, divided
1½ tablespoons sugar
2 cups sushi rice
3 cups water, divided
3 sheets seaweed for sushi (nori)
1 (½-pound) salmon fillet, cut into thin strips
1 cup cream cheese
¼ cup chopped scallions
1 large egg
2 cups all-purpose flour
½ teaspoon baking powder
2 cups panko or very fine bread crumbs
Vegetable oil, for frying

1. Place the vinegar, ½ teaspoon salt, and sugar in a small saucepan and heat over low heat until sugar is dissolved. Remove from heat and let cool.

2. Rinse the rice with water until water runs clear. Place the rice in a heavy saucepan or rice cooker and add 2 cups of water. Bring to a simmer over medium heat, reduce heat to low, cover, and cook for 15–20 minutes, or until water is absorbed. Remove from heat and leave covered for 5 minutes.

3. Transfer the rice to a shallow bowl and toss gently with the vinegar/sugar mixture.

4. Place a piece of seaweed (shiny side down) onto a bamboo mat for rolling sushi. Spread a thin layer of rice over the seaweed, leaving 2" at the top (the long side) free of rice.

5. Place a strip of salmon down the center of the rice (parallel to the long side). Place a strip of cream cheese alongside the salmon. Sprinkle some of the scallions along the length of the salmon and cream cheese.

6. Roll up the sushi tightly with the bamboo mat. Moisten the top of the seaweed with water to help seal and trim off any excess. Repeat with remaining 2 pieces of seaweed.

7. In a shallow bowl, whisk together the egg, 1 cup of cold water, flour, remaining ½ teaspoon salt, and baking powder until you have a smooth paste. Dip each sushi roll into the paste, letting the excess drip off, and dip the rolls into the bread crumbs to coat.

8. Heat 3" inches of vegetable oil to 350°F in a wok or deep skillet that is wide enough to fit the rolls. Fry the rolls one at a time until golden brown.

9. Use a sharp knife moistened with water to cut each roll into 8 pieces. Serve immediately while still warm.

German-Style Pineapple Cake (*Cuca de Abacaxi*)

This cake is a cross between pineapple upside-down cake and coffee cake, and it's great for breakfast or dessert.

INGREDIENTS | SERVES 10

1 small pineapple, peeled, cored, and cut into small cubes

1¼ cups sugar, divided

1 cinnamon stick

1 teaspoon salt, divided

3¾ cups all-purpose flour, divided

1 teaspoon ground cinnamon

4 tablespoons cold butter

1 tablespoon active dry yeast

1½ cups warm milk

2 large eggs

4 tablespoons vegetable oil

1 teaspoon vanilla

1. Butter and flour a 9" or 10" springform pan.

2. Place the pineapple, ½ cup sugar, cinnamon stick, and ½ teaspoon salt in a large saucepan. Cook over low heat until pineapple is golden brown and syrup is thick, about 5 minutes. Remove cinnamon stick.

3. In a small bowl, mix ¾ cup flour, ½ cup sugar, pinch of salt, and 1 teaspoon ground cinnamon. Mix in cold butter using a pastry cutter or your fingers, until mixture is crumbly.

4. In the bowl of a standing mixer, sprinkle the yeast over the warm milk and set aside for 5 minutes. Add the eggs and remaining ¼ cup sugar and mix well. Add the vegetable oil, vanilla, remaining ½ teaspoon salt, and remaining 3 cups flour and mix until smooth. Set aside in a warm place to rise for 1 hour.

5. Preheat oven to 350°F. Spread yeasted batter into prepared pan. Top with pineapples (and syrup) and sprinkle cinnamon-crumb mixture on top.

6. Bake for 35–40 minutes, or until topping is browned and bubbly and cake springs back lightly to the touch.

Brazilian-Style Stroganoff (*Estrogonofe*)

Serve Brazilian-Style Stroganoff topped with potato sticks for crunch and with white rice on the side.

INGREDIENTS | SERVES 8

2 pounds beef (filet mignon) or chicken breasts

1½ teaspoons salt

1 teaspoon freshly ground black pepper

4 tablespoons all-purpose flour, divided

3 tablespoons butter, divided

1 cup sliced mushrooms

2 tablespoons Worcestershire sauce

1 small onion, peeled and finely chopped

2 cloves garlic, minced

⅓ cup ketchup

3 tablespoons Dijon mustard

2½ cups heavy cream

Potato sticks, for garnish

1. Cut the meat against the grain into small strips, about ½" × 2". Season the meat with the salt and pepper, and toss with 3 tablespoons of flour until well coated.

2. Melt 1 tablespoon butter in a stockpot over medium-high heat. Add the meat, in batches if necessary, and cook until browned on all sides. If using steak, cook to desired doneless. If using chicken, cook until chicken strips are cooked through. Remove meat from pot and set aside on a plate.

3. Add another tablespoon of butter to the same pot. Add the mushrooms and Worcestershire sauce and cook until liquid evaporates and mushrooms are lightly browned, about 5 minutes. Remove mushrooms from pot and set aside with the meat.

4. Add the remaining tablespoon of butter to the pot with the onions and cook until onions are soft, about 5–8 minutes. Add the garlic and cook for 1 minute. Add the meat, mushrooms, ketchup, mustard, and remaining tablespoon of flour and mix well.

5. Add the cream and cook over medium-low heat until mixture simmers and thickens, about 3–4 minutes. Taste for seasoning.

6. Serve garnished with potato sticks.

Manioc Gnocchi with Brazil Nut Sauce
(*Nhoque de Mandioca*)

A classic Italian dish gets a makeover with Brazilian ingredients. Manioc is an important staple in the Brazilian diet, and it adds a subtle but unique flavor to the gnocchi.

INGREDIENTS | SERVES 8

1 pound manioc, peeled, inner fibrous core removed

1 tablespoon butter

2 tablespoons grated Parmesan cheese

1 large egg

1½ teaspoons salt, divided

1 cup all-purpose flour

½ cup coarsely chopped Brazil nuts

2 cups vegetable broth

⅓ cup lemon juice

2 teaspoons dried oregano, divided

1 teaspoon freshly ground black pepper

1 small onion, peeled and minced

1 tablespoon olive oil

2 cloves garlic, minced

1 cup thinly sliced collard greens or kale

2 tablespoons cornstarch

1. Cook the manioc in boiling salted water until very tender when pierced with a fork. Drain, and pass manioc through a potato ricer into a large bowl.

2. Add the butter, Parmesan, egg, 1 teaspoon of salt, and ½ cup flour to the manioc, and mix well. Knead in the remaining flour a little bit at a time, until mixture comes together into a soft dough.

3. On a floured surface, roll out the dough into several 1"-thick ropes, and cut the ropes into 1" pieces to create gnocchi.

4. Bring a pot of salted water to a boil and cook the gnocchi, in batches if necessary, until they float to the surface. Remove them with a slotted spoon to a lightly oiled bowl and set aside.

5. Place the nuts in a microwave-safe bowl, cover them with water, and microwave them for 1 minute on high to soften. Drain and add them to a blender with the vegetable broth, lemon juice, 1 teaspoon oregano, remaining ½ teaspoon salt, and pepper. Blend until smooth.

6. In a medium skillet, sauté the onion in the olive oil until soft, about 5 minutes. Add the garlic and kale and cook for 1 minute. Add the cornstarch and mix well. Add the Brazil nut sauce, bring to a simmer, and cook for several minutes until heated through.

7. Serve the gnocchi with the sauce, and garnish with remaining oregano.

Stuffed Gnocchi (*Nhoque Recheado*)

Bolinhos (spherical foods) are everywhere in Brazilian cuisine and are often stuffed with a filling, such as an olive or a piece of cheese. So it's natural that Brazilians enjoy these large Italian-style gnocchi filled with seasoned ground beef.

INGREDIENTS | SERVES 6

1 tablespoon olive oil

½ cup minced onion

2 cloves garlic, peeled and minced

½ pound ground beef

1½ teaspoons salt, divided

2 tablespoons tomato paste

½ cup beef broth

1 pound potatoes, boiled and drained

2 tablespoons butter

½ cup grated Parmesan, divided

1 large egg

1 cup all-purpose flour

¼ cup butter, melted

2 cups tomato sauce

½ cup grated mozzarella cheese

1. Heat the olive oil in a medium skillet over medium heat. Add the onion and cook until soft, about 5–8 minutes. Add the garlic, ground beef, and 1 teaspoon salt and cook, stirring frequently, until beef is well browned. Stir in the tomato paste and the beef broth and simmer until most of the liquid has evaporated, about 5 minutes. Set aside to cool.

2. Pass the potatoes through a potato ricer into a large bowl.

3. Add 2 tablespoons butter, ¼ cup Parmesan, egg, remaining ½ teaspoon salt, and ½ cup flour to the potatoes and mix well. Knead in the remaining flour a little bit at a time, until mixture comes together into a soft dough.

4. Take golf ball–size pieces of dough with floured hands and roll into balls. Press an opening into each ball with your fingers and fill with 2 teaspoons of ground beef. Close dough over the filling and reshape. Set aside.

5. Bring a pot of salted water to a boil and cook the gnocchi, in batches if necessary, until they float to the surface. Remove them with a slotted spoon to a lightly oiled casserole dish. Preheat the oven to 350°F.

6. Drizzle the melted butter over the gnocchi. Spoon the tomato sauce over the gnocchi, and sprinkle the mozzarella and remaining Parmesan over the sauce.

7. Bake until cheese is melted and gnocchi are heated through.

Shrimp and Coconut Risotto
(*Risoto de Camarão à Moda Baiana*)

This tasty risotto is rich with the classic flavors of Bahian cuisine—shrimp, coconut, and dendê (palm) oil. If you can't find dendê, substitute ¼ cup olive oil mixed with 1 teaspoon annatto seed powder.

INGREDIENTS | SERVES 6

1 pound shrimp, cleaned

Juice of 1 lime

2 teaspoons salt, divided

2 teaspoons freshly ground black pepper, divided

4 tablespoons *dendê* oil, divided

½ cup minced onion

2 cloves garlic, minced

1 tomato, seeded and diced

1 medium orange bell pepper, seeded and chopped

2 cups Arborio rice

½ cup white wine

2½ cups vegetable stock

½ cup coconut milk

2 tablespoons cream cheese

1 scallion, chopped

2 tablespoons minced fresh cilantro

1. Place the shrimp in a bowl and toss with the lime juice, 1 teaspoon salt, and 1 teaspoon pepper.

2. Place 2 tablespoons of the oil in a heavy skillet over medium heat. Add the shrimp and sauté until shrimp turn pink. Remove shrimp from the skillet and set aside.

3. Add the onions to the same skillet and cook until soft, about 5–8 minutes. Add the garlic, tomato, bell pepper, ½ teaspoon salt, and ½ teaspoon pepper and cook until vegetables are soft and all of the liquid evaporates, about 6–8 minutes. Remove vegetables from skillet and set aside.

4. Add the remaining oil to the same skillet. Add the rice and cook for 2 minutes, stirring. Add the white wine and cook, stirring, until liquid is absorbed.

5. Add the vegetable stock ½ cup at a time and simmer over low heat, stirring, until liquid is absorbed. Add the coconut milk and stir until rice is creamy and most of the liquid is absorbed. Add the shrimp, the vegetables, and the cream cheese and stir well. Taste for seasoning and add remaining ½ teaspoon salt and pepper as needed.

6. Garnish with scallion and cilantro and serve.

Polenta Cakes with Sausage and Okra (*Angu com Quiabo*)

Angu is a creamed cornmeal dish, similar to polenta, that can be molded into round cakes, which are delicious topped with linguiça *sausage, tomatoes, and okra.*

INGREDIENTS | SERVES 6

4 ounces thick-cut bacon, cubed

2 cups chicken stock

1½ cups water

1 teaspoon salt, divided

1½ cups cornmeal

4 tablespoons butter, divided

2 tablespoons olive oil

½ pound *linguiça* or other smoked sausage, diced

1½ cups fresh or frozen okra, cut into ½" pieces

1 small onion, peeled and minced

2 cloves garlic, minced

2 medium tomatoes, seeded and diced

¼ cup chopped scallions

1. Place the bacon in a heavy saucepan and cook over medium heat until crispy. Remove bacon from saucepan and set aside.

2. Add the chicken stock, water, and ½ teaspoon salt to the same saucepan and bring to a boil. Slowly stir in the cornmeal. Cook over low heat, stirring constantly, until cornmeal mixture thickens and pulls away from the sides of the pot, about 30–40 minutes. Remove from heat, stir in 2 tablespoons butter, and chill until ready to use.

3. Add 2 tablespoons olive oil to a skillet and cook the sausage until browned. Remove sausage and set aside with the bacon.

4. Add the okra to the same skillet and sauté over medium heat until okra starts to brown at the edges. Remove okra from skillet and set aside on a plate lined with paper towels.

5. Add the onion to the same skillet and cook until soft and fragrant, about 5–8 minutes. Add the garlic and the tomato and cook until tomato is soft and most of the liquid has evaporated, about 5 minutes. Add scallions. Transfer vegetable mixture to a bowl, and add the sausage, bacon, okra, and remaining salt to taste. Set aside.

6. Shape the cornmeal mixture into 6 (1"-thick) patties. Add remaining 2 tablespoons butter to the same skillet. Cook the cornmeal patties until they are browned on each side and heated through. Spoon sausage and vegetable mixture over the patties and serve.

Black Forest Trifle (*Pavé Floresta Negra*)

Pavé is a wonderful Brazilian dessert—a cross between a trifle and tiramisu. This version of pavé is inspired by the flavors of a German black forest cake.

INGREDIENTS | SERVES 8

16 ounces bittersweet chocolate, chopped

12 ounces milk chocolate, chopped

3 cups heavy cream, divided

2 teaspoons vanilla, divided

Pinch of salt

1 (16-ounce) can dark sweet cherries in syrup

¼ cup sugar

¾ cup brandy or cherry liqueur

2 packages ladyfingers or Maria cookies (about 8 ounces)

Maraschino cherries, for decoration

½ cup chocolate chips or chocolate curls, for decoration

Chocolate Curls

Place 4 ounces of chopped semisweet chocolate and 1 tablespoon of vegetable shortening in a microwave-safe bowl. Microwave for 30 seconds, or until chocolate is melted. Spread chocolate onto a baking sheet. Place chocolate in the freezer until it's almost firm (if you press on it your finger should leave a slight mark). Remove from freezer and use a spatula to scrape chocolate into curls. If it breaks instead of curling, let it soften a bit. Place chocolate curls on a plate and refrigerate until ready to use.

1. Place the bittersweet and milk chocolates in a double boiler with 1½ cups cream and heat over medium-low heat until chocolate is melted. Remove from heat, stir in 1 teaspoon vanilla and a pinch of salt, and let cool, stirring occasionally.

2. Drain the cherries, reserving the syrup. Fold the cherries into the chocolate mixture.

3. Whip the remaining cream, adding the sugar gradually, until soft peaks form. Stir in remaining teaspoon vanilla. Chill until ready to use.

4. Lightly grease a 9" or 10" springform pan. In a small bowl, mix together the reserved cherry syrup and the brandy or cherry liqueur.

5. Place all of the cookies in a bowl and pour the syrup/brandy mixture over them. Line the bottom and sides of the pan with two-thirds of the moistened cookies.

6. Place half of the chocolate cherry mixture in the bottom of the pan. Top with half of the whipped cream. Make a layer with the remaining cookies. Spread the remaining chocolate mixture over the cookies, then top with the rest of the whipped cream. Decorate the top layer with maraschino cherries and chocolate chips or chocolate curls. Chill thoroughly before serving.

7. To serve, gently loosen and remove the ring of the springform pan.

CHAPTER 20

Holidays (*Feriados e Festas*)

Tuna and Vegetable Couscous Ring (*Cuscuz Paulista*)

This unusual and striking dish originated in São Paulo. This dish is not hard to make, but it has a very attractive presentation and is therefore often served at holiday meals and celebrations.

INGREDIENTS | SERVES 10

2 tablespoons butter

1 medium onion, peeled and finely diced

1 medium red bell pepper, seeded and diced

2 cloves garlic, minced

1 (14-ounce) jar hearts of palm, drained and sliced crosswise into rings

1 cup frozen peas

1 cup frozen corn

½ cup chopped green olives

¼ cup diced scallions

1 teaspoon salt

1 teaspoon fresh ground black pepper

1 (12-ounce) can tuna fish, drained

½ cup tomato sauce

1½ cups chicken stock

2 (18-ounce) tubes precooked polenta, cut into cubes

1 plum tomato, sliced

6 parsley sprigs

2 large hard-cooked eggs, peeled and sliced

1. Melt the butter in a stockpot over medium heat. Add the onion and bell peppers and cook until onion is soft, about 5–8 minutes.

2. Add the garlic, hearts of palm (reserve ¼ cup for decoration), peas, corn, green olives, scallions, salt, and pepper and sauté for 3–4 minutes, stirring constantly.

3. Add the tuna and the tomato sauce and cook for 2–3 minutes.

4. Add the chicken stock and bring to a simmer. Add the polenta cubes and cook, stirring constantly, until mixture thickens and liquid is absorbed, about 5–10 minutes. The mixture should be thick enough that it pulls away from the sides of the pot.

5. Lightly oil the inside of a ring mold. Line the mold decoratively with the reserved hearts of palm slices, tomato slices, parsley sprigs, and sliced hard-cooked eggs.

6. Spoon the cornmeal mixture into the mold (covering the decorative garnishes). Use a spatula to press and pack the cornmeal down evenly into the mold. Chill the mold for 1 hour.

7. When ready to serve, place the serving plate upside down over the mold. Invert the mold and plate, and knock mold lightly with your hands to loosen the *cuscuz*. Gently lift mold off of the *cuscuz* and serve.

Holiday Roast Stuffed Turkey
(*Peru Recheado Assado com Molho de Cachaça*)

Turkey is called peru *in Portuguese, presumably because the bird is native to the Americas. Roast turkey, often stuffed with* farofa, *is the centerpiece of the Christmas Eve meal in Brazil.*

INGREDIENTS | SERVES 10

1 (10–12-pound) turkey
2 oranges, halved
2 limes, halved
1½ gallons water
1 cup kosher salt
1 cup orange juice
1 recipe Toasted Manioc (*Farofa*) Stuffing (see sidebar)

3 large onions, peeled and quartered
6 medium carrots, peeled and cut into 1" pieces
4 medium potatoes, peeled and quartered
8 tablespoons butter, divided
½ cup *cachaça*
2½ cups chicken stock
4 tablespoons all-purpose flour
Salt and pepper, to taste

1. Place turkey in a large zip-top bag with oranges, limes, water, kosher salt, and orange juice. Marinate the turkey in the refrigerator overnight.

2. Preheat oven to 350°F. Remove turkey from marinade and rinse well. Pat the turkey dry and fill the cavity with half of the stuffing.

3. Line the bottom of a roasting pan with onions, carrots, and potatoes. Place turkey breast side up on top of the vegetables. Brush the skin with 2 tablespoons butter. Loosely cover with foil and roast for 2 hours. Remove foil, brush with 2 tablespoons butter, and raise oven temperature to 425°F. Roast turkey for 1 hour more, until the temperature in the middle of the thigh reaches 165°F.

4. Transfer turkey and vegetables to a serving platter, with the remaining stuffing. Set aside.

5. Place the roasting pan over medium heat. Add the *cachaça* and cook, scraping the bottom of the pan with a wooden spoon. Add the stock and bring to a simmer.

6. Place remaining butter in a large saucepan. Whisk flour into the butter. Strain the stock mixture into the saucepan. Bring gravy to a simmer and cook, stirring, until gravy thickens. Season with salt and pepper.

Toasted Manioc (*Farofa*) Stuffing

Melt 1 stick of butter in a large skillet over medium heat. Add 8 ounces sliced smoked sausage and 6 ounces diced bacon and cook until bacon is crispy. Add 1 cup minced onion and cook until soft. Add 4 minced cloves garlic, 1 cup golden raisins, and 1 cup cashews and cook for 2 minutes. Mix 4 cups manioc meal with 4 eggs and ½ cup chopped parsley and add to the skillet. Cook until light brown. Season with salt and pepper to taste.

Roasted Pork Tenderloin with Prunes
(*Lombo de Porco Assado com Molho de Ameixa Seca*)

Roast pork is a popular main course for festive holiday meals, especially during Christmas and New Year's.

INGREDIENTS | SERVES 8

1 (2-pound) pork tenderloin
1 teaspoon kosher salt
1 teaspoon freshly ground black pepper
2 tablespoons butter
3 tablespoons balsamic vinegar
1½ cups prune juice
2 tablespoons brown sugar
½ cup dried plums (prunes)
½ cup golden raisins

1. Season the pork tenderloin with salt and pepper. Preheat the oven to 400°F.

2. Melt the butter in a large skillet over medium-high heat. Place the tenderloin in the skillet and brown on all sides. Place the pork in a roasting pan.

3. In a small bowl, whisk together the vinegar, prune juice, and brown sugar. Pour mixture over the pork. Cover pan with foil.

   Roast pork for 20 minutes, then remove foil and roast for 10 minutes more, or until internal temperature reaches 145°F–150°F. Remove from oven and transfer pork to a cutting board.

4. Transfer the juices and marinade to a medium saucepan. Add the prunes and the raisins and simmer over medium heat until liquid is reduced by half.

5. Slice the pork into medallions and arrange on a serving platter. Drizzle prune sauce over the sliced pork and serve.

Christmas Rice (*Arroz de Natal*)

This savory rice with nuts and raisins is a typical festive side dish for the big late-night holiday meal on Christmas Eve and on New Year's Eve.

INGREDIENTS | SERVES 8

2 tablespoons butter

¼ cup minced onion

2 cloves garlic, minced

½ cup coarsely chopped walnuts

½ cup chopped roasted salted cashews

½ cup roasted salted peanuts

¾ cup raisins

6 ounces smoked ham, diced

2½ cups white rice

½ teaspoon ground black pepper

4 cups chicken stock

¼ cup chopped fresh parsley

¼ cup chopped scallions

Molded Rice

For special occasions, rice dishes are often molded into a ring shape. Generously oil a ring mold with vegetable oil. Once the rice is cooked, just after stirring in half of the parsley and scallions, spoon the rice into the ring mold, packing it down firmly and evenly with a spatula. Place serving platter upside down over the ring mold, and then flip the mold and plate over. Give the bottom of the mold a few sharp raps to loosen the rice, and lift mold off of rice. Garnish with remaining scallions and parsley.

1. Melt the butter in a stockpot over medium heat. Add the onion and cook until soft, about 5–8 minutes. Add the garlic, nuts, raisins, and ham and sauté for 3–4 minutes. Add the rice and pepper and stir for 2–3 minutes.

2. Add the chicken stock and bring to a simmer, stirring frequently. Reduce heat to low, cover, and simmer until rice is cooked and liquid is absorbed, about 20 minutes.

3. Fluff rice with a fork, stirring in half of the parsley and scallions.

4. Place rice in a serving bowl and garnish with remaining parsley and scallions.

Good Luck Lentil Soup (*Sopa de Lentilha*)

Brazilians eat lentils on New Year's (Réveillon) for good luck, a tradition brought over from Italy.

INGREDIENTS | SERVES 6

3 pieces bacon, chopped

6 ounces *linguiça* or similar sausage (*chouriço*, Italian-style sausage), sliced

1 medium onion, peeled and finely chopped

2 cloves garlic, minced

1 bay leaf

1 medium tomato, seeded and chopped

2 tablespoons tomato paste

½ teaspoon salt

1 teaspoon freshly ground black pepper

1½ cups lentils

4 cups chicken or vegetable stock

1 cup thinly sliced kale or collard greens (optional)

Chopped parsley, for garnish

1. Place the bacon in a stockpot over medium heat and cook until crispy. Remove bacon and reserve. Add the sliced sausage to the pot and sauté until browned.

2. Add the onion and cook until soft, about 5 minutes. Add the garlic, bay leaf, tomato, tomato paste, salt, and pepper and cook until tomato is soft and liquid has evaporated, about 5–7 minutes.

3. Add the lentils and stir for 1 minute. Add the stock and bring to a simmer. Lower heat and cover. Simmer until lentils are tender, about 30–40 minutes.

4. Transfer half of the lentils to a blender and process until smooth. Add them back to the pot. Stir in the greens and cook for 2–3 minutes.

5. Serve soup warm, garnished with reserved bacon and parsley.

Panettone with Truffle Filling (*Panetone Trufeado*)

Panettone is a yeasted sweet bread with candied fruit. Brazilians like to enhance store-bought panettone by adding a creamy chocolate ganache filling and decorative icing.

INGREDIENTS | SERVES 8

1 store-bought standard size (about 1.6 pounds) panettone

16 ounces milk or dark chocolate (or mixed), chopped

1½ cups heavy cream

1 teaspoon instant espresso powder

1 teaspoon vanilla

1 cup coarsely chopped walnuts, divided

1 cup raisins or other dried fruit (cranberries, cherries, chopped apricots), divided

1. Slice the rounded top off of the panettone horizontally and reserve. Use a knife to cut out the middle of the panettone, leaving 1" thickness on the bottom and sides. Crumble the cake that was removed from the center and set aside.

2. Place the chocolate in a heatproof bowl. Place the cream and instant espresso powder in a small saucepan and heat over medium-low heat until almost boiling.

3. Pour hot cream/espresso mixture over the chocolate and set aside for 2 minutes. Stir very gently with a spatula, just until mixture is smooth and glossy. If chocolate does not melt, place mixture over a pot of simmering water (do not let bowl touch the water) until all of the chocolate melts. Stir in the vanilla. Reserve 1 cup of the chocolate mixture and set aside.

4. Mix the remaining chocolate ganache with the reserved cake crumbs, half of the walnuts, and half of the dried fruit. Use cake/chocolate mixture to fill the cavity in the panettone.

5. Replace top of panettone and place cake in a plastic bakery bag. Drizzle reserved chocolate over the panettone and garnish with remaining fruits and nuts.

6. Chill panettone for 2–3 hours in the refrigerator. Slice vertically into wedge-shaped slices to serve.

Panettone Trifle (*Pavé de Panetone*)

Serve this delicious merengue-topped trifle on New Year's Eve.
It's a great way to use up leftover panettone from Christmas.

INGREDIENTS | SERVES 10

1 store-bought panettone

1 cup sweetened condensed milk

1 cup brandy

3 teaspoons vanilla, divided

4 egg yolks

¼ cup cornstarch

2 tablespoons cocoa powder

3 cups milk

¼ teaspoon salt

¾ cup sugar, divided

3 tablespoons butter

6 ounces semisweet chocolate, finely chopped

3 cups heavy cream

Chocolate sprinkles or chocolate shavings, for garnish

Chopped nuts, for garnish

1. Cut the panettone into 1" cubes and place in a large bowl. Whisk together 1 cup condensed milk with 1 cup brandy and 1 teaspoon vanilla, and toss mixture with the panettone. Set aside.

2. In a medium heatproof bowl, beat the egg yolks with the cornstarch and the cocoa powder until well mixed.

3. In a large saucepan, heat the milk with the salt and ½ cup sugar over medium-low heat. Bring to a simmer. Gradually pour half of the milk mixture into the egg/cocoa powder mixture, stirring constantly. Add the egg/cocoa powder mixture to the saucepan with the remaining hot milk and cook, stirring constantly, until mixture thickens.

4. Remove from heat and stir in the butter, 1 teaspoon vanilla, and chopped chocolate. Cover surface with plastic wrap and chill.

5. Beat cream with remaining ¼ cup sugar until soft peaks form. Fold remaining teaspoon of vanilla into the cream. Fold a third of the whipped cream into the chilled chocolate cream.

6. Place half of the chocolate cream in a large glass bowl or casserole dish. Top with half of the panettone and half of the whipped cream. Repeat layers, ending with a layer of whipped cream.

7. Garnish with chocolate sprinkles or chocolate shavings and chopped nuts.

Portuguese Fried Bread (*Rabanadas*)

Rabanadas are traditionally served at Christmas in both Portugal and Brazil. This delicious dessert is similar to Spanish torrijas, which are eaten during Easter Week.

INGREDIENTS | SERVES 8

1 (14-ounce) can sweetened condensed milk

2 cups milk (optional: substitute 1 cup of red wine or port for 1 cup of milk)

1 cup heavy cream

1 teaspoon vanilla

½ teaspoon salt

1 cinnamon stick

16 (1"-thick) slices stale bread (French, Italian, challah, brioche)

6 large eggs, lightly beaten

Olive oil or vegetable oil, for frying

1 cup sugar

2 tablespoons ground cinnamon

Maple syrup or honey (optional)

1. Place the condensed milk, milk (and wine or port, if using), cream, vanilla, salt, and cinnamon stick in a large saucepan. Simmer for 2–3 minutes over medium heat, then remove from heat. Remove cinnamon stick.

2. Place the bread slices in a single layer in a pan or casserole dish. Pour milk mixture over the bread and set aside for 20–30 minutes, so that bread can soak up the milk.

3. Heat 3" of oil in a deep skillet or pot to 350°F, or until it sizzles when a piece of bread is dipped into it.

4. Place the beaten eggs in a shallow bowl. Gently pick up slices of the bread with tongs and dip them into the beaten eggs, coating both sides in the mixture. Transfer the pieces to the oil, cooking them in batches. Cook until bread is golden brown on one side, then flip to cook the other side. Transfer bread to a plate lined with paper towels.

5. Stir the sugar and cinnamon together and sprinkle over both sides of the pieces of bread while they are still warm.

6. Serve warm, with syrup or honey if desired.

King Cake (*Bolo de Reis*)

*Brazilians serve this pretty fruitcake from Christmas until January 5 (Twelfth Night).
Two items are hidden inside the cake: a fava bean and a small trinket. The person who discovers
the bean will have good luck for the year but must buy next year's king cake. The person
who finds the trinket can look forward to a prosperous new year.*

INGREDIENTS | SERVES 10

1½ cups mixed dried fruits (regular and/
or golden raisins, dried apricots, dates),
chopped

1 cup very hot water

½ cup brandy, divided

2 sticks butter, softened

1 cup sugar

4 large eggs

2 teaspoons vanilla, divided

1 teaspoon almond extract

¾ teaspoon salt

1½ cups all-purpose flour

2 teaspoons baking powder

⅓ cup chopped maraschino cherries

1 cup coarsely chopped walnuts

¼ cup candied orange peel

3 tablespoons honey

1¼ cups powdered sugar

2–3 tablespoons milk

6–8 whole or halved maraschino
cherries, for decoration

6–8 walnut halves, for decoration

1. Place the dried fruit in a small bowl and cover with hot water and 2 tablespoons brandy. Set aside for 30 minutes.

2. Preheat the oven to 350°F. Grease and flour a ring pan, angel food cake pan, bundt pan, or springform pan.

3. In the bowl of a standing mixer, beat the butter with the sugar until fluffy. Add eggs one at a time, beating well after each. Add 1 teaspoon vanilla, almond extract, 2 tablespoons brandy, and salt and mix well.

4. In a large bowl, whisk the flour and baking powder together. Toss in the cherries and add it to the batter, mixing until just incorporated.

5. Drain the dried fruits and fold them into the batter. Fold in the chopped walnuts and orange peel. Spread the batter into the cake pan. Hide one fava bean and one trinket (wrapped in tinfoil) in the batter if desired.

6. Bake cake for 35–40 minutes, or until toothpick inserted into the center comes out clean. Let cool for 15 minutes before unmolding.

7. In a small saucepan, heat remaining 4 tablespoons brandy with 3 tablespoons honey over low heat until well blended. Use a wooden skewer to poke holes in the cake, and brush brandy syrup over the top of the cake, letting it soak into the holes.

8. In a small bowl, whisk together the powdered sugar, remaining teaspoon vanilla, and milk to make a glaze of desired consistency. Drizzle glaze over the top of the cake and decorate with cherries and walnut halves.

Salt Cod and Potato Gratin (*Bacalhau Gratinado*)

This cheesy potato gratin with salt cod is very rich and filling, perfect for family gatherings.
Salt cod must be soaked for 24 hours in water to remove the excess salt, so plan ahead.

INGREDIENTS | SERVES 10

2 tablespoons olive oil

1 medium onion, peeled and chopped

1 medium tomato, seeded and diced

1½ pounds salt cod, soaked (to remove salt) and dried

¼ cup chopped fresh parsley

½ cup coconut milk

8 ounces cream cheese, softened

4 pounds potatoes, peeled

½ cup grated Parmesan cheese, divided

½ cup heavy cream

½ teaspoon salt

1 teaspoon freshly ground black pepper

1 cup grated cheese (Cheddar, Monterey jack, or mozzarella)

1. Place the olive oil in a large skillet. Add the onion and cook over medium heat until onion is soft, about 5–8 minutes. Add the tomato and the salt cod, and cook until tomato is soft, about 10 minutes. Add the parsley, coconut milk, and cream cheese. Mix well and set aside.

2. Cut the potatoes into large chunks and place in a pot of boiling water. Simmer until potatoes are very tender, about 15–20 minutes. Drain. Pass potatoes through a potato ricer, into the bowl of a standing mixer. Add ¼ cup of the Parmesan, cream, salt, and pepper, and beat until well mixed and fluffy. Set aside.

3. Preheat the oven to 350°F. Butter a 9" × 13" baking pan. Spread half of the mashed potatoes to cover the bottom of the pan. Place the fish mixture over the potatoes, then cover with remaining potatoes. Sprinkle grated cheese and remaining Parmesan over the top.

4. Bake for 30–40 minutes, until cheese is melted and slightly browned and casserole is heated through.

Hominy Corn Pudding (*Canjica Doce*)

Canjica is a creamy pudding made from white hominy corn, very similar to rice pudding.

INGREDIENTS | SERVES 8

2 cups dried hominy corn

¼ teaspoon salt

1 cinnamon stick

3 or 4 whole cloves

2½ cups milk

1 (14-ounce) can sweetened condensed milk

½ teaspoon ground cinnamon

¼ cup toasted peanuts

Coconut *Canjica*

Coconut is often added to this dish. Substitute 1 cup of milk with 1 cup of coconut milk. Add 1 cup of grated fresh coconut to the pudding during the last 5 minutes of cooking time.

1. Place the corn in a large saucepan. Cover with water (enough to cover the corn by 1") and soak overnight.

2. Add the salt to the corn, and bring to a boil. Cover and simmer over low heat until the corn is tender, about 1 hour.

3. Add the cinnamon stick, cloves, milk, and condensed milk to the corn. Bring to a gentle simmer and cook, stirring often with a wooden spoon, until mixture thickens and becomes very creamy, and the corn is very tender. Remove cinnamon stick and cloves.

4. When ready to serve, garnish with the ground cinnamon and toasted peanuts.

Coconut Squares (*Bombocado de Coco*)

These sweet coconut bars have a creamy, pudding-like texture and are especially delicious when they are warm from the oven. In Brazil they are served at parties or enjoyed as an afternoon snack.

INGREDIENTS | SERVES 12

1 tablespoon butter, melted

2 cups sugar, divided

1 cup coconut milk

1 cup sweetened condensed milk

¼ cup ricotta cheese

3 large eggs

1 cup grated fresh (or frozen) coconut

5 tablespoons all-purpose flour

1 teaspoon salt

1 teaspoon baking powder

2 tablespoons dried sweetened coconut flakes

1. Preheat the oven to 350°F. Brush a 9" × 9" baking pan with melted butter and sprinkle with 1 tablespoon sugar.

2. Place the coconut milk, condensed milk, ricotta, eggs, grated coconut, flour, salt, baking powder, and remaining sugar in a blender and process until smooth.

3. Pour the batter into the baking pan. Sprinkle the dried coconut flakes over the batter.

4. Bake for 25–30 minutes until batter has risen and coconut is lightly browned on top.

5. Let cool for 20–30 minutes before cutting into squares.

Peanut Brittle (*Pé-de-moleque*)

This peanut candy is popular throughout Brazil, and is associated with the Festa Junina *(June Festival).*

INGREDIENTS | SERVES 16

3 cups peanuts (with or without skins)

3 cups sugar

½ teaspoon salt

1 (14-ounce) can sweetened condensed milk

1. Butter a baking sheet or place a silpat on the counter.

2. Place the peanuts in a heavy saucepan with the sugar and the salt. Heat over medium heat, stirring, until sugar melts and turns sticky and medium brown.

3. Add the condensed milk (be careful; mixture will boil up high) and cook, stirring constantly, until mixture thickens. The candy is ready when you can scrape a spoon along the bottom of the pan and it takes several seconds for the mixture to close back over the bottom.

4. Transfer hot candy to buttered baking sheet or silpat, and spread into an even layer with a spatula.

5. When mixture has cooled somewhat but is still soft enough to cut, cut the candy into rectangular pieces. Let cool completely until candy is firm.

Mulled Red Wine (*Vinho Quente*)

This warm, sweet red wine is especially popular during Festa Junina.

INGREDIENTS | SERVES 4

1½ cups sugar, divided

6 cinnamon sticks, divided

4–6 whole cloves

1 liter red wine (about 4 cups)

2 cups water

1 tablespoon orange zest

1 tablespoon orange juice

1 red or green apple, peeled and diced

1. Place 1 cup sugar, 2 cinnamon sticks, and cloves in a heavy saucepan. Heat over medium-low heat, stirring occasionally, until sugar melts and very lightly caramelizes.

2. Add wine, water, remaining sugar, orange zest, orange juice, and apple. Heat until mixture is almost at a simmer.

3. Strain mixture and divide mixture between 4 mugs, adding some of the apple to each mug.

4. Garnish each mug with a cinnamon stick and serve hot.

Chocolate Cake Roll with Dulce de Leche
(*Rocambole de Chocolate*)

This elegant chocolate cake roll is a popular dessert for birthdays, Father's Day, and Easter.

INGREDIENTS | SERVES 8

8 large eggs, separated

2¼ cups sugar, divided

1 cup unsweetened cocoa powder, divided

1 tablespoon all-purpose flour

½ teaspoon cinnamon

½ teaspoon salt

6 tablespoons powdered sugar

2 teaspoons instant espresso powder

1½ cups water, divided

2 cups dulce de leche, softened

⅓ cup heavy cream

Pinch of salt

1 teaspoon vanilla

Chocolate sprinkles, for decoration

1. Line an 11" × 18" rimmed baking sheet with greased parchment paper. Preheat the oven to 325°F

2. Place the egg whites in the bowl of a standing mixer and beat until soft peaks form. Gradually add ¼ cup sugar and beat until stiff peaks form. Add the egg yolks and beat until mixed.

3. In a medium bowl, whisk ⅓ cup cocoa powder, flour, cinnamon, and salt together. Gently fold dry ingredients into the egg mixture. Use a spatula to spread batter on the baking sheet in an even layer. Bake for 15–20 minutes, or until cake just springs back to the touch.

4. Flip cake out of the pan onto a clean dishtowel dusted with 3 tablespoons powdered sugar. Peel off parchment paper and dust top of cake with 3 tablespoons powdered sugar. Roll up cake loosely in the dishtowel, starting with a short side. Let cool.

5. In a small saucepan, bring 1 cup sugar, instant espresso powder, and ¾ cup water to a boil. Simmer for 2–3 minutes, or until sugar is dissolved. Let cool.

6. Gently unroll cake. Brush with espresso syrup and spread with dulce de leche. Reroll cake and refrigerate for 30 minutes, wrapped loosely in plastic wrap.

7. Add the cream, remaining cocoa powder, and water, 1 cup sugar, and salt to a medium saucepan. Stir well and bring to a simmer over medium-low heat. Simmer for 5 minutes, stirring, until mixture becomes slightly thickened. Remove from heat and stir in vanilla.

8. Place cake on a serving platter, and spread glaze over cake. Decorate with chocolate sprinkles.

Chicken Salad Sandwich "Cake" (*Bolo Salgado*)

This clever old-fashioned dish, often served at birthday parties, looks like a beautifully decorated cake but is actually a savory dish of chicken salad layered with mashed potatoes.

INGREDIENTS | SERVES 10

6 tablespoons olive oil, divided

1 small onion, peeled and chopped

2 cloves garlic, minced

1 medium tomato, seeded and diced

2 poached boneless, skinless chicken breasts, shredded

1 cup corn (canned or frozen)

½ cup chopped olives

1 teaspoon salt, divided

1½ teaspoons ground black pepper, divided

¼ cup chicken stock

2 tablespoons minced fresh parsley

1 cup mayonnaise, divided

1½ loaves sandwich bread, crusts removed

⅔ cup cream cheese, softened

2½ cups mashed potatoes prepared with butter and heavy cream

2 tablespoons fresh lime juice

Potato sticks, cooked peas, olives, parsley leaves, and shredded carrots, for decoration

1. Line a 9" × 11" cake pan with foil.

2. Heat the 2 tablespoons olive oil in a large saucepan over medium-low heat and cook onion until soft. Add garlic and tomato and cook until tomato is soft, about 5 minutes. Add chicken, corn, olives, ½ teaspoon salt, 1 teaspoon pepper, and chicken stock and cook for 5–8 minutes until most of the liquid is absorbed. Remove from heat and stir in the parsley and ½ cup mayonnaise. Set aside.

3. Place a layer of bread slices in the bottom of the prepared pan. Spread half of the cream cheese over the bread. Top with half of the chicken mixture.

4. Place another layer of bread slices over the chicken. Spread remaining cream cheese over the bread. Top with the rest of the chicken mixture.

5. Make a final layer of bread slices. Close foil over the bread and place in the refrigerator to chill for 2–3 hours or overnight.

6. Invert cake onto serving platter and remove foil. Spread cake with a thin layer of mayonnaise.

7. Microwave the mashed potatoes until they are softened and warm. Season potatoes with ½ teaspoon salt and pepper to taste. Stir lime juice and remaining 4 tablespoons olive oil into potatoes. Smooth the potatoes over the top and sides of the cake like frosting.

8. Press potato sticks into the sides of the cake. Decoratively arrange peas, olives, parsley, and shredded carrots on top of the cake as desired. Refrigerate until ready to serve.

Coconut Birthday Cake (*Bolo de Coco*)

This layer cake is filled with coconut cream and frosted with a fluffy meringue icing.
Perfect for birthdays and other celebrations.

INGREDIENTS | SERVES 10

1 store-bought white cake mix, prepared according to package directions but not baked

4 large eggs, separated

1½ cups sugar, divided

4 tablespoons cornstarch

¼ teaspoon salt

1 cup milk

1 (14-ounce) can coconut milk, divided

2 cups sweetened coconut flakes, divided

2 teaspoons vanilla, divided

¼ cup heavy cream

⅓ cup water

1 tablespoon corn syrup

1. Divide cake batter between 2 greased 9" cake pans and bake according to package directions.

2. Place the egg yolks in a heatproof bowl and whisk until pale yellow and creamy.

3. Place ½ cup sugar, cornstarch, salt, milk and 1 cup coconut milk in a large saucepan. Heat over medium heat, stirring, until mixture boils and thickens.

4. Gradually stir half of the hot milk mixture into the egg yolks. Add egg mixture back to the saucepan and cook over medium heat until thickened. Remove from heat and stir in 1 cup coconut flakes and 1 teaspoon vanilla. Cover with plastic wrap and chill for 1 hour.

5. Mix together the remaining coconut milk, cream, and remaining teaspoon vanilla. Poke cake layers with a wooden skewer, and brush milk mixture over the 2 cake layers, letting it soak in.

6. Place the egg whites in the bowl of a standing mixer. Place remaining 1 cup sugar, ⅓ cup water, and corn syrup in a large saucepan. Bring to a boil. When the syrup reaches 238°F, turn on the mixer to beat the egg whites. When the syrup reaches 244°F, remove from heat. Gradually add syrup to the egg whites (egg whites should form soft peaks before adding syrup). Beat until stiff peaks form and meringue cools slightly.

7. Place one cake layer on serving plate. Spread coconut cream over the cake layer and top with the second layer. Frost tops and side of cake with meringue.

8. Sprinkle remaining coconut flakes over cake and serve.

Chicken and Sausage Pie (*Empadão Goiano*)

Empanadas are typically snacks or appetizers, but this giant empadão *is more of a main course dish, served at family gatherings and special occasions.*

INGREDIENTS | SERVES 8

1½ cups warm milk
1 teaspoon sugar
1 tablespoon active dry yeast
4 cups all-purpose flour
¼ cup vegetable oil
1 tablespoon butter
1 teaspoon salt
4 tablespoons olive oil, divided
1 pound *linguiça* or other sausage, diced
1½ pounds chicken breasts, cut into small cubes
1 teaspoon salt
1 teaspoon freshly ground black pepper
1½ pounds pork tenderloin, cut into small cubes

1 large onion, peeled and finely chopped
3 cloves garlic, minced
3 tablespoons tomato paste
1 teaspoon paprika
1 cup sweet corn kernels (fresh or frozen)
1 cup sliced hearts of palm
1 medium boiled potato, cut into small cubes
½ cup sliced olives
3 tablespoons cornstarch
2 cups chicken stock
½ cup chopped fresh parsley
4 ounces mozzarella cheese, diced
2 large hard-cooked eggs, peeled and diced
1 large egg, beaten

1. Place milk and sugar in a large bowl. Sprinkle yeast on top. Set aside for 5 minutes. Stir in 1 cup flour, vegetable oil, butter, and salt and mix well. Add remaining flour and knead until mixture is a smooth dough. Set aside in a warm place to rise for 1 hour.

2. Add the olive oil to a large skillet or stockpot and brown the sausage over medium heat. Transfer sausage to a large bowl and set aside.

3. Season the chicken with salt and pepper. Add to the skillet and sauté until just browned on all sides. Place chicken in the bowl with the sausage. Repeat procedure with the pork, adding more oil to the skillet if needed.

4. Add remaining olive oil to the skillet and cook the onion over medium heat until soft and translucent, about 5–8 minutes. Add garlic and cook for 1 minute. Add tomato paste and paprika and mix well. Add corn, hearts of palm, potato, and olives and cook until heated through.

5. Add sausage, chicken, and pork to the skillet, Add cornstarch and mix well. Add stock and simmer until thickened, about 5–8 minutes. Stir in parsley. Remove from heat and cool.

6. Preheat oven to 350°F. On a floured surface, roll out ⅔ of the dough into a 12" circle. Use it to line a 9" deep-dish pie pan. Roll out the remaining dough into a 9" or 10" circle.

7. Add the filling to the pie pan. Scatter cheese and hard-cooked egg over filling. Top with second circle of dough. Seal and crimp edges. Brush pie lightly with beaten egg.

8. Bake until golden brown, about 30–40 minutes. Cool for 15–20 minutes.

Chocolate Popcorn (*Pipoca Doce de Chocolate*)

This is a simple way to make delicious chocolate-covered popcorn that is ready as soon as it pops. Make it really Brazilian by topping it with a drizzle of condensed milk.

INGREDIENTS | SERVES 6

4 tablespoons oil

4 tablespoons sugar

4 tablespoons cocoa powder

½ cup popcorn kernels

1 teaspoon kosher salt (not traditional, but good)

1. Place the oil, sugar, cocoa powder, and popcorn kernels in a stovetop popcorn popper or a large pot with a lid. Mix everything well.

2. Heat over medium heat, stirring occasionally until kernels start popping, then start stirring constantly. If using a pot, place the lid on the pot to keep the kernels inside and shake the pot to stir it.

3. When popping slows, remove pot from heat (don't try to wait for every piece to pop or it will burn).

4. Toss popcorn with salt and serve.

Sausage Rolls (*Enroladinho de Salsicha e Queijo*)

No child can resist these little sausage rolls, and most adults love them as well.
They are a must-have snack for parties.

INGREDIENTS | MAKES 36

1 cup warm milk

1 tablespoon sugar

1 tablespoon active dry yeast

4½ cups all-purpose flour

1 teaspoon salt

2 large eggs, divided

¼ cup oil

12 hot dogs or cooked sausages

12 slices cheese

1 teaspoon dried oregano (optional)

1. Add the milk and the sugar to the bowl of a standing mixer. Sprinkle the yeast over the milk and let stand for 5 minutes.

2. Add 3 cups of flour, salt, 1 egg, and oil to the bowl. Knead mixture with the dough hook attachment until smooth. Add remaining flour gradually, and continue to knead until you have a smooth dough that is not sticky. Cover dough with plastic wrap and let rise in a warm place until doubled in bulk, about 1 hour.

3. Cut the hot dogs or sausages into thirds. Cut each cheese slice into 3 strips. Wrap a strip of cheese around each piece of hot dog.

4. On a lightly floured surface, roll out the dough into a large rectangle. Use a pizza cutter or sharp knife to cut the dough into strips as wide as the hot-dog pieces are long.

5. Place a piece of sausage (with the cheese) at the end of a strip of dough. Roll the sausage up in the dough, until it is covered (about twice around). Cut the dough and press the cut edge down onto the hot dog to seal. Place on a baking sheet, seam side down. Repeat until all of the hot-dog pieces are wrapped in dough.

6. Whisk the remaining egg in a small bowl. Brush sausage rolls with egg and sprinkle lightly with oregano (if using). Preheat oven to 375°F, and set rolls aside for 15 minutes in a warm place.

7. Place sausage rolls in the oven and lower temperature to 350°F. Bake until golden brown, about 25–30 minutes.

8. Serve warm.

Rainbow Cake (*Bolo Arco-Íris*)

This colorful cake is fun for birthday celebrations, and it is especially perfect for Carnaval.

INGREDIENTS | SERVES 10

1 cup sour cream
½ cup vegetable oil
4 large eggs
½ cup water
2 teaspoons vanilla, divided
1 store-bought plain white cake mix
Food color (blue, red, yellow, green)
4 egg whites
1 cup sugar
½ teaspoon cream of tartar
¼ teaspoon salt
Colored candies or sprinkles, for decoration

1. Place sour cream, oil, eggs, water, and 1 teaspoon vanilla in a blender and pulse briefly to mix. Add the cake mix in 3 parts, blending after each. Batter should be pourable but not too runny. Add more water if needed.

2. Divide the cake batter between 6 small bowls, putting about ⅓ of the batter in the first bowl, and a little bit less in each of the remaining bowls. The last bowl should have the least amount of batter.

3. Use the food coloring to tint the first bowl of batter dark purple. Color the second bowl blue, the next bowl green, then yellow, orange, and the last one red.

4. Grease two 8" or 9" cake pans. Preheat oven to 350°F.

5. Divide the purple batter between the two pans, pouring it in a circle around the perimeter of the pan. Add the blue batter next, making a small circle just inside of the purple one. Tap cake pans on counter to settle the batter, then repeat with remaining colors, adding the red batter last to the center of the pans.

6. Bake cakes for 20–25 minutes or until cakes have risen. Remove from oven and let cool.

7. Place the egg whites, sugar, cream of tartar, and salt in a heatproof bowl over a pot with 1" of boiling water, making sure the bowl does not touch the boiling water. Whisk egg-white mixture until sugar is dissolved and mixture is hot to the touch (120°F).

8. Transfer mixture to the clean mixing bowl of a standing mixer and beat with whisk attachment until stiff peaks form. Fold in remaining vanilla.

9. Frost cake layers with the meringue frosting and decorate with candies or sprinkles.

APPENDIX A

Glossary of Brazilian Ingredients

Abóbora (Squash)

Abóbora is the general term in Portuguese for pumpkins and squash. Brazilians cook with many varieties of squash, some indigenous and others that came to Brazil through immigration. Brazilian recipes that call for *abóbora* are usually referring to a large green tubular squash with orange flesh. This sweeter squash is often used to make *doce de abóbora* (candied pumpkin), a popular dessert. Butternut squash makes a good substitute. When a recipe calls for *moranga* (such as the famous shrimp dish *camarão na moranga*), it is referring to a round pumpkin-like squash, similar to the North American sugar pumpkin.

Açaí (Acai Berry)

This purple "berry" is actually the fruit of a particular species of South American palm tree (*Euterpe oleracea*). Açaí is valued for its high content of antioxidants and other nutrients. Açaí even has a legend about its origin—the story goes that the daughter of a village chief, whose child died during a famine, wandered off into the Amazon forest distraught with grief. Her body was found lying under a tree laden with the fruit, thus saving the village from starvation. The word *açaí* is

her name, Iaça, spelled backwards, and the village supposedly became the city of Bélem. *Açaí na Tigela* is a famous Brazilian breakfast treat—it's a bowl of frozen açaí purée, banana, and *guaraná* syrup, topped with granola and banana slices. Açaí is too perishable to export, but you can find frozen açaí pulp in grocery stores.

Amendoim (Peanuts)

Peanuts are native to South America, and the European immigrants quickly adapted them as a substitute for the walnuts and almonds that they missed from home. The Portuguese used peanuts to make candies and sweets, which remains a tradition today. Brazil's most well-known peanut candy is a crumbly confection of peanuts, manioc starch, and sugar called *pé-de-moleque*.

Bacalhau (Salt Cod)

The tradition of salting and drying cod as a method of preservation may have originated in Newfoundland. European explorers brought it back with them to the Old World, and it became a popular staple in Mediterranean cuisine. The Portuguese brought salt cod to Brazil, where it is still enjoyed in Portuguese-style dishes, and especially in the deep-fried croquettes called *bolinho de bacalhau*. Salt cod must be soaked in water for at least 24 hours to remove the excess salt before it is edible.

Banana-de-terra (Plantain)

The literal translation of the Portuguese word for plantain is "banana of the earth" (perhaps to distinguish it from less starchy, sweeter bananas). Plantains are a type of banana, but they differ from so-called "dessert" bananas in that they must be cooked before they are eaten. Interestingly the plantain is not native to South America, and was brought to Brazil by the Portuguese from Southeast Asia.

Batata-doce (Sweet Potato)

The sweet potato (*Ipomoea batatas*) is a root vegetable, native to South America, and actually belongs to a different plant family (*Convolvulaceae*, or morning glory family) than the regular potato (of the *Solanaceae*, or nightshade family). The Portuguese and Spanish explorers incorporated the indigenous Taíno name for the sweet potato—*batata*—into their own language. Eventually *batata* became the general term for all potatoes in Portuguese (though it remains a distinct term for sweet potato in Spanish), and the sweet potato became the *batata-doce*. Brazilian sweet potatoes have dark purple skin and light yellow flesh (not bright orange like North American varieties). Brazilians also eat yams (*inhame*), which were brought to Brazil by African immigrants.

Cachaça (Brazilian Rum)

Cachaça is one of Brazil's most famous products—a white rum–like spirit made from fermented and distilled fresh (unprocessed) sugarcane juice. (Most other rums are made from molasses, a byproduct of sugarcane processing.) *Cachaça* is also referred to as *pinga* in Brazilian recipes. *Cachaça* can be bottled immediately after distillation (white *cachaça*) or aged in wooden barrels (dark or premium *cachaça*). It is the key ingredient in a *caipirinha*, Brazil's national cocktail.

Camarão Seco (Dried Shrimp)

Small, intensely flavored dried shrimp are commonly used in the cooking of northeastern Brazil. They are essential ingredients in the famous black-eyed pea fritters called *acarajé*, and they are often ground and sprinkled onto dishes or added to stews and sauces.

Carne Seca/Carne-de-sol (Dried Beef)

Carne seca is salted dried beef, similar to beef jerky but not smoked, that is often rehydrated and used in many traditional dishes, particularly in southern Brazil. *Carne-de-sol* ("beef of the sun") is a specialty of northeastern Brazil, which has a very hot, dry, and windy climate that is ideal for drying and preserving thin cuts of lightly salted beef. *Carne seca* is much drier and saltier than *carne-de-sol*, and keeps longer at room temperature. *Carne seca* must be soaked overnight in water before it is used in a dish, to remove the excess salt. Both forms of dried beef are hard to find in the United States. The closest substitutes might be lightly seasoned beef jerky or chipped beef.

Castanhas-do-pará (Brazil Nuts)

The Portuguese name for these large, creamy Amazonian nuts translates literally to "chestnuts from Pará," which is what the Portuguese immigrants called them. The export of Brazil nuts is one of the Amazon's potential sustainable resources. Brazil nut trees can live to be 500 years old, and their pollination (and nut production) depends on the presence of a particular species of orchid that attracts a particular bee. Brazil nuts can be harvested each year without damaging the trees, but the nut production requires a delicate environmental balance that is recently threatened by deforestation.

Cheiro-verde (Cilantro and Green Onions)

The term cheiro-verde translates literally to "smell-green," and it is the name for the fragrant mixture of chopped fresh cilantro and green onions that is added to so many Brazilian dishes. The two herbs are often packaged together at the grocery in Brazil— you can buy a bag of ready-to-use green-smelling cilantro and green onions.

Chuchu (Chayote Squash)

Chayote is native to Central America and Mexico, and consumed throughout Latin America. Though it is sometimes chopped thinly and added raw to salads, Brazilians typically boil chuchu until it is just tender. It is a key ingredient in the famous shrimp dish camarão com chuchu.

Coco (Coconut)

Coconuts grow on the Cocos nucifera species of palm tree. Coconut water (from green coconuts) is a popular beach beverage in Brazil, and coconut milk (processed from the white coconut meat of mature coconuts) is used in Brazilian cooking, especially in the seafood dishes from Bahia. Grated coconut is used to make many sweets and desserts.

Coentro (Cilantro)

Cilantro is not native to South America— the Portuguese brought this unique herb to Brazil. Cilantro is associated with the Afro-Brazilian cuisine of Bahia and is especially used to season seafood dishes.

Couve (Collard Greens)

Thinly shredded, garlicky, sautéed collard greens are one of the key accompaniments of Brazil's national dish feijoada. Collard greens are also an important ingredient in the Brazilian-Portuguese soup caldo verde.

Dendê (Palm Oil)

This bright reddish oil is obtained from the fruit of an African palm tree. The color comes from beta-carotene, and the oil has a distinctive flavor that is one of the identifying characteristics of Bahian cuisine.

Doce de Leite (Dulce de Leche)

This creamy confection is made of milk and sugar that has been cooked very slowly until it is lightly caramelized and thick enough to spread. Dulce de leche is popular throughout Latin America and is used in pastries, cakes, and frozen desserts.

Farofa (Toasted Manioc)

Farofa is an essential condiment in Brazil. It is made of ground manioc that has a bread crumb–like texture and has been toasted in a skillet and seasoned with other ingredients, such as butter, onions, bacon or other meats, eggs, and vegetables. Brazilians sprinkle *farofa* over beans, rice, stews, barbecue, and especially on *feijoada*, the national dish of smoked meats and black beans.

Feijão (Beans)

Beans are one of the main staples of Brazilian cuisine. Many people associate black beans with Brazilian food, probably because one of the most famous Brazilian dishes, *feijoada*, is made with them. But Brazilians eat many different kinds of beans, including the popular carioca beans (*feijão carioca*), which are similar to pinto beans, and black-eyed peas (*feijão-fradinho*).

Goiabada (Guava Paste)

The Portuguese discovered that the tropical fruit guava made a great substitute for quince, and they quickly began using it to make a sweet candied fruit paste. Guava paste is typically served with cheese in Brazil, a combination that is often called *Romeu e Julieta* (Romeo and Juliet). Guava paste is also used in pastries and desserts.

Guaraná

This fruit grows on a climbing plant that is native to the Amazon. The fruit contains even more caffeine than coffee, and is used to make sweetened beverages and soft drinks that are quite popular sources of caffeine in Brazil.

Jambu (Toothache Plant)

Jambu (*Acmella oleracea*) is an interesting Amazonian plant that causes a tingling and numbing sensation in the mouth. The leaves are used in certain Brazilian dishes, especially in *tacacá*, a unique soup from northern Brazil made with shrimp and manioc. *Jambú* leaves are hard to find in the United States, but you can order dried flower buds ("buzz buttons") online. You can also order seeds to grow your own *jambu*, which is also prized as an ornamental plant.

Limão (Lime)

Brazilians do not typically cook with lemons. The small green limes that are typical of South America are used instead, in any dish that might need tart citrus flavor. These extra tart and juicy limes are a key component of the famous *caipirinha* cocktail.

Linguiça (Portuguese-Style Sausage)

Linguiça is Portuguese smoked sausage that is seasoned with garlic and paprika. Brazilians enjoy several kinds of *linguiça*, including a spicier, Italian-style version called *linguiça calabresa*. *Linguiça calabresa* is similar to pepperoni.

Mamão (Papaya)

Papayas are one of the most popular tropical fruits in Brazil, and there are many different varieties. Papaya is eaten fresh, especially for breakfast, and is commonly used in desserts, such as mousses and ice cream. Eat a ripe papaya like you would eat cantelope: Cut it in half, remove the seeds, and then scoop the flesh with a spoon.

Mandioca (Manioc)

Manioc is a starchy tuber, also known as *cassava, aipim,* and *yuca,* that is native to Brazil and is a staple food of the indigenous people of South America. Certain varieties require proper processing because they contain small amounts of cyanide. Manioc is used in many different forms in Brazilian cuisine. The pulp is pressed to produce a liquid. A fine powdery starch can be extracted from this liquid (*polvilho,* or tapioca starch). When the liquid is fermented, the starch acquires a slightly sour taste (*polvilho azedo*); otherwise, it is sweet starch (*polvilho doce*). Tapioca starch can also be processed into small gelantinous pearls (tapioca pearls). The pulp is processed into dough that is dried and ground into meal (*farinha de mandioca*), which is used in many ways but especially to make the popular condiment *farofa.* Manioc root can also be boiled like potatoes, or boiled and mashed, or fried (*mandioca frita*).

Maracujá (Passion Fruit)

This tropical fruit is native to Brazil and the surrounding regions of South America. Its exotic flavor is used in a variety of Brazilian desserts and pastries.

Milho (Corn)

Corn is another staple of South American cuisine. In Brazil fresh corn is used to make certain traditional indigenous dishes, like the *pamonha* (a fresh corn tamale). Cornmeal, or *fubá,* is used to make cakes and breads, and to make Italian-style polenta (*angu*). Brazil has another form of cornmeal called *milharina* (or *farinha de milho flocada*), which is dried corn that has been processed into a flake-like texture. *Milharina* is steamed and served like couscous. *Canjica* is dried white hominy corn, and it is cooked into a creamy, sweet porridge that is also called *canjica.*

Palmito (Hearts of Palm)

This unusual vegetable comes from the tender inner core of certain palm tree varieties, and is considered a delicacy because of the labor required to harvest it. Brazilians enjoy eating and cooking with fresh hearts of palm, which are quite different from the jarred variety available in the United States. Many wild palm trees have a single stem, meaning that in order to harvest the palm heart the tree has to be sacrificed. Cultivated palm trees are clonal, or have several stems, which allows for sustainable harvesting over time.

Pequi (Souari Nut)

Pequi is an unusual fruit of the Brazilian Cerrado (the tropical savannah in central western Brazil). The small fruit has very sharp spines on its pit and must be eaten very carefully. The seeds are often roasted and consumed as a snack. *Pequi* is used in the local cuisine of this region of Brazil, and it has a strong flavor that can be an acquired taste for some.

Pimenta (Chili Peppers)

Brazilians have a wide variety of chili peppers from which to choose. *Pimenta-de-cheiro* are small, round, green peppers with a mild and aromatic flavor. *Dedo-de-moça* (girl's finger) is a popular thin green (finger-shaped) pepper that turns red when fully ripe and is slightly milder than a jalapeño. *Pimento-de-bode* (goat pepper) is a small, round, yellow, medium hot pepper that is important in the cuisine of the state of Goiás. *Pimenta-malagueta* is the hottest Brazilian pepper, and is widely used in the Afro-Brazilian cuisine of Bahia. It is not related to (but is named after) the West African chili pepper of the same name.

Presunto (Ham)

Presunto is technically Portuguese dry-cured ham, similar to Italian prosciutto. In most of Brazil, the word *presunto* is used to describe all different kinds of ham, including deli-style ham. *Tender* is another Brazilian word for dry-cured ham.

Quiabo (Okra)

West African slaves introduced okra to Brazil, and thereby introduced it into Brazilian cuisine. Several iconic Brazilian dishes are made with okra, including *caruru* (a shrimp and okra stew/sauce) from Bahia, and *frango com quiabo* (chicken and okra stew) from Minas Gerais.

Queijo Coalho (Coalho Cheese)

Queijo coalho is a firm white cheese that is similar to Greek halloumi cheese. It's a "squeaky" cheese that holds its shape when heated and can even be placed on a skewer and grilled (a popular beach snack).

Queijo Minas (Minas Cheese)

This is the signature cheese from the state of Minas Gerais. It is made from cow's milk, and is available fresh (similar to *queso fresco*), slightly matured, or aged. The aged version is used to make the famous cheese rolls, *pão de queijo*.

Requeijão (Cream Cheese)

This creamy cheese is also known by a popular brand name, *Catupiry*. It is a white creamy cheese, spreadable or sometimes even pourable, that is used on everything from pastries to pizza.

Torresmos (Fried Pork Rinds)

Torresmos are fried pieces of pork rind—also known as cracklings. Pork skin is cooked to render the lard, producing crispy leftovers that are a popular bar snack in Brazil. *Torresmos* are customarily served with certain dishes such as *feijão tropeiro* (cattle drover beans).

Cooking Techniques and Equipment

Tips and Techniques

There are a few kitchen tricks and techniques that come in handy when cooking Brazilian food. Certain Brazilian ingredients that might be unfamiliar are easy to use once you know how to peel, process, or prepare them.

Bacalhau

Bacalhau is cod fillet that has been dried and preserved in salt. Bacalhau has a unique flavor and is a traditional ingredient in Portuguese-Brazilian cuisine. Salt cod must be soaked in water before it is consumed, in order to remove the excess salt. Rinse the fillets under cold water to remove the salty crust. Cut the fish into 2" pieces, and place them in a bowl. Cover the pieces with cold water and refrigerate for 24 hours, changing the water every 4–6 hours. Taste a piece of the fish for saltiness. Soak longer if needed. When desired flavor is obtained, drain the fish, pat dry with paper towels, and shred.

Choosing and Peeling Papayas

Choose a papaya that is not too firm (but not mushy) with skin that is turning from green to yellow. Cut the papaya in half lengthwise and scoop out the seeds. Use a vegetable peeler or sharp knife to peel the skin from the fruit. Slice the fruit crosswise into wedges, then cut each wedge into bite-size pieces.

Churrasco Dining

A visit to Brazil will almost certainly include a meal at a *churrascaria*, a restaurant that serves Brazilian-style grilled meat. The meat is slow-roasted over a fire (traditional) or charcoal, and brought to the table on skewers. Slices of meat are then served to the diners. Different cuts of beef and other types of meat keep coming to the table, until the diner signals that he or she has had enough. The cuts of beef are quite particular, supposedly perfected by the *gaúchos* (cowboys), and are slightly different than the cuts of beef available in U.S. supermarkets. *Picanha* (known as the "rump cap" or "top sirloin cap" in the United States) is one of the most popular cuts. Specifically, the *picanha* is the other side of the rump cap from the tri tip. *Picanha* is typically cut into thin slices that include a layer of fat, which are placed on a skewer and grilled. Another popular cut is *alcatra*, which is a long piece cut from the top of the sirloin, perfect for placing on a skewer. *Fraldinha* is the Brazilian term for flank steak.

In addition to steak, a typical *churrascaria* might serve grilled spicy sausages, grilled chicken and chicken hearts, lamb, beef short ribs, and pork ribs.

Cooking with Clay Pots

Many Brazilian dishes like *moqueca* (seafood stew) and *feijoada* (black beans with smoked meats) are cooked (and served) in beautiful black clay pots. Clay pots give dishes a special flavor, especially when they have been used over time. Clay pots do not tolerate extreme temperatures or rapid changes in temperature well. They are perfect for dishes that are cooked for a long time at a low temperature (beans, stews). You can heat a clay pot directly on the stove, but you must warm it up slowly. For baking, place the pot in a cold oven and let it warm up as the oven does. The first time you use an unglazed clay pot, season it: Soak it in water overnight, dry it, rub it all over with vegetable oil, and bake in the oven at a low temperature for an hour. Or use it to fry some bacon (remember to start at a low temperature)—the bacon fat will help to season it. Over time, with frequent use, the pot will become sturdier and more heat tolerant.

Cooking with Condensed Milk

Condensed milk is the base for many Brazilian desserts. One Brazilian technique is to cook the condensed milk in a saucepan with a bit of butter until it thickens enough to shape into truffle-like balls when cool. The mixture is cooked for about 10 minutes, or until "*até desgrudar do fundo da panela*"—when the mixture stops sticking to the pan and begins to pull away slightly from the bottom. If you scrape the bottom of the pan with a spatula, it will take a couple of seconds for the mixture to close over the path of the spatula. This is the technique used to make the chocolate fudge candy *brigadeiro*, so some recipes will say to cook the condensed milk to the point of a *brigadeiro*.

Cracking Coconuts

There is a lot you can do with a fresh coconut, once you get it open! Choose a coconut that feels heavy. You should hear liquid sloshing when you shake it. To crack the coconut open, pierce one of the "eyes" (one of the three eyes will be a soft spot) and drain out the liquid. That liquid is coconut water, and it should be relatively clear and sweet (not oily). You can drink it, or add it to a smoothie. Place the coconut in a 350°F oven for 15 minutes. Use a hammer to break open the shell. With a knife, peel the white flesh away from the shell. Peel any brown skin off of the white flesh with a vegetable peeler. Grate the coconut with a box grater or food processor. Store in the refrigerator for 1 week, or freeze for up to 3 months. To make coconut milk, place the shredded coconut in a bowl and add 1½ cups hot (not boiling) water. Let the coconut steep for 10 minutes, then pour the mixture through a colander lined with cheesecloth. Squeeze the cheesecloth to remove all of the liquid. Store coconut milk in the refrigerator for up to 1 week.

Homemade Lime Mayonnaise

Lime and mayo make a popular combo in South America. Add 1 egg, 1 teaspoon prepared mustard, ½ teaspoon salt, and 2 tablespoons fresh lime juice to a food processor or blender. Process the mixture while very slowly adding ¾ cup of olive oil or vegetable oil, until the mixture emulsifies and becomes thick. Store in refrigerator for 2–3 days.

Homemade Requeijão Cheese

Requijão is a very smooth and creamy Brazilian cheese that is something like a combination of ricotta and cream cheese. It is available in various consistencies, from spreadable to pourable. Brazilians enjoy it on bread, and it is used in many recipes as well. It's difficult to find commercial *requeijão* in the United States, but it is quite easy to make a homemade version. To make your own, place 5 tablespoons butter, 3 tablespoons cornstarch, and 1 teaspoon of salt in a saucepan, and heat over low-medium heat until just bubbling. Add 2 cups whole milk and cook, stirring constantly, until mixture thickens. Remove from heat and let cool. Place mixture in a blender with ⅓ cup cream and 1 cup ricotta cheese, and blend until very smooth. Store in the refrigerator. To make a firmer *requeijão*, stir 6 ounces grated mozzarella cheese and 2 ounces grated Monterey jack cheese into the hot milk/cornstarch mixture, omit cream, and decrease ricotta to ¼ cup. Pour melted cheese into a ramekin lined with plastic wrap, chill until firm enough to spread, then unmold and serve.

Juicing Limes

There are a couple of tricks for coaxing the maximum amount of juice from limes. First heat the limes in the microwave for 20–30 seconds, or until they just start to feel warm. Next roll the limes around on a flat surface, pressing down on them with the palms of your hands. Then juice the limes as usual.

Notes on Brazilian Measurements

If you read Brazilian recipes, you will notice a variety of different measurements, more than could possibly correlate with the standard U.S. cup, teaspoon, and tablespoon. If you watch cooking videos, particularly the homemade variety, you will see cooks measuring with plastic drinking cups and glasses and using terms like "*copo*" and "*colher de café*." A quick explanation of terms is helpful. One U.S. cup is equivalent to the Brazilian *xícara*, or *xícara de chá* (teacup). A Brazilian *copo* is slightly larger, equivalent to 1 cup plus 2 teaspoons. A *colher de sopa* ("soup spoon") is equal to the U.S. tablespoon, and a *colher de chá* ("teaspoon") is the same as the U.S. teaspoon. A *colher de café* (coffee spoon) is equal to a half teaspoon, and a *colher de sobremesa* ("dessert spoon") is equal to 2 teaspoons. A *pitada* is a "pinch," or about ¼ teaspoon. A *litro* is a measure of liquid (same as a U.S. liter) of about 4 cups, and a *garafa* is 600 millileters, or about 2½ cups. One *dose* of an alcoholic beverage such as *cachaça* is equivalent to 1 shot, or about 1½ ounces.

Oven-Dried Tomatoes

These Italian-style roasted tomatoes are a popular addition to salads, pasta, and pizza. Slice ripe plum tomatoes in half lengthwise. Place the tomatoes cut side up on a baking sheet lined with parchment paper. Sprinkle with coarse salt, oregano, and black pepper. Place in a low-temperature oven (200°F) and bake for 2–3 hours until dry and somewhat shriveled. Place in a jar with 1 or 2 peeled garlic cloves, cover with olive oil, and store in refrigerator.

Passion Fruit Pulp

Passion fruit is a slightly oblong fruit, green or dark red in color, with a pulp that is yellow, gelatinous, and full of green seeds. Before it ripens, passion fruit is stringent and tart. As it ripens, the skin of the fruit becomes wrinkled and brownish, and the pulp becomes fragrant and sweet. To extract the juice, scoop out the pulp and seeds from a ripe passion fruit, and heat pulp over low heat in a small saucepan, until fruit becomes more liquid and less gummy. Strain pulp before using, reserving the (edible) seeds for decoration if desired.

Perfect Rice

Brazilians cook rice by first sautéing an aromatic vegetable or herb, and then adding the rice. Garlic is the simplest, but minced onions and tomatoes are nice additions. To make 3 cups of cooked rice, place ¼ cup minced onion and 3 tablespoons vegetable oil in heavy saucepan. Sauté for 2 minutes, until the onion is fragrant. If using tomatoes, add ¼ cup chopped tomatoes and cook until soft. Add 2 teaspoons of minced garlic and 1 teaspoon of salt and cook for 1 minute. Add 1½ cups rice and stir well. Add water to cover the rice by almost 1". Cover and cook over low heat for 15 minutes, then turn off heat and let rest, covered, for 10 minutes. Uncover and fluff before serving.

Pressure Cooker Beans

Beans are a staple of Brazilian cuisine, consumed on a daily basis. Beans take a long time to cook, however, so most Brazilian households have a pressure cooker, which saves a lot of time. Beans will cook in 30 minutes in a pressure cooker (including the time needed for the pressure to release on its own). If the beans are not presoaked, they might take a few minutes longer to become tender. Modern pressure cookers have many built-in safety features to prevent the storied explosions and food-on-the-ceiling catastrophes of the past. Follow the instructions for your particular pressure cooker for details, but in general you can cook 1 pound of beans in 3 quarts of water, with a bit of vegetable oil to prevent foaming, and salt to taste. Other possible additions include bay leaves, pieces of onion, bouillon, and/or bacon/ham hock. Once the beans are cooked, add the *refogado* (onions, garlic, and/ or tomatoes and sausage, sautéed separately in a skillet) to the beans and simmer everything together in the pot with the lid off (not pressurized) for 5–10 minutes.

Refogado

A *refogado* (also called *sofrito* in Spanish) is a traditional Portuguese method of seasoning dishes that is widely used in Brazil. A mixture of finely chopped aromatic vegetables, usually onions, garlic, and tomatoes (also bay leaves and herbs), is sautéed in oil until soft and fragrant. Only then are the remaining ingredients (meat, rice, beans, etc.) added. Many Brazilian recipes start by sautéing the onion, then adding the garlic, then adding the tomatoes.

Tools for the Brazilian Kitchen

There are few pieces of kitchen equipment, some basic and some more unusual, that are useful when cooking Brazilian food.

Blender

The blender may be the most used piece of equipment in a Brazilian kitchen. Brazilians use blenders in place of standing mixers or food processors for many kitchen tasks, which can be a convenient alternative (especially if you need to free up counter space in your kitchen).

Couscoussier (Cuscuzeira)

Often used in Moroccan cooking, a couscous steamer both cooks the couscous and molds it for serving. In Brazil these steamers are used to cook flaked cornmeal (*milharina*), and they are designed so that you can lift out the *cuscuz* in the shape of a tall wheel.

Deep-Fat Fryer

Brazilians love fried snacks such as *bolinho de bacalhau* and *coxinha*. A deep-fat fryer maintains the proper temperature for frying and makes cleanup much simpler.

Lime Juicer

This small tool is just the right size for squeezing juice from small South American limes. These limes have thin skins and lots of juice, and are used in place of lemons in Brazilian cooking.

Muddler

A muddler is a piece of bartending equipment, similar to a pestle, which is used to "muddle" the lime and sugar when making the famous Brazilian *caipirinha* cocktail.

Muffin Pan

A muffin pan is useful for making *empandinhas*, which are little muffin-shaped tarts filled with various savory fillings.

Potato Ricer

This is a handy tool to have for working with manioc root. The cooked manioc is pressed through the small holes of the ricer, removing any remaining stringy pieces or lumps. Great for potatoes as well, of course!

Pressure Cooker

Nearly every Brazilian household has a pressure cooker for cooking beans and stews.

Tube Pan

Most Brazilian cakes are baked in a tube pan, so that the cake comes out in the shape of a ring. An angel food cake pan, especially one with a removeable base, works well too.

Online Resources for Brazilian Foods

BrazilianShop.com
Ingredients (including frozen foods), books, seasonal items, clothes, and more.
www.brazilianshop.com

BrazilianFoodsOnline.com
Ingredients, candy, coffee, tea, seasonal products, snacks, beauty products.
www.brazilianfoodsonline.com

Brazil by the Bay Market
Brazilian specialty ingredients
www.brazilbythebaymarket.com

Brasil Mania
Ingredients, sausages, and frozen snacks.
www.brasilmania.com

AmigoFoods.com
South American ingredients, including many Brazilian products.
www.amigofoods.com

Seamless—Brazilian Food
Find Brazilian food delivery and takeout restaurants in certain U.S. cities.
www.seamless.com/brazilian-food-delivery

Standard U.S./Metric Measurement Conversions

VOLUME CONVERSIONS

U.S. Volume Measure	Metric Equivalent
⅛ teaspoon	0.5 milliliter
¼ teaspoon	1 milliliter
½ teaspoon	2 milliliters
1 teaspoon	5 milliliters
½ tablespoon	7 milliliters
1 tablespoon (3 teaspoons)	15 milliliters
2 tablespoons (1 fluid ounce)	30 milliliters
¼ cup (4 tablespoons)	60 milliliters
⅓ cup	90 milliliters
½ cup (4 fluid ounces)	125 milliliters
⅔ cup	160 milliliters
¾ cup (6 fluid ounces)	180 milliliters
1 cup (16 tablespoons)	250 milliliters
1 pint (2 cups)	500 milliliters
1 quart (4 cups)	1 liter (about)

WEIGHT CONVERSIONS

U.S. Weight Measure	Metric Equivalent
½ ounce	15 grams
1 ounce	30 grams
2 ounces	60 grams
3 ounces	85 grams
¼ pound (4 ounces)	115 grams
½ pound (8 ounces)	225 grams
¾ pound (12 ounces)	340 grams
1 pound (16 ounces)	454 grams

OVEN TEMPERATURE CONVERSIONS

Degrees Fahrenheit	Degrees Celsius
200 degrees F	95 degrees C
250 degrees F	120 degrees C
275 degrees F	135 degrees C
300 degrees F	150 degrees C
325 degrees F	160 degrees C
350 degrees F	180 degrees C
375 degrees F	190 degrees C
400 degrees F	205 degrees C
425 degrees F	220 degrees C
450 degrees F	230 degrees C

BAKING PAN SIZES

U.S.	Metric
8 × 1½ inch round baking pan	20 × 4 cm cake tin
9 × 1½ inch round baking pan	23 × 3.5 cm cake tin
11 × 7 × 1½ inch baking pan	28 × 18 × 4 cm baking tin
13 × 9 × 2 inch baking pan	30 × 20 × 5 cm baking tin
2 quart rectangular baking dish	30 × 20 × 3 cm baking tin
15 × 10 × 2 inch baking pan	30 × 25 × 2 cm baking tin (Swiss roll tin)
9 inch pie plate	22 × 4 or 23 × 4 cm pie plate
7 or 8 inch springform pan	18 or 20 cm springform or loose-bottom cake tin
9 × 5 × 3 inch loaf pan	23 × 13 × 7 cm or 2 lb narrow loaf or pâté tin
1½ quart casserole	1.5 liter casserole
2 quart casserole	2 liter casserole

Index

Note: Page numbers in **bold** indicate recipe category lists.